CULLEN BUNN   JONAS SCHARF   ALEX GUIMARÃES

BASILISK™

VOLUME TWO

BASILISK Vol. 2, June 2022. Published by BOOM! Studios, a division of Boom Entertainment, Inc. Basilisk is ™ & © 2022 Cullen Bunn & Jonas Scharf. Originally published in single magazine form as BASILISK No. 5 - 8. ™ & © 2021, 2022 Cullen Bunn & Jonas Scharf. All rights reserved. BOOM! Studios™ and the BOOM! Studios logo are trademarks of Boom Entertainment, Inc., registered in various countries and categories. All characters, events, and institutions depicted herein are fictional. Any similarity between any of the names, characters, persons, events, and/or institutions in this publication to actual names, characters, and persons, whether living or dead, events, and/or institutions is unintended and purely coincidental. BOOM! Studios does not read or accept unsolicited submissions of ideas, stories, or artwork.

BOOM! Studios, 5670 Wilshire Boulevard, Suite 400, Los Angeles, CA, 90036-5679. Printed in China. First Printing.

ISBN: 978-1-68415-834-8, eISBN: 978-1-64668-733-6

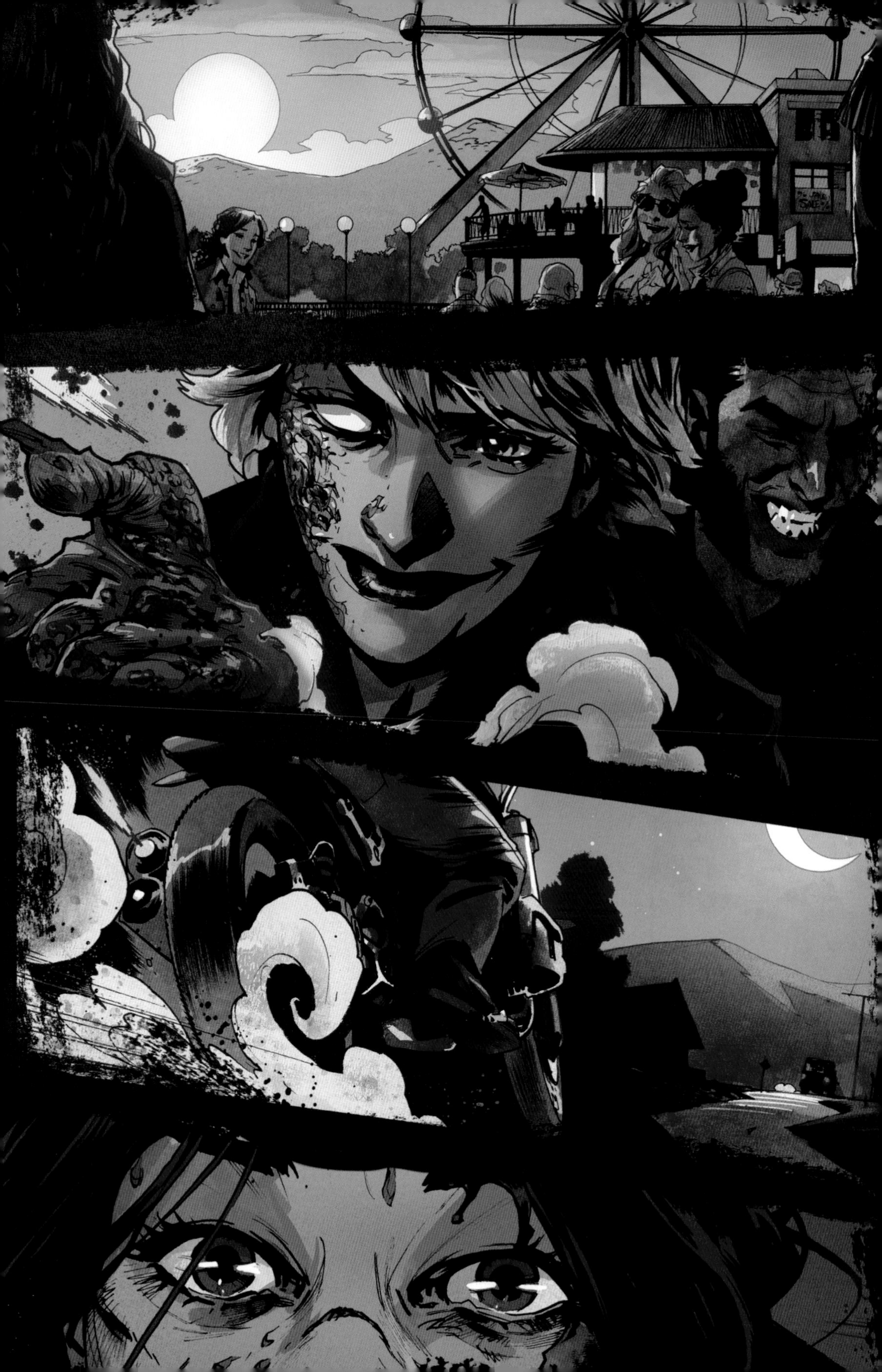

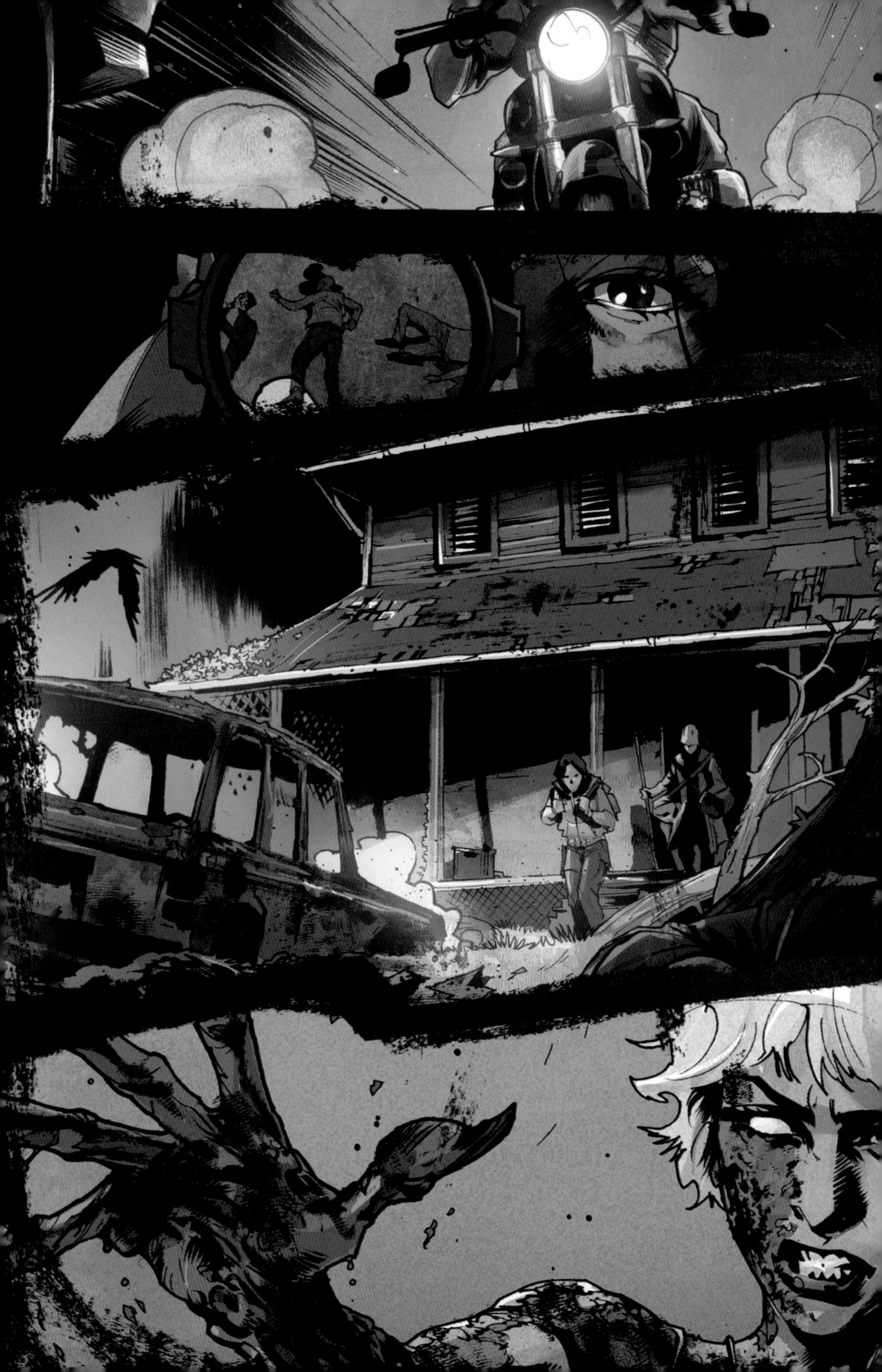

Written by
CULLEN BUNN

Illustrated by
JONAS SCHARF

Colored by
ALEX GUIMARÃES

Lettered by
ED DUKESHIRE

Cover by
JONAS SCHARF

Series Designer
GRACE PARK

Collection Designers
**CHELSEA ROBERTS
& MARIE KRUPINA**

Assistant Editor
RAMIRO PORTNOY

Associate Editor
JONATHAN MANNING

Editor
ERIC HARBURN

BASILISK Created by
CULLEN BUNN & JONAS SCHARF

CHAPTER FIVE

THE VOICE

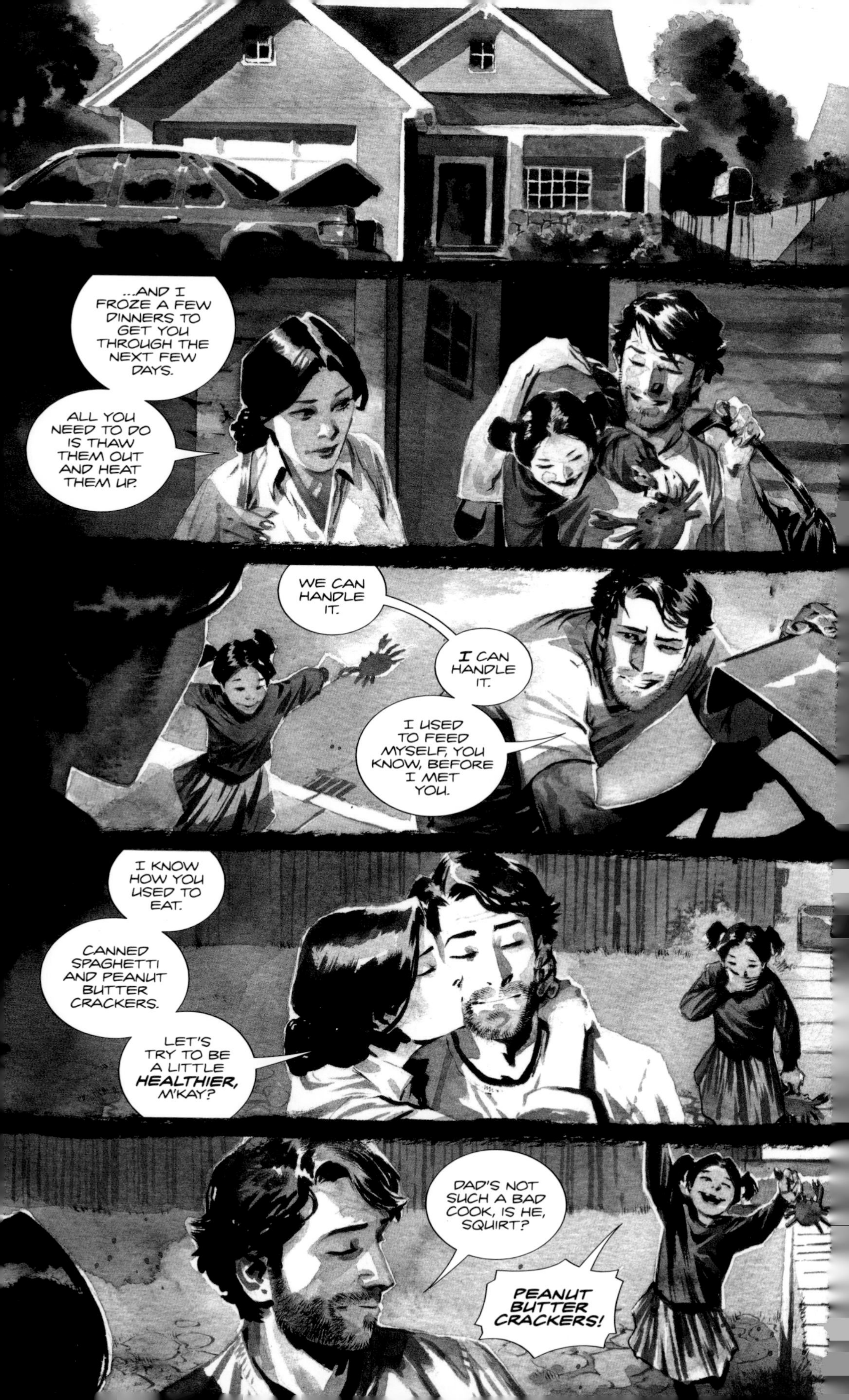

...AND I FROZE A FEW DINNERS TO GET YOU THROUGH THE NEXT FEW DAYS.
ALL YOU NEED TO DO IS THAW THEM OUT AND HEAT THEM UP.
WE CAN HANDLE IT.
I CAN HANDLE IT.
I USED TO FEED MYSELF, YOU KNOW, BEFORE I MET YOU.
I KNOW HOW YOU USED TO EAT.
CANNED SPAGHETTI AND PEANUT BUTTER CRACKERS.
LET'S TRY TO BE A LITTLE HEALTHIER, M'KAY?
DAD'S NOT SUCH A BAD COOK, IS HE, SQUIRT?
PEANUT BUTTER CRACKERS!

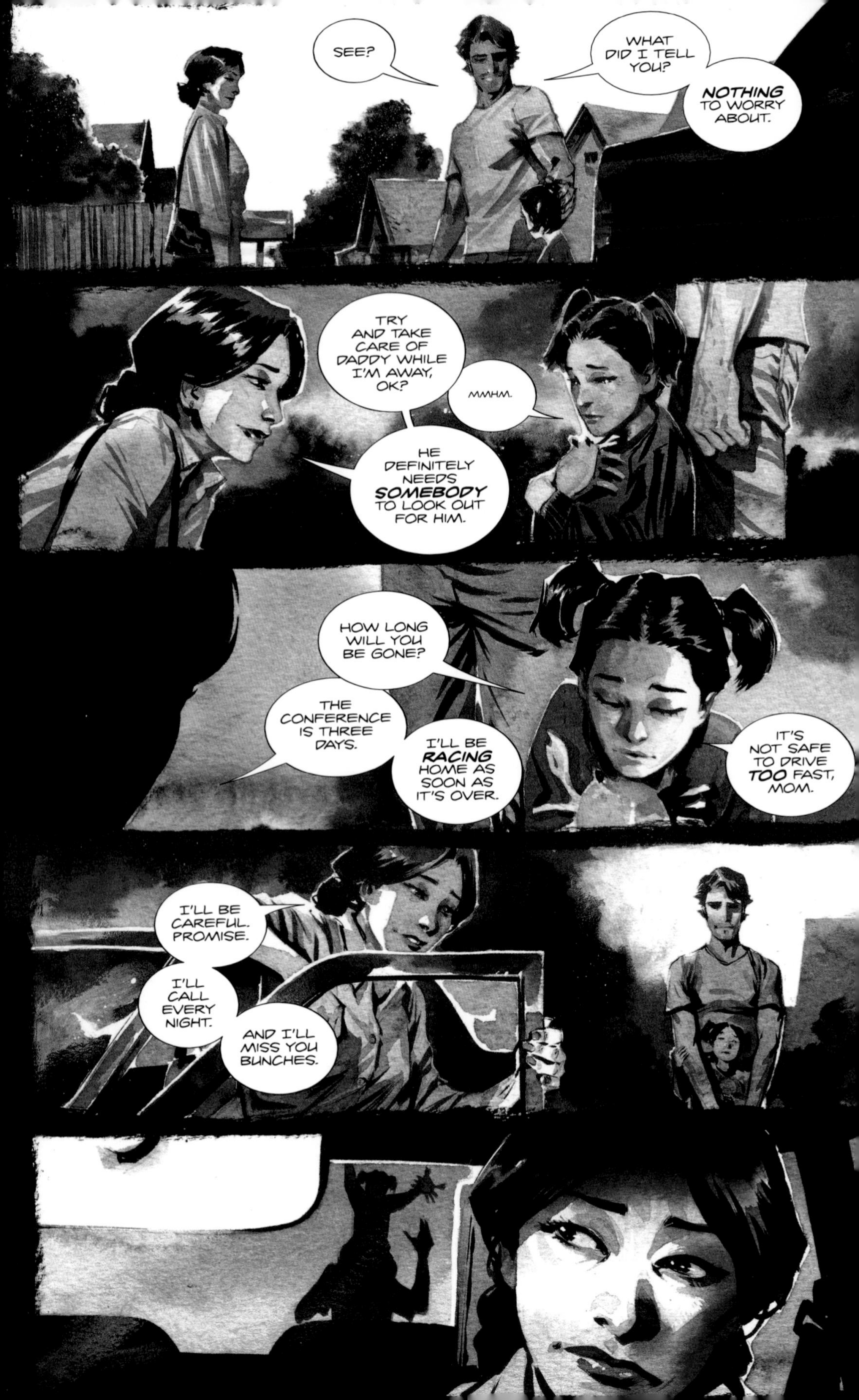
SEE?
WHAT DID I TELL YOU?
NOTHING TO WORRY ABOUT.
TRY AND TAKE CARE OF DADDY WHILE I'M AWAY, OK?
HE DEFINITELY NEEDS SOMEBODY TO LOOK OUT FOR HIM.
MMHM.
HOW LONG WILL YOU BE GONE?
THE CONFERENCE IS THREE DAYS.
I'LL BE RACING HOME AS SOON AS IT'S OVER.
IT'S NOT SAFE TO DRIVE TOO FAST, MOM.
I'LL BE CAREFUL. PROMISE.
I'LL CALL EVERY NIGHT.
AND I'LL MISS YOU BUNCHES.

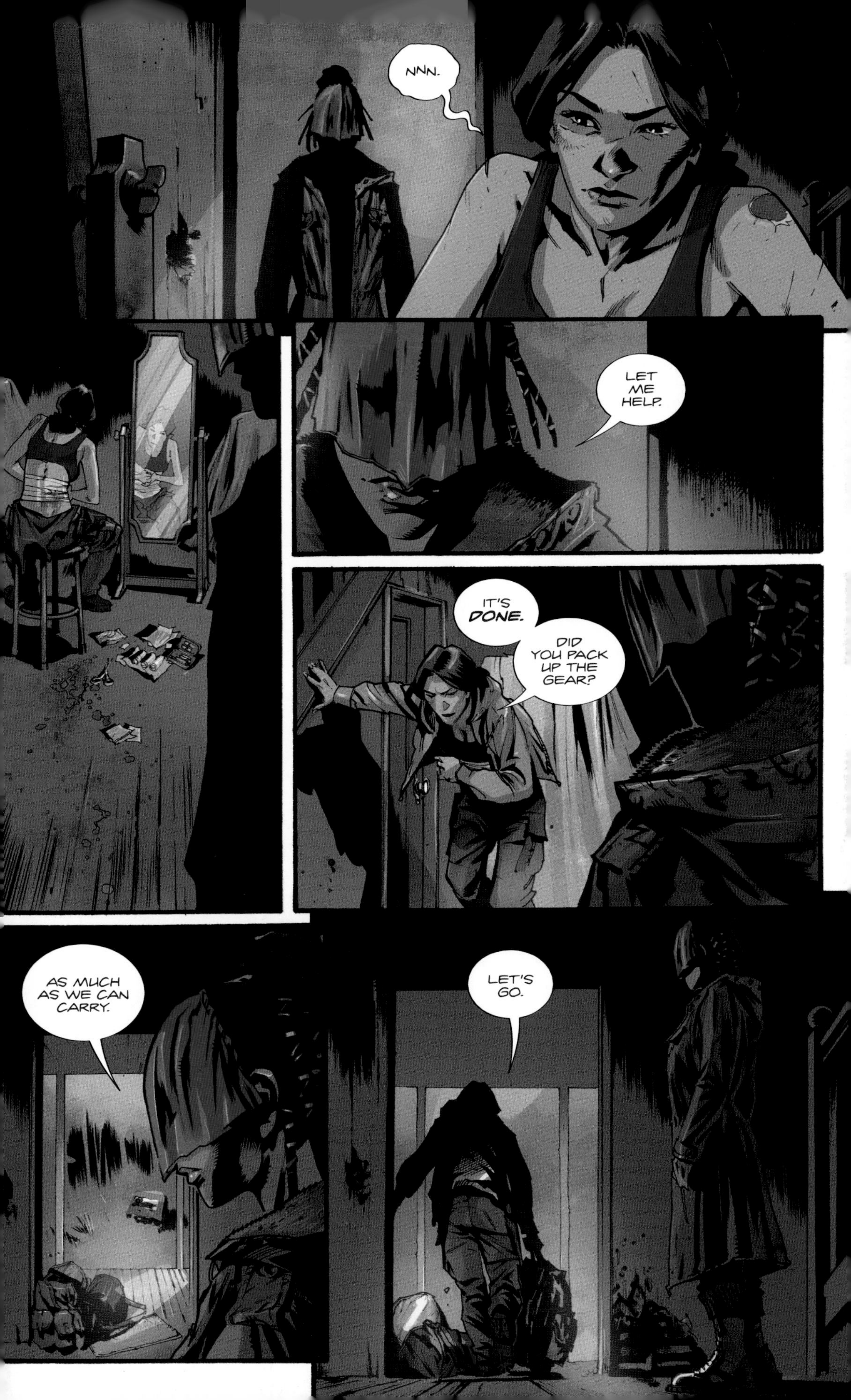
NNN.
LET ME HELP.
IT'S DONE.
DID YOU PACK UP THE GEAR?
AS MUCH AS WE CAN CARRY.
LET'S GO.

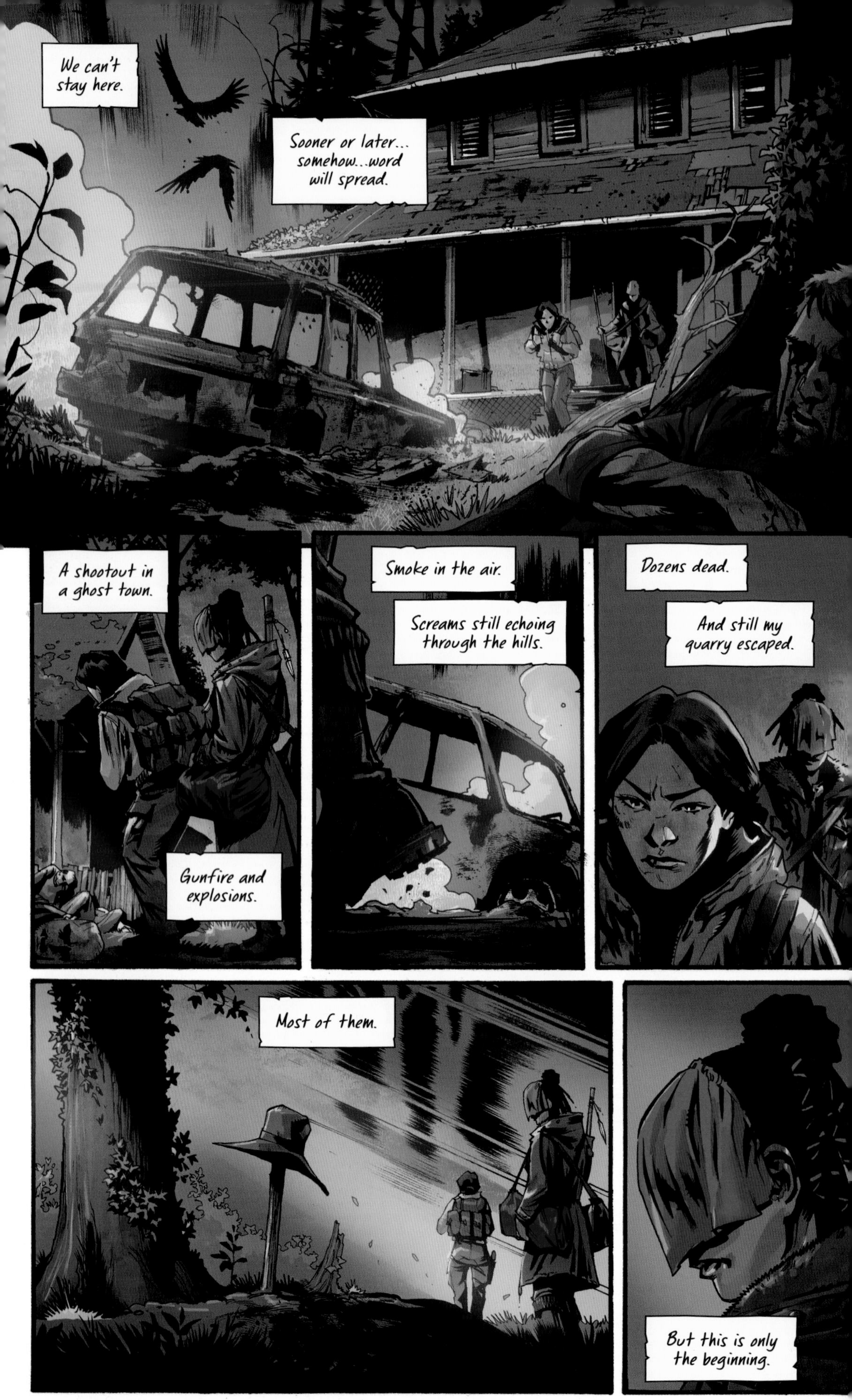
We can't stay here.
Sooner or later... somehow...word will spread.
A shootout in a ghost town.
Gunfire and explosions.
Smoke in the air.
Screams still echoing through the hills.
Dozens dead.
And still my quarry escaped.
Most of them.
But this is only the beginning.

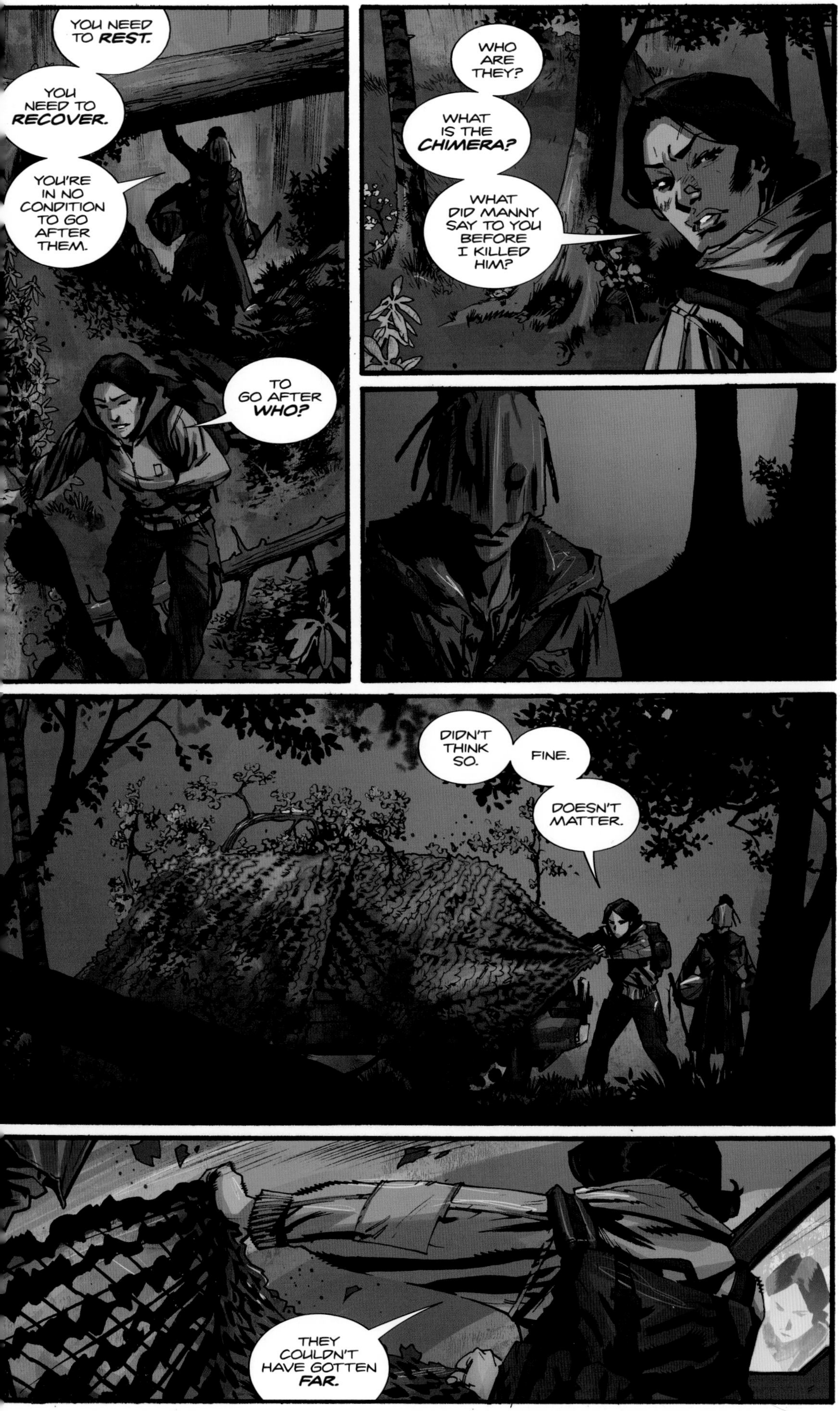

YOU NEED TO **REST.**
YOU NEED TO **RECOVER.**
YOU'RE IN NO CONDITION TO GO AFTER THEM.
TO GO AFTER **WHO?**
WHO ARE THEY?
WHAT IS THE **CHIMERA?**
WHAT DID MANNY SAY TO YOU BEFORE I KILLED HIM?
DIDN'T THINK SO.
FINE.
DOESN'T MATTER.
THEY COULDN'T HAVE GOTTEN **FAR.**

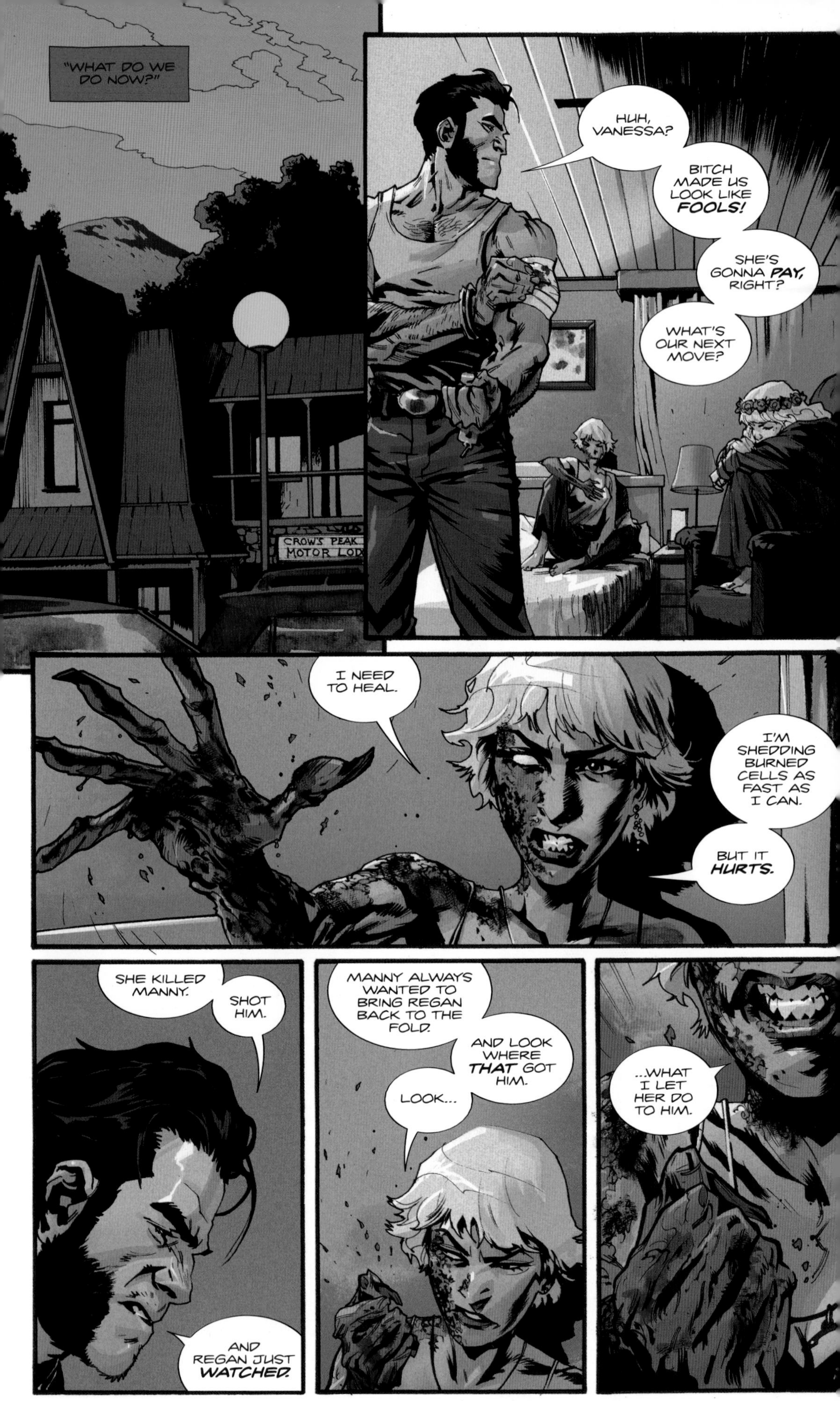
"WHAT DO WE DO NOW?"
CROW'S PEAK MOTOR LOD
HUH, VANESSA?
BITCH MADE US LOOK LIKE *FOOLS!*
SHE'S GONNA *PAY,* RIGHT?
WHAT'S OUR NEXT MOVE?
I NEED TO HEAL.
I'M SHEDDING BURNED CELLS AS FAST AS I CAN.
BUT IT *HURTS.*
SHE KILLED MANNY.
SHOT HIM.
AND REGAN JUST *WATCHED.*
MANNY ALWAYS WANTED TO BRING REGAN BACK TO THE FOLD.
AND LOOK WHERE *THAT* GOT HIM.
LOOK...
...WHAT I LET HER DO TO HIM.

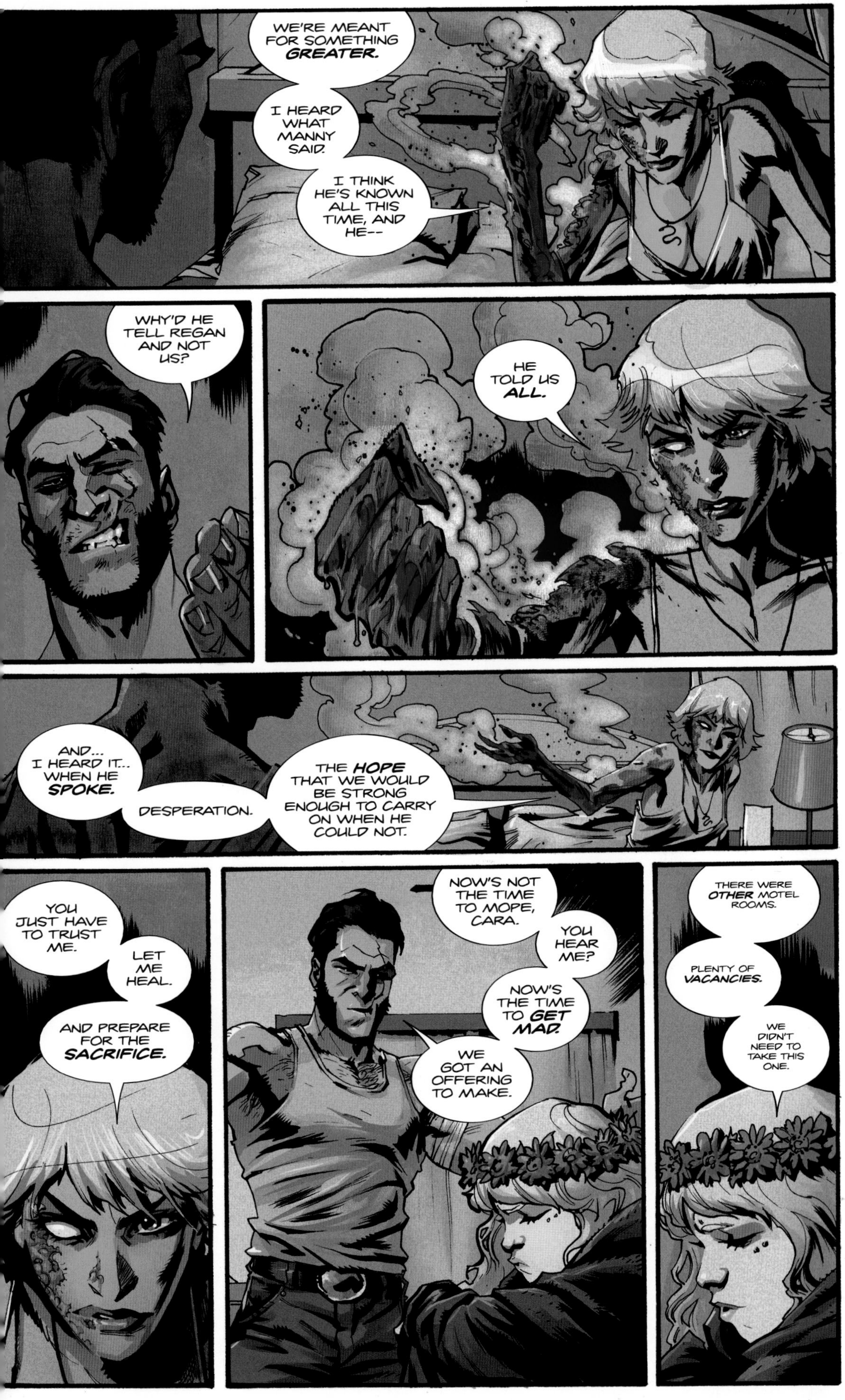

WE'RE MEANT FOR SOMETHING GREATER.
I HEARD WHAT MANNY SAID.
I THINK HE'S KNOWN ALL THIS TIME, AND HE--
WHY'D HE TELL REGAN AND NOT US?
HE TOLD US ALL.
AND... I HEARD IT... WHEN HE SPOKE.
DESPERATION.
THE HOPE THAT WE WOULD BE STRONG ENOUGH TO CARRY ON WHEN HE COULD NOT.
YOU JUST HAVE TO TRUST ME.
LET ME HEAL.
AND PREPARE FOR THE SACRIFICE.
NOW'S NOT THE TIME TO MOPE, CARA.
YOU HEAR ME?
NOW'S THE TIME TO GET MAD.
WE GOT AN OFFERING TO MAKE.
THERE WERE OTHER MOTEL ROOMS.
PLENTY OF VACANCIES.
WE DIDN'T NEED TO TAKE THIS ONE.

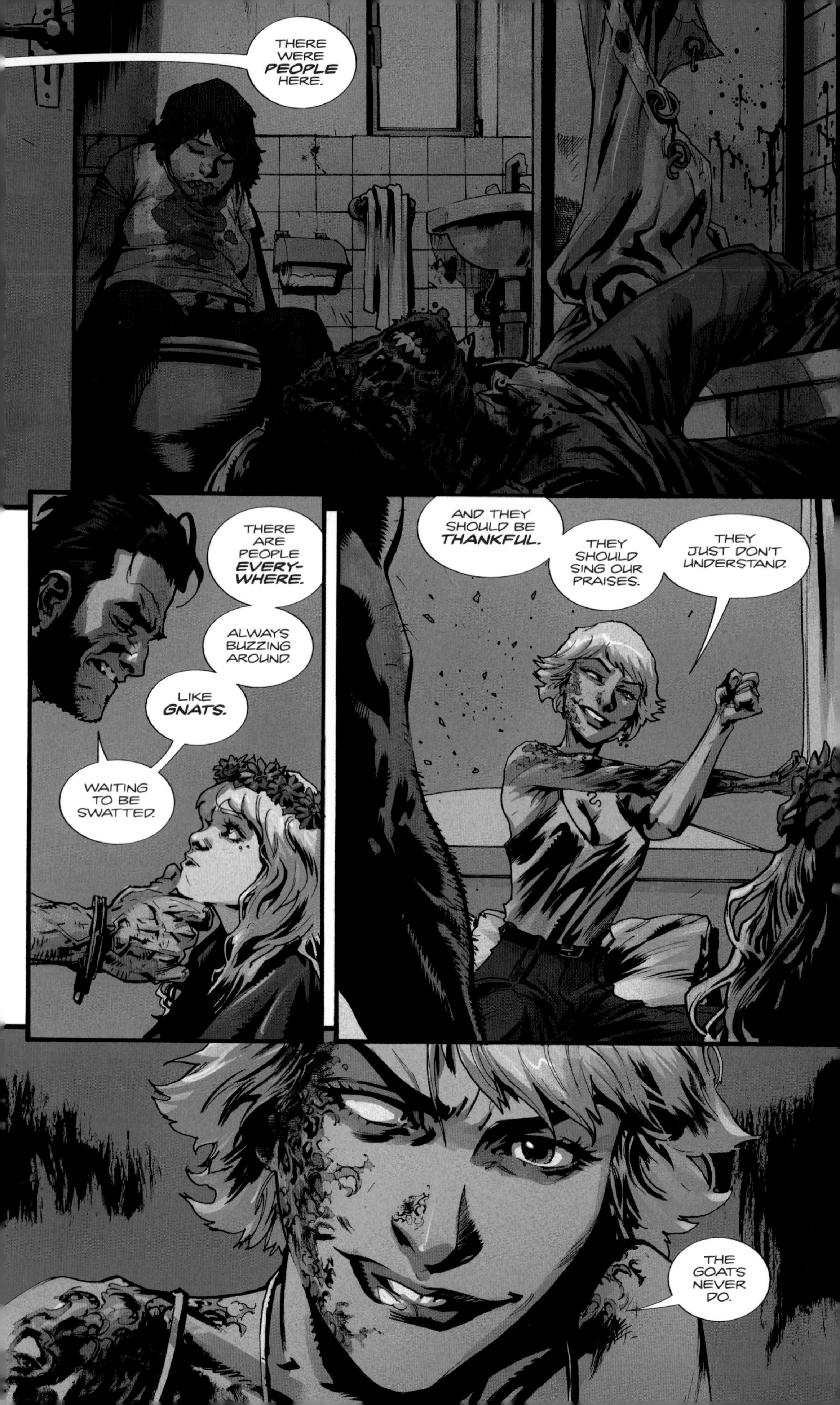

THERE WERE **PEOPLE** HERE.
THERE ARE PEOPLE **EVERY-WHERE.**
ALWAYS BUZZING AROUND.
LIKE **GNATS.**
WAITING TO BE SWATTED.
AND THEY SHOULD BE **THANKFUL.**
THEY SHOULD SING OUR PRAISES.
THEY JUST DON'T UNDERSTAND.
THE GOATS NEVER DO.

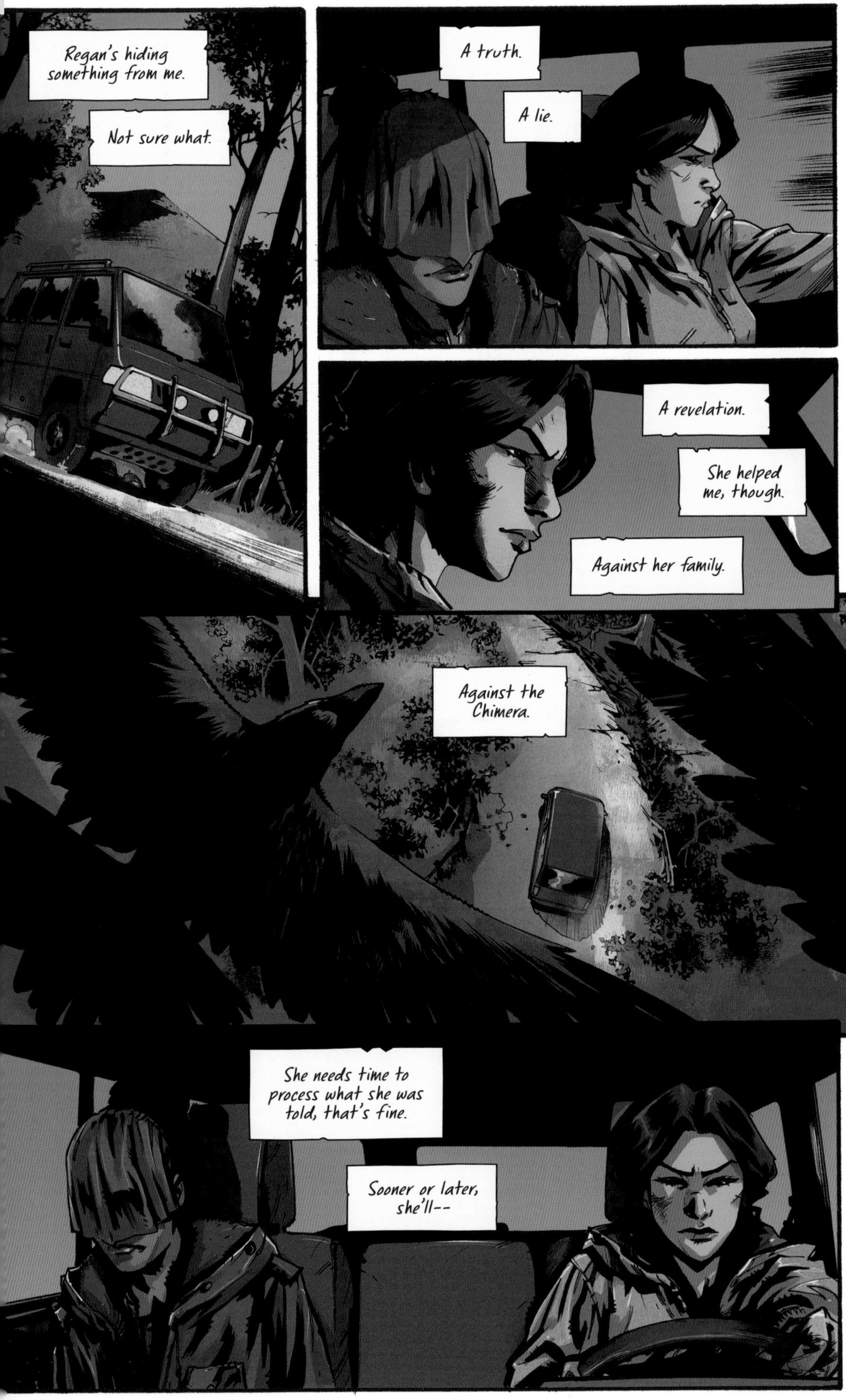
Regan's hiding something from me.
Not sure what.
A truth.
A lie.
A revelation.
She helped me, though.
Against her family.
Against the Chimera.
She needs time to process what she was told, that's fine.
Sooner or later, she'll--

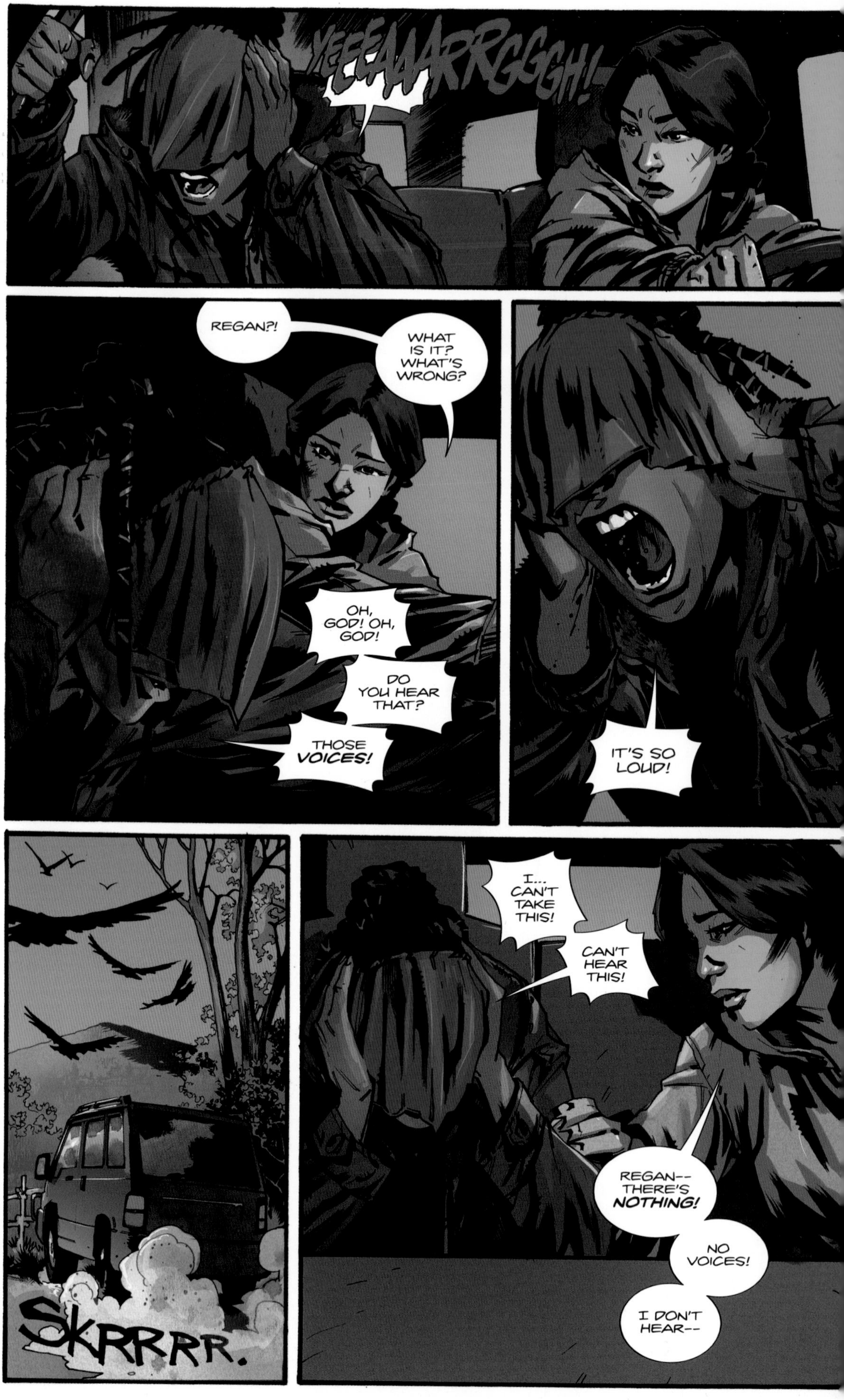
YEEEAAARRGGGH!
REGAN?!
WHAT IS IT? WHAT'S WRONG?
OH, GOD! OH, GOD!
DO YOU HEAR THAT?
THOSE VOICES!
IT'S SO LOUD!
SKRRRR.
I... CAN'T TAKE THIS!
CAN'T HEAR THIS!
REGAN-- THERE'S NOTHING!
NO VOICES!
I DON'T HEAR--

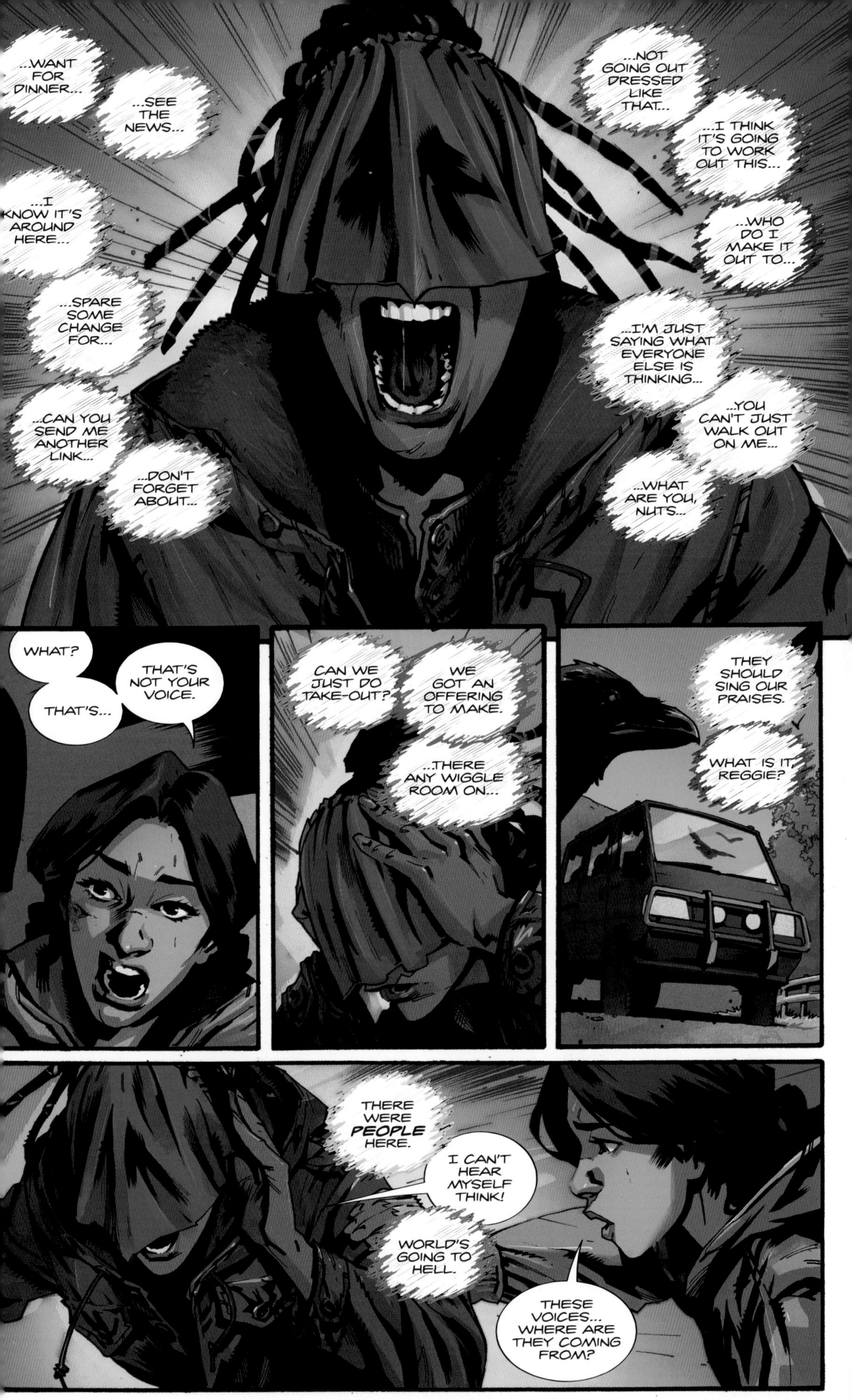
...WANT FOR DINNER...
...SEE THE NEWS...
...I KNOW IT'S AROUND HERE...
...SPARE SOME CHANGE FOR...
...CAN YOU SEND ME ANOTHER LINK...
...DON'T FORGET ABOUT...
...NOT GOING OUT DRESSED LIKE THAT...
...I THINK IT'S GOING TO WORK OUT THIS...
...WHO DO I MAKE IT OUT TO...
...I'M JUST SAYING WHAT EVERYONE ELSE IS THINKING...
...YOU CAN'T JUST WALK OUT ON ME...
...WHAT ARE YOU, NUTS...
WHAT?
THAT'S...
THAT'S NOT YOUR VOICE.
CAN WE JUST DO TAKE-OUT?
WE GOT AN OFFERING TO MAKE.
...THERE ANY WIGGLE ROOM ON...
THEY SHOULD SING OUR PRAISES.
WHAT IS IT, REGGIE?
THERE WERE PEOPLE HERE.
I CAN'T HEAR MYSELF THINK!
WORLD'S GOING TO HELL.
THESE VOICES... WHERE ARE THEY COMING FROM?

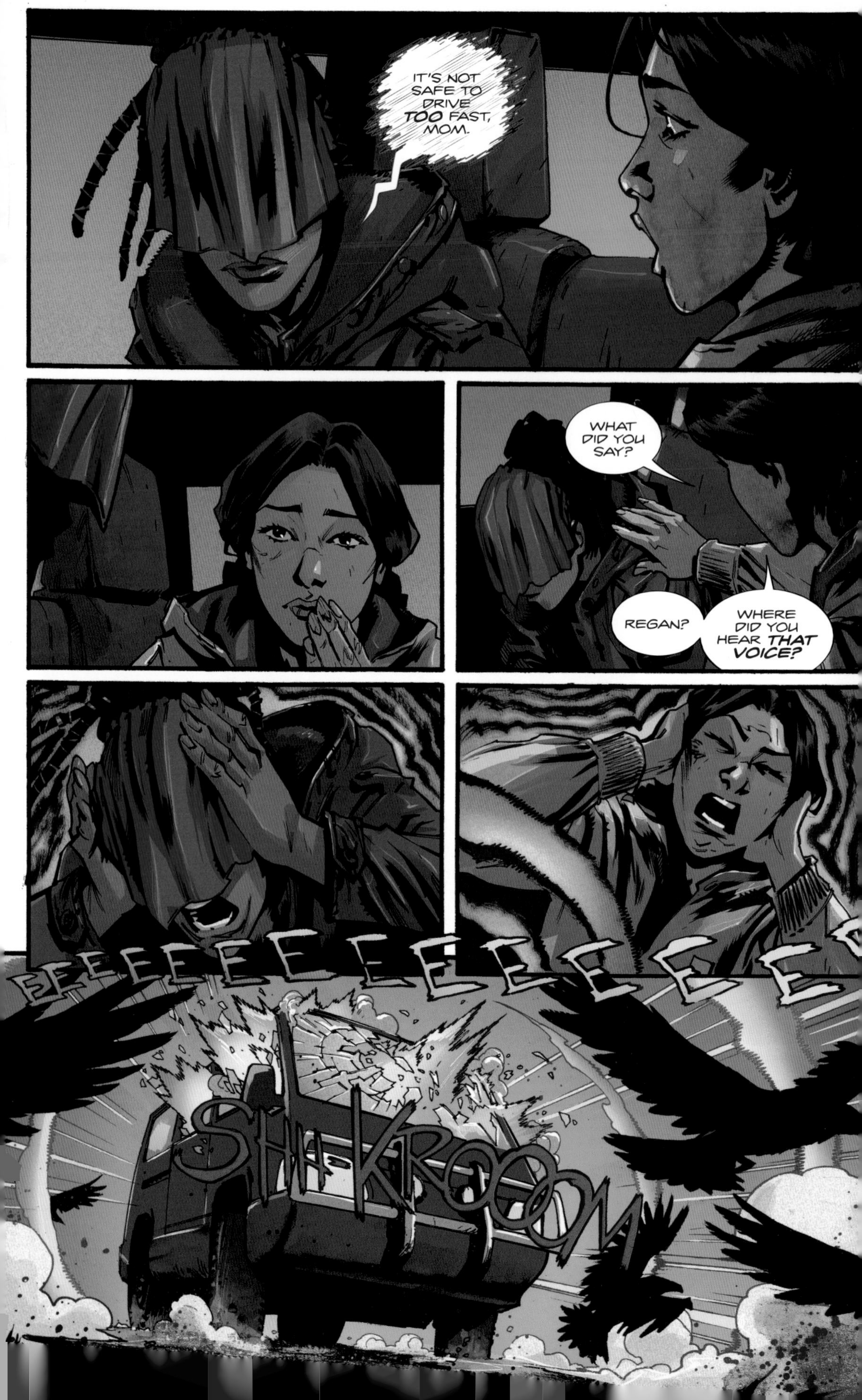
IT'S NOT SAFE TO DRIVE TOO FAST, MOM.
WHAT DID YOU SAY?
REGAN?
WHERE DID YOU HEAR THAT VOICE?
EEEEEEEEEEEEEE
SHHKROOOM

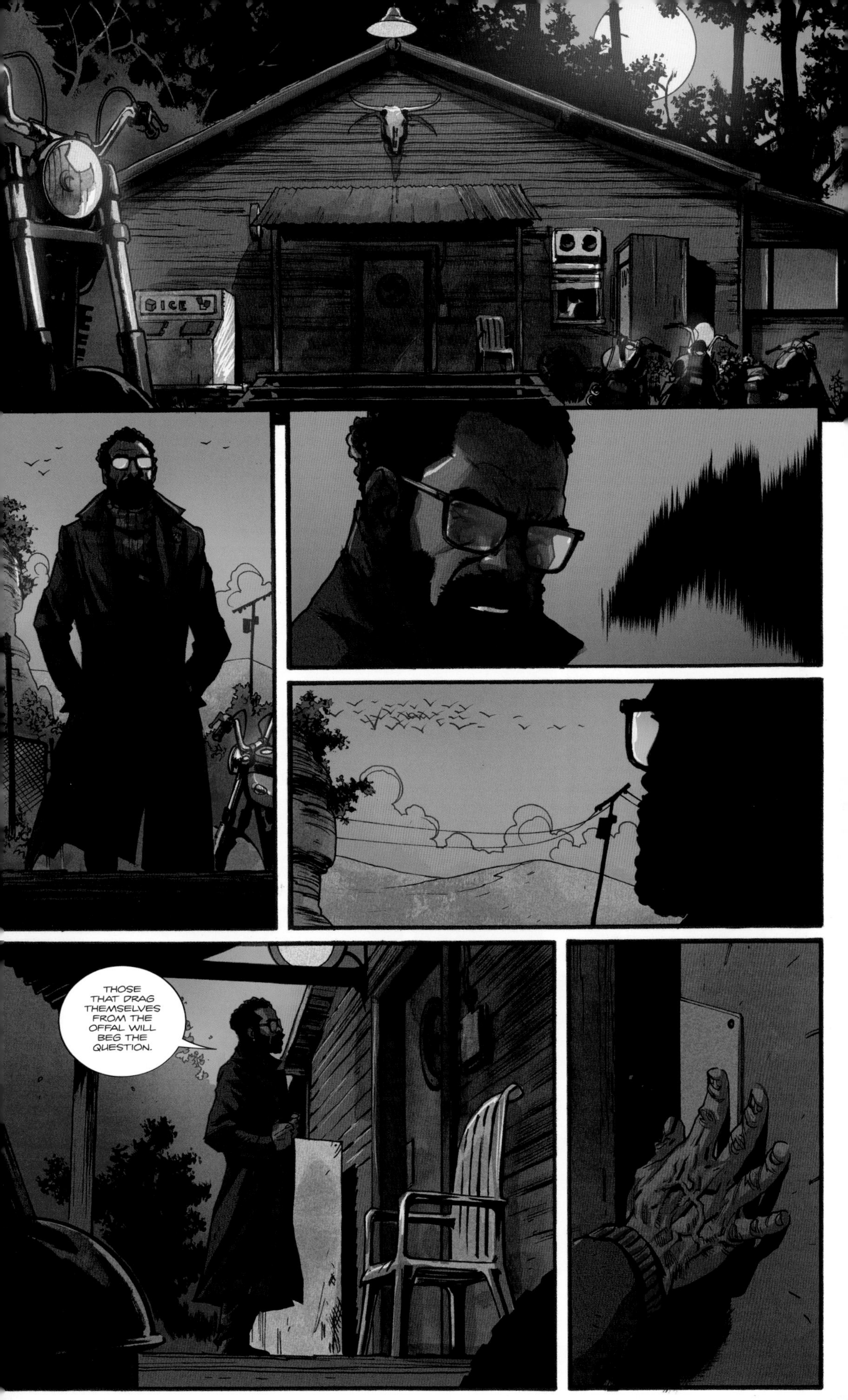
ICE
THOSE THAT DRAG THEMSELVES FROM THE OFFAL WILL BEG THE QUESTION.

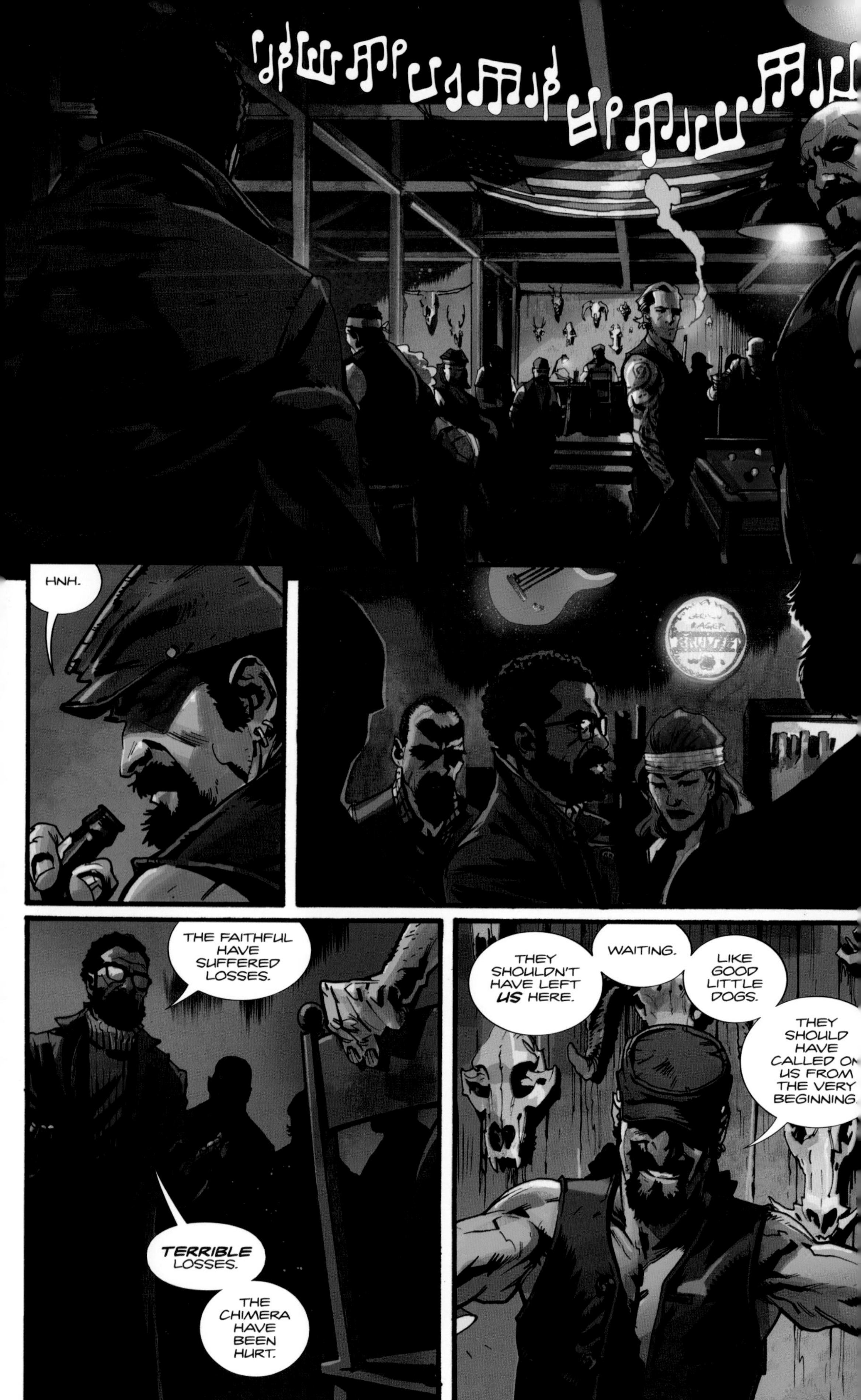
HNH.
THE FAITHFUL HAVE SUFFERED LOSSES.
TERRIBLE LOSSES.
THE CHIMERA HAVE BEEN HURT.
THEY SHOULDN'T HAVE LEFT US HERE.
WAITING.
LIKE GOOD LITTLE DOGS.
THEY SHOULD HAVE CALLED ON US FROM THE VERY BEGINNING.

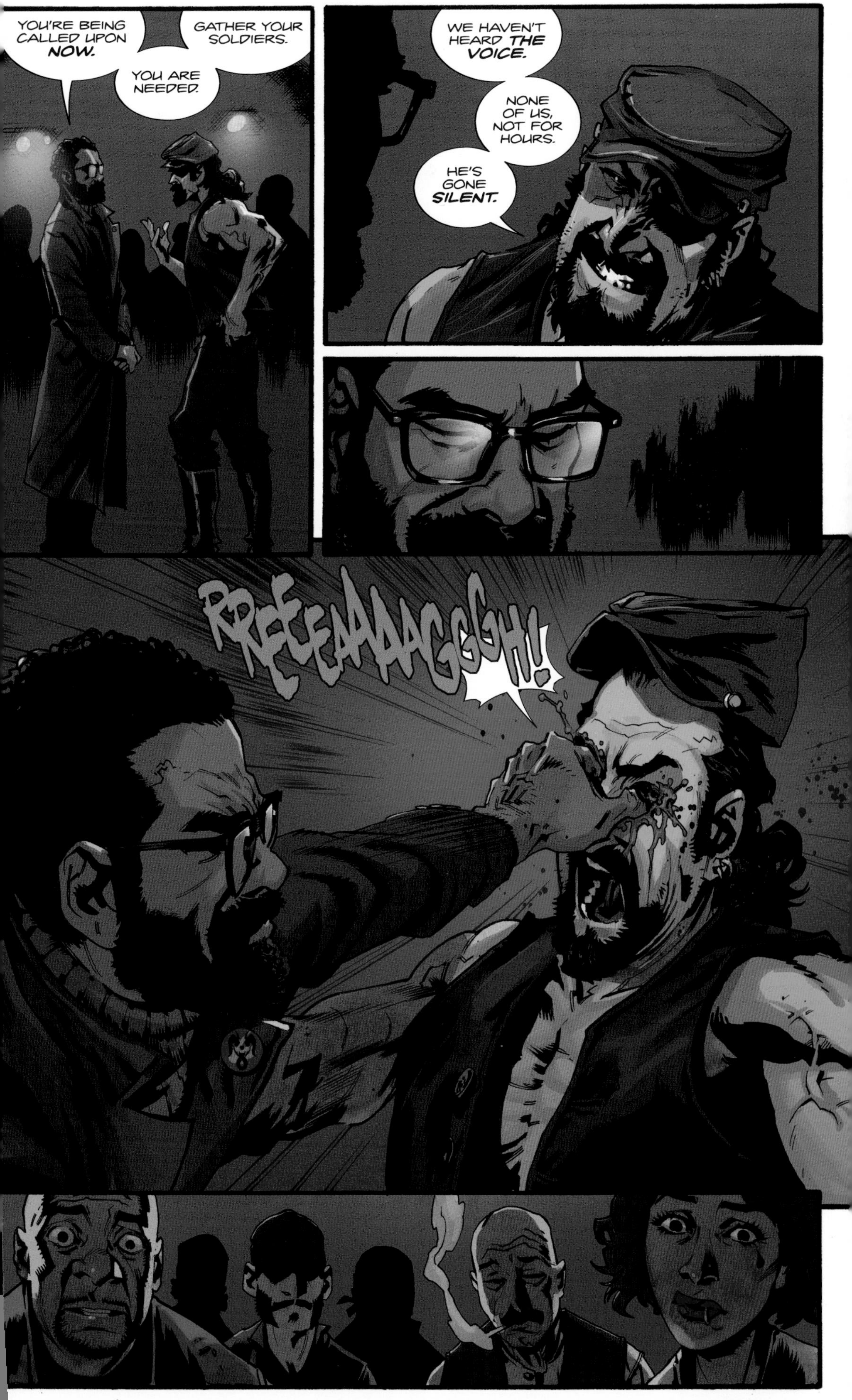
YOU'RE BEING CALLED UPON NOW.
YOU ARE NEEDED.
GATHER YOUR SOLDIERS.
WE HAVEN'T HEARD THE VOICE.
NONE OF US, NOT FOR HOURS.
HE'S GONE SILENT.
RREEEAAAAGGGH!!

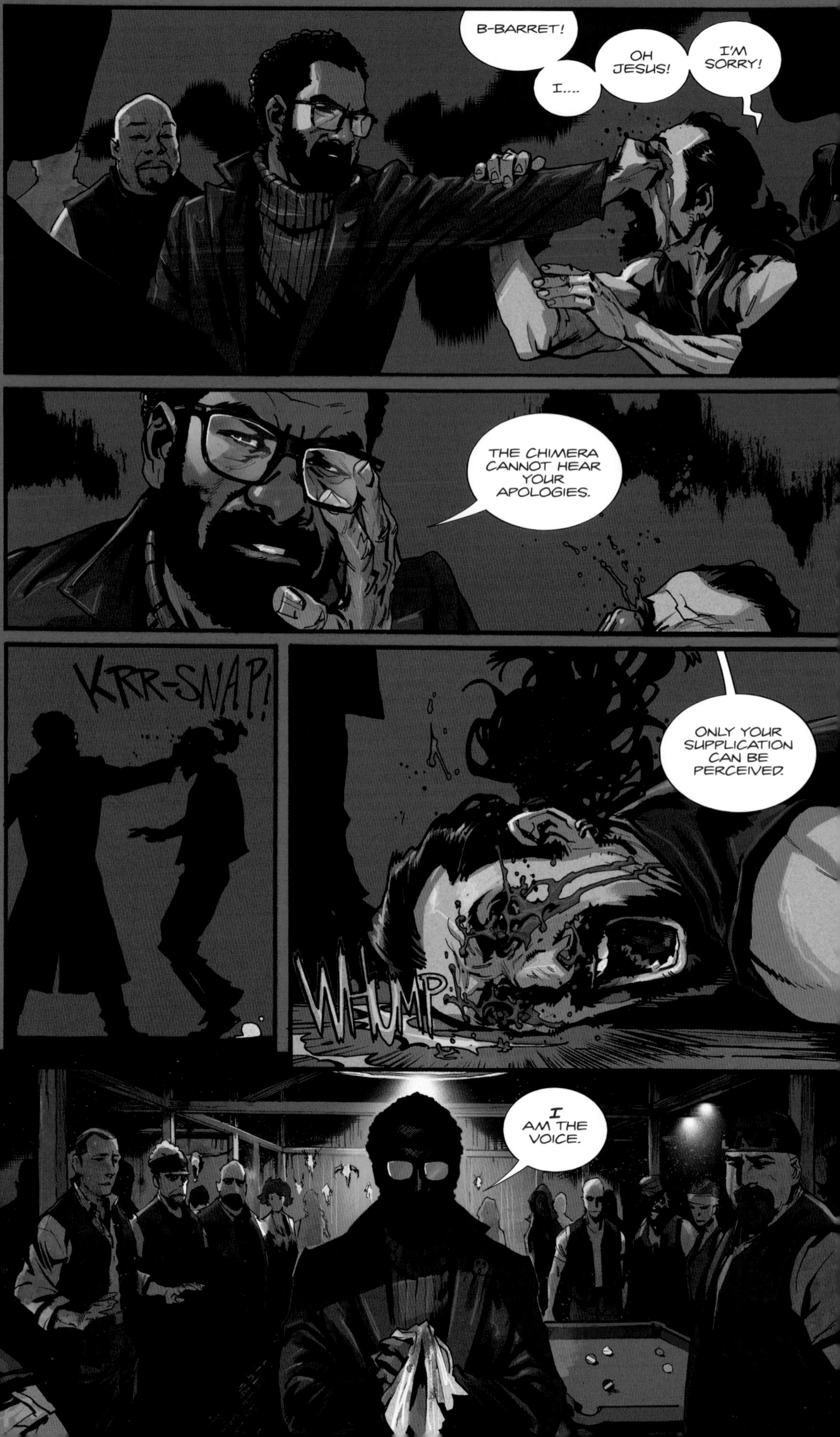
B-BARRET!
I....
OH JESUS!
I'M SORRY!
THE CHIMERA CANNOT HEAR YOUR APOLOGIES.
KRR-SNAP!
ONLY YOUR SUPPLICATION CAN BE PERCEIVED.
WHUMP
I AM THE VOICE.

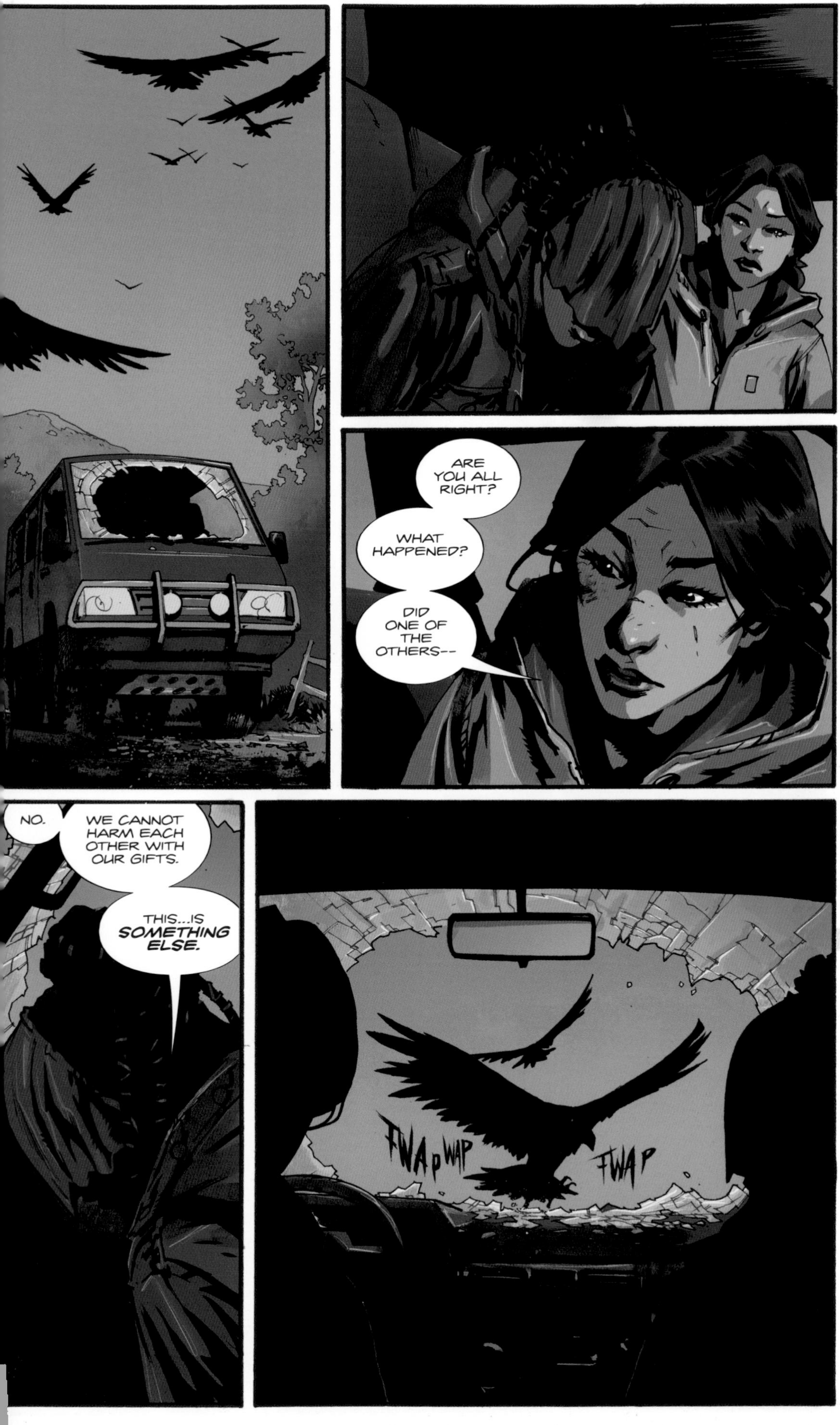

ARE YOU ALL RIGHT?
WHAT HAPPENED?
DID ONE OF THE OTHERS--
NO.
WE CANNOT HARM EACH OTHER WITH OUR GIFTS.
THIS...IS **SOMETHING ELSE.**
FWAP WAP
FWAP

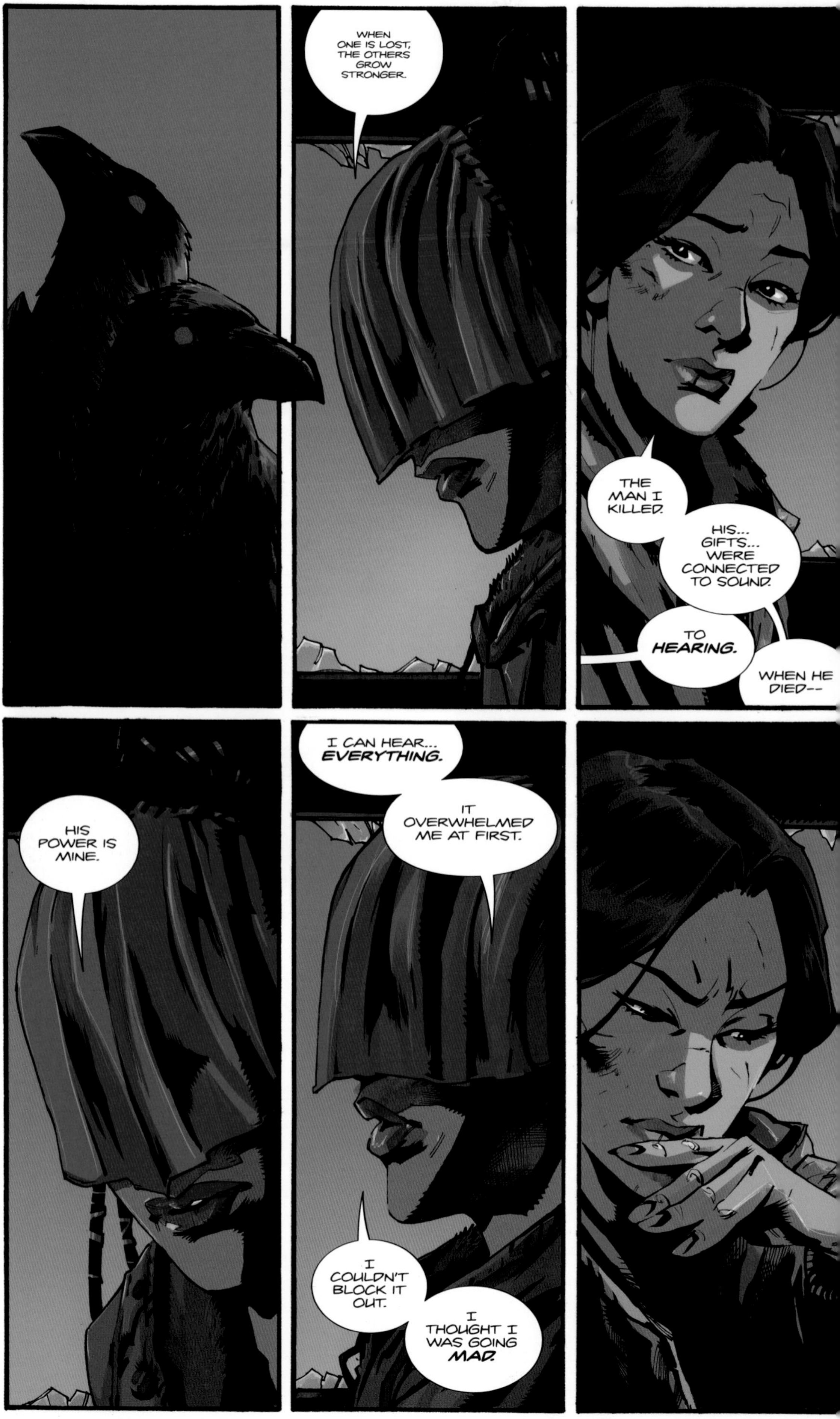
WHEN ONE IS LOST, THE OTHERS GROW STRONGER.
THE MAN I KILLED.
HIS... GIFTS... WERE CONNECTED TO SOUND.
TO *HEARING.*
WHEN HE DIED--
HIS POWER IS MINE.
I CAN HEAR... *EVERYTHING.*
IT OVERWHELMED ME AT FIRST.
I COULDN'T BLOCK IT OUT.
I THOUGHT I WAS GOING *MAD.*

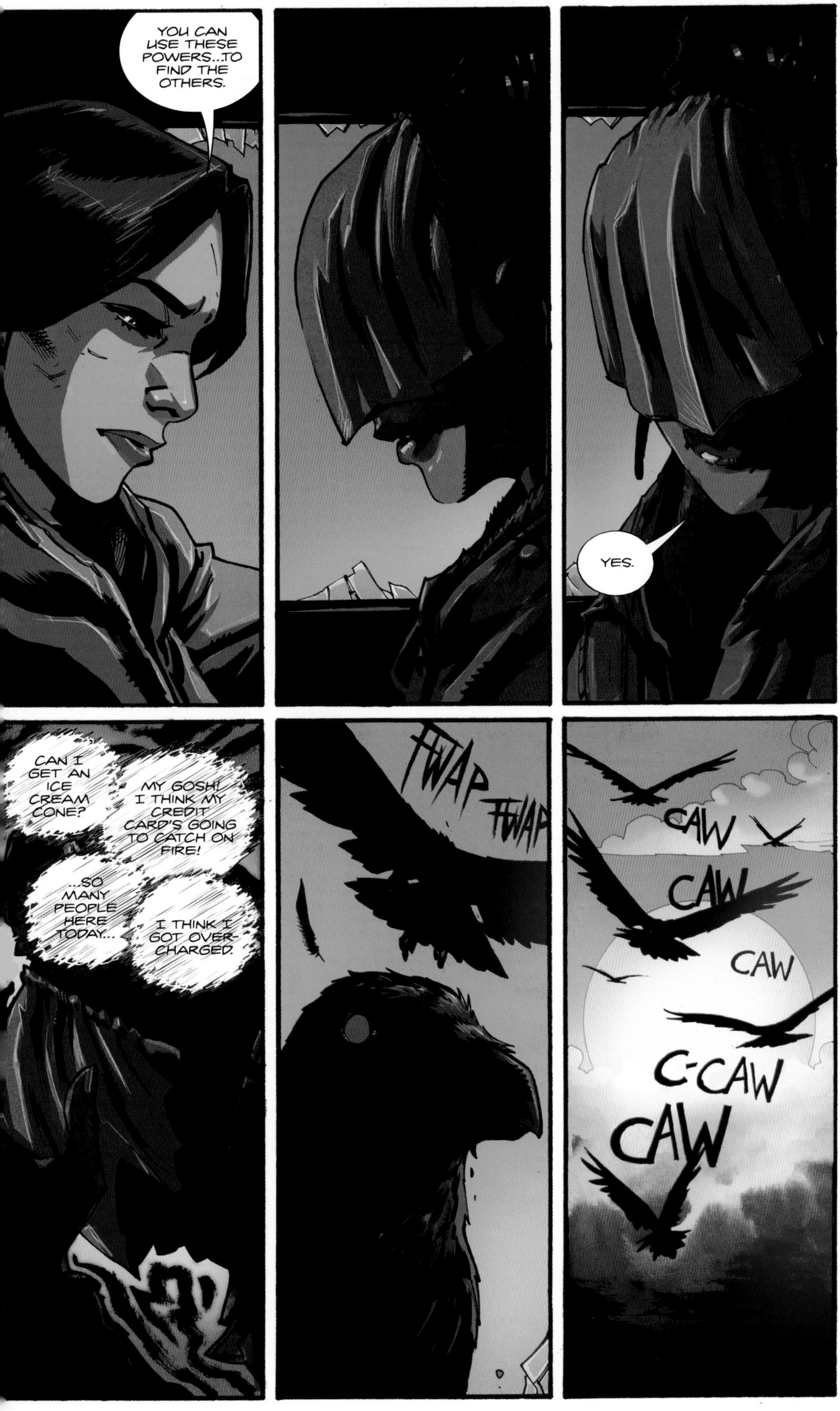
YOU CAN USE THESE POWERS...TO FIND THE OTHERS.
YES.
CAN I GET AN ICE CREAM CONE?
MY GOSH! I THINK MY CREDIT CARD'S GOING TO CATCH ON FIRE!
...SO MANY PEOPLE HERE TODAY...
I THINK I GOT OVER-CHARGED.
FWAP
FWAP
CAW
CAW
CAW
C-CAW
CAW

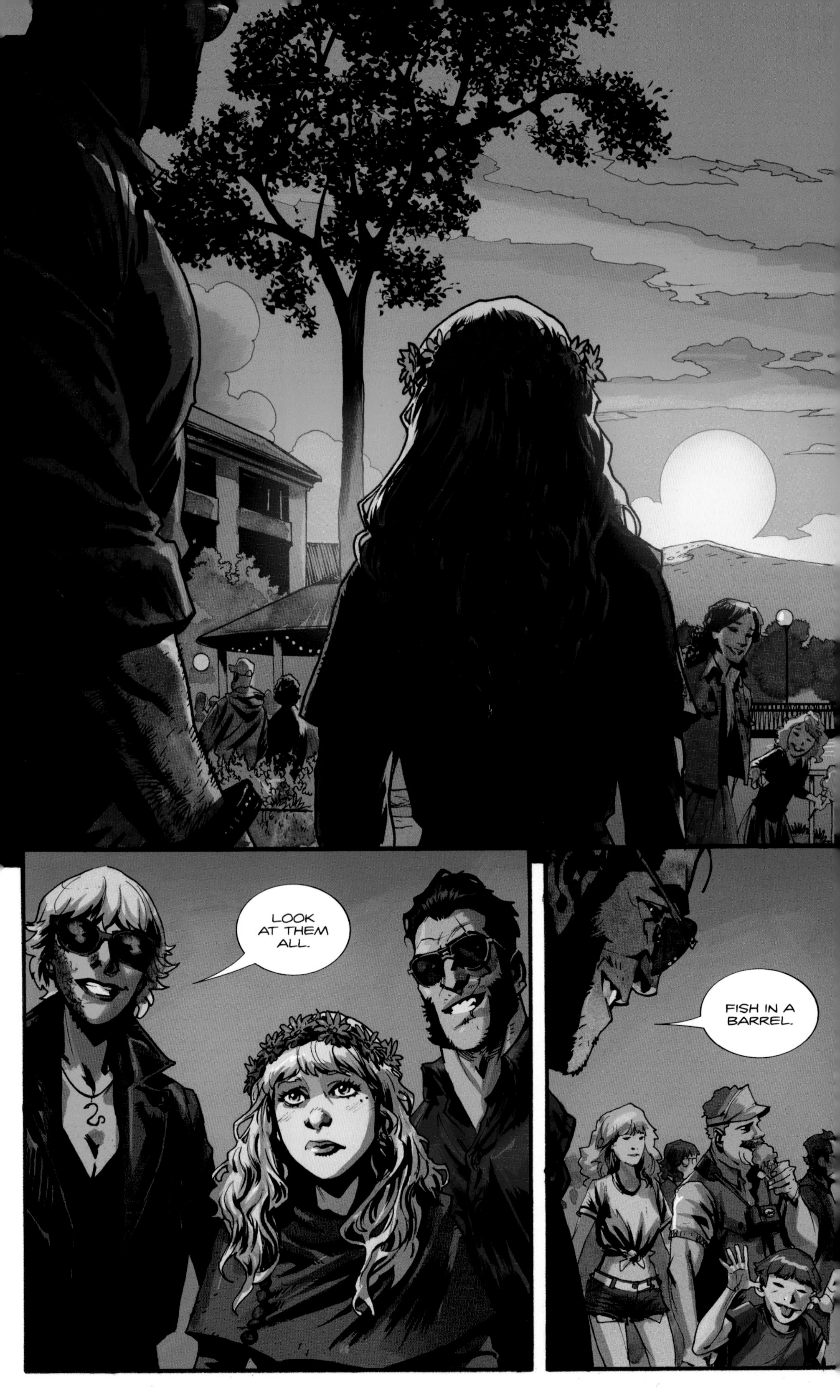
LOOK AT THEM ALL.
FISH IN A BARREL.

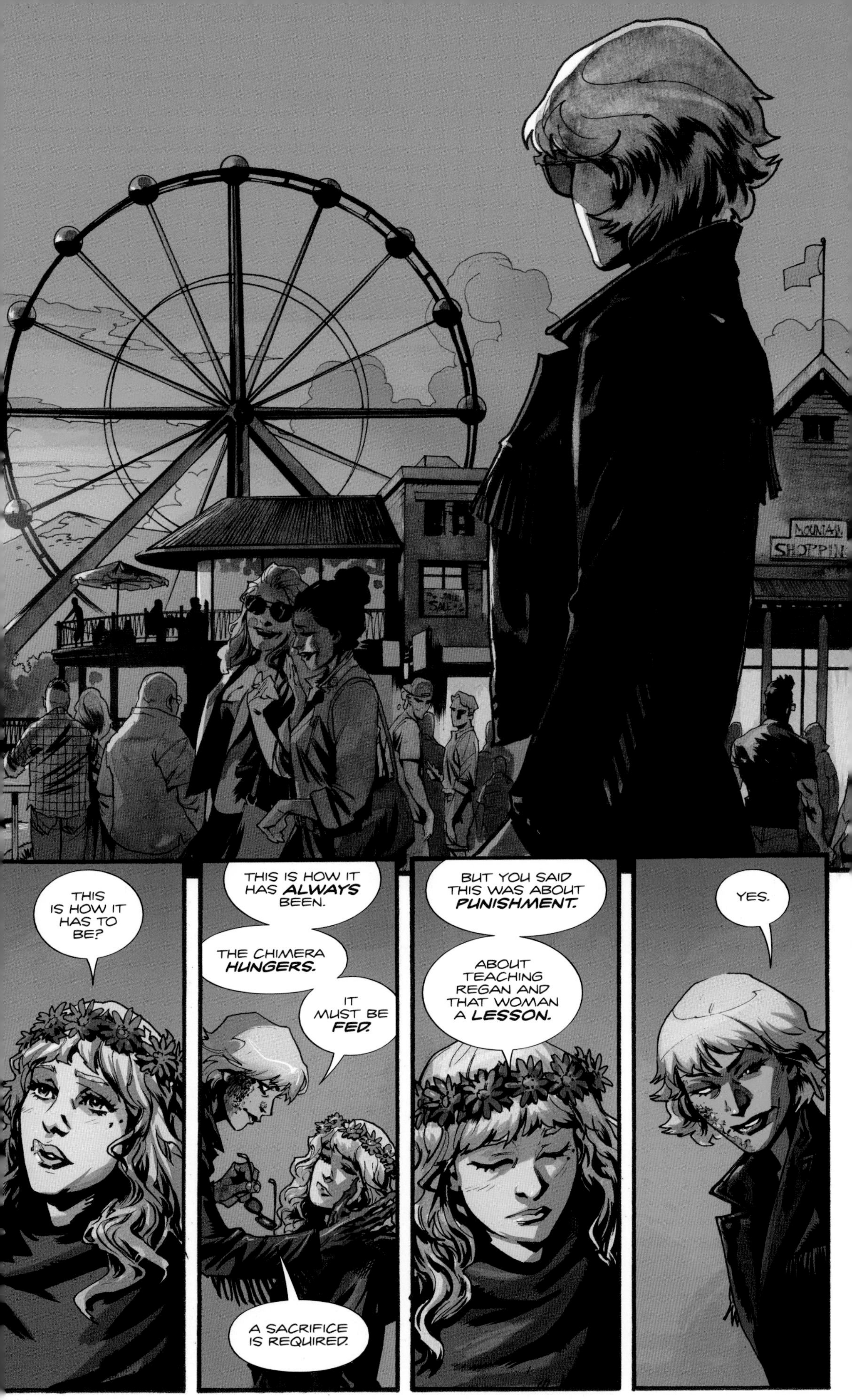

MOUNTAIN
SHOPPIN
SALE
THIS IS HOW IT HAS TO BE?
THIS IS HOW IT HAS ALWAYS BEEN.
THE CHIMERA HUNGERS.
IT MUST BE FED.
A SACRIFICE IS REQUIRED.
BUT YOU SAID THIS WAS ABOUT PUNISHMENT.
ABOUT TEACHING REGAN AND THAT WOMAN A LESSON.
YES.

CHAPTER SIX

SHOWDOWN

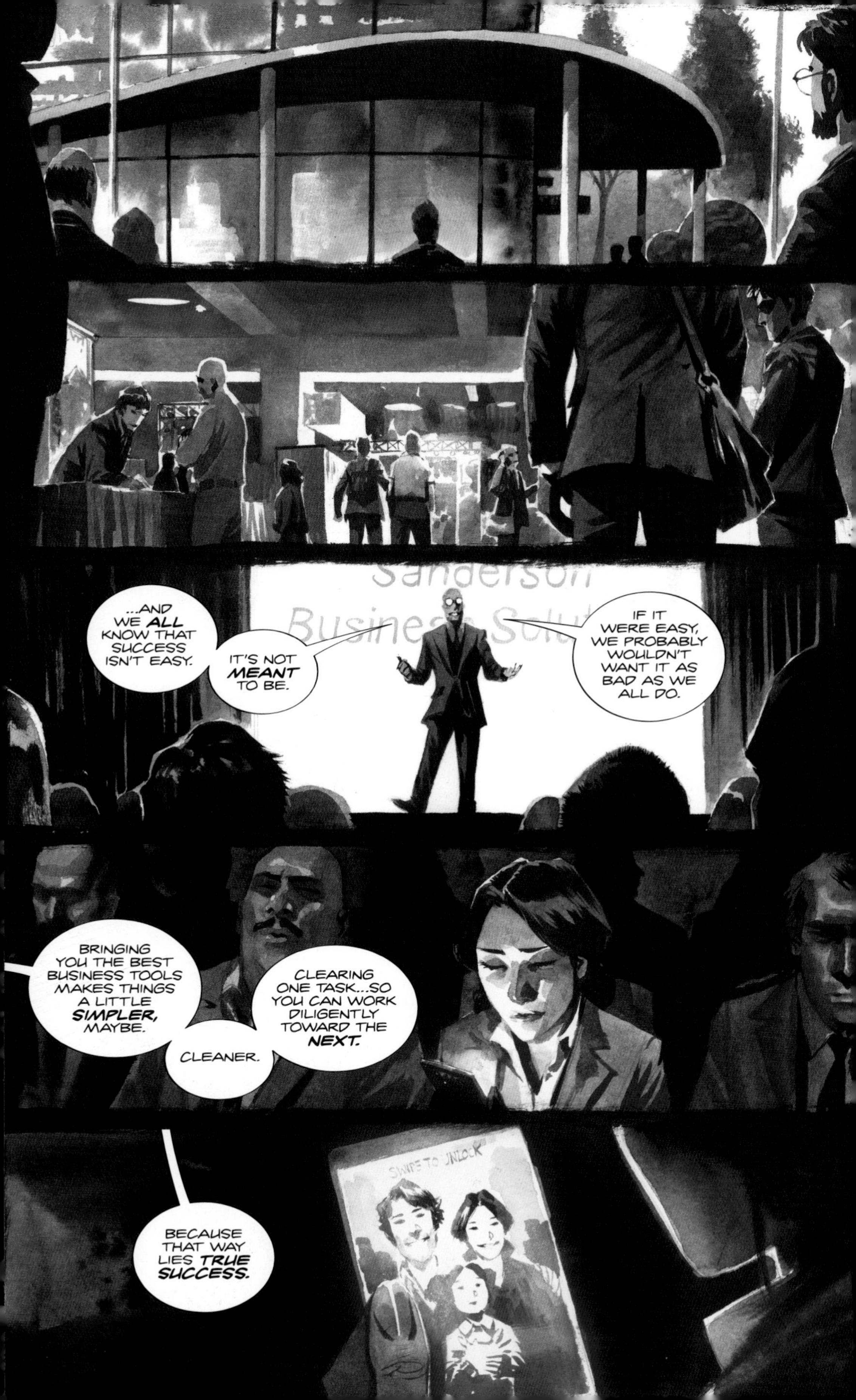
Sanderson
Business Solut
...AND WE ALL KNOW THAT SUCCESS ISN'T EASY.
IT'S NOT MEANT TO BE.
IF IT WERE EASY, WE PROBABLY WOULDN'T WANT IT AS BAD AS WE ALL DO.
BRINGING YOU THE BEST BUSINESS TOOLS MAKES THINGS A LITTLE SIMPLER, MAYBE.
CLEANER.
CLEARING ONE TASK...SO YOU CAN WORK DILIGENTLY TOWARD THE NEXT.
BECAUSE THAT WAY LIES TRUE SUCCESS.
SWIPE TO UNLOCK

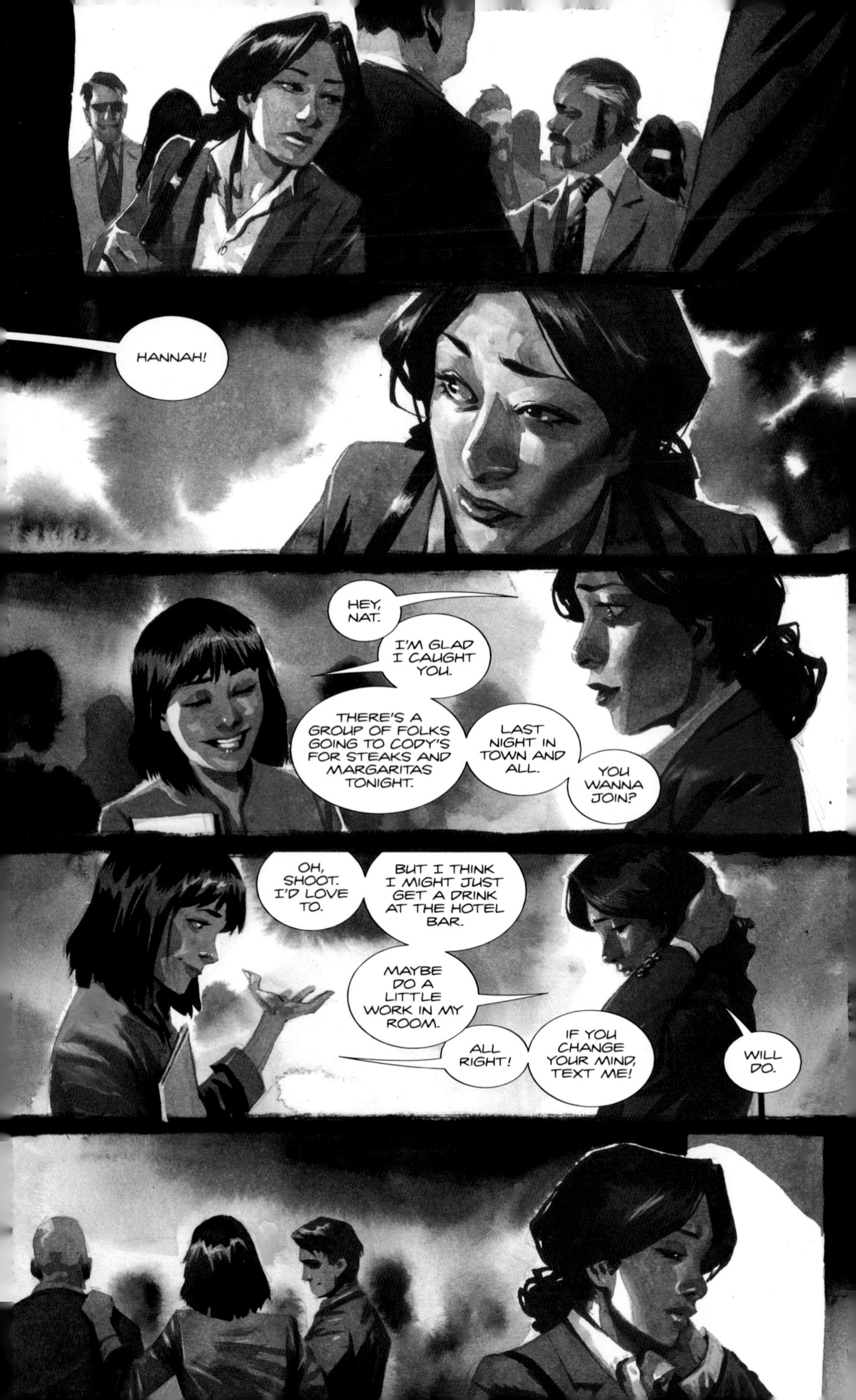
HANNAH!
HEY, NAT.
I'M GLAD I CAUGHT YOU.
THERE'S A GROUP OF FOLKS GOING TO CODY'S FOR STEAKS AND MARGARITAS TONIGHT.
LAST NIGHT IN TOWN AND ALL.
YOU WANNA JOIN?
OH, SHOOT. I'D LOVE TO.
BUT I THINK I MIGHT JUST GET A DRINK AT THE HOTEL BAR.
MAYBE DO A LITTLE WORK IN MY ROOM.
ALL RIGHT!
IF YOU CHANGE YOUR MIND, TEXT ME!
WILL DO.

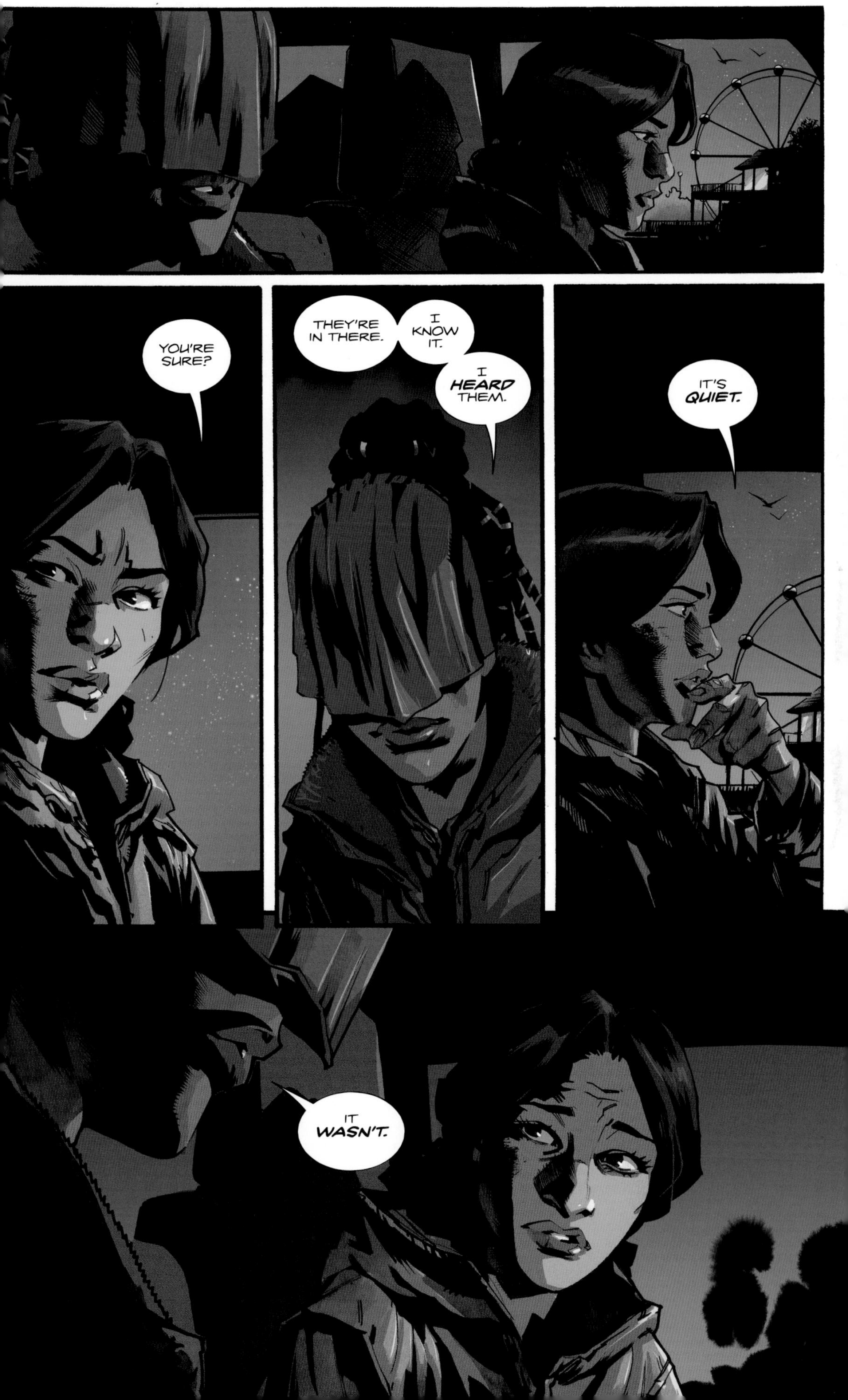
YOU'RE SURE?
THEY'RE IN THERE.
I KNOW IT.
I **HEARD** THEM.
IT'S **QUIET.**
IT **WASN'T.**

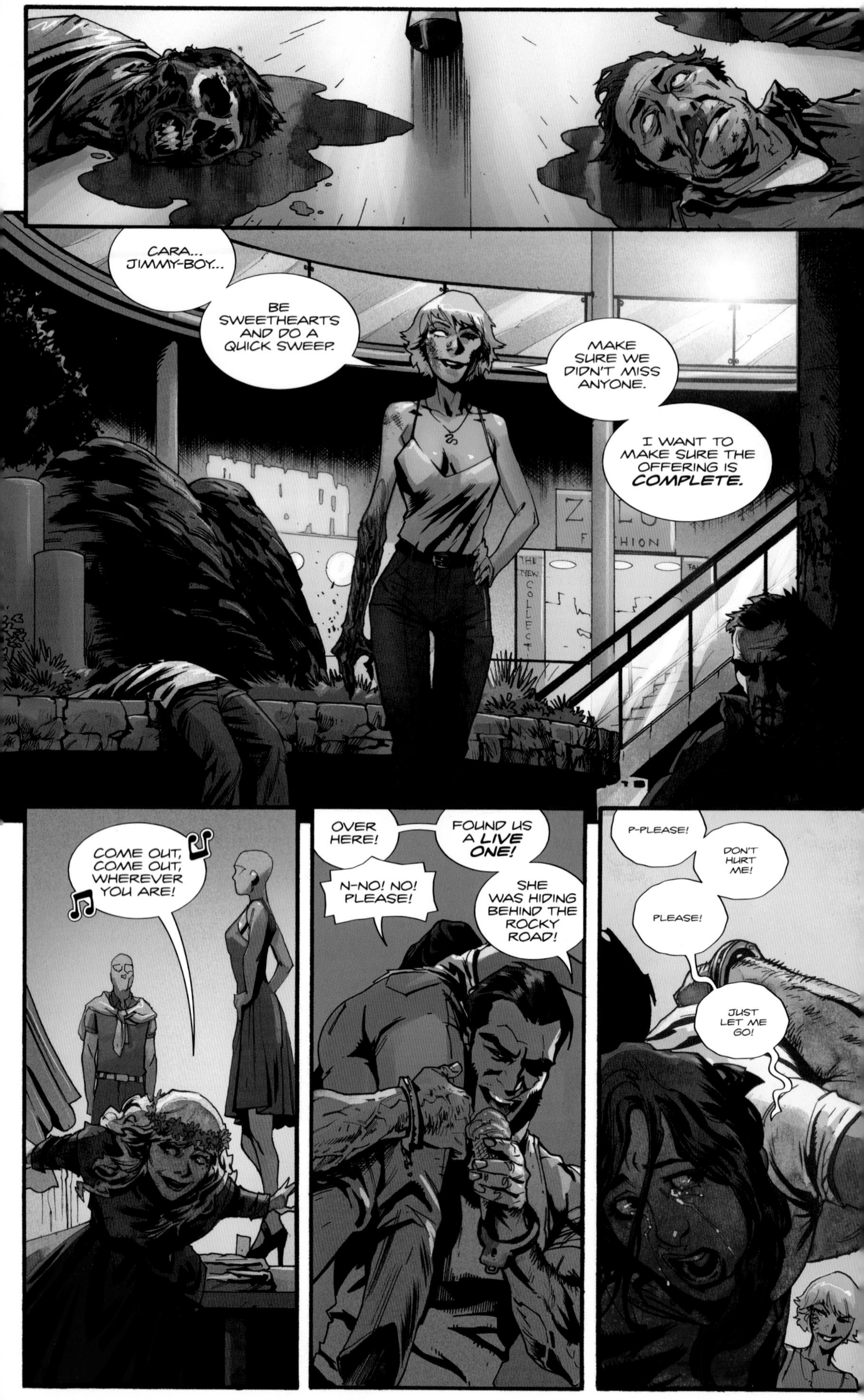
CARA... JIMMY-BOY...
BE SWEETHEARTS AND DO A QUICK SWEEP.
MAKE SURE WE DIDN'T MISS ANYONE.
I WANT TO MAKE SURE THE OFFERING IS COMPLETE.
COME OUT, COME OUT, WHEREVER YOU ARE!
OVER HERE!
FOUND US A LIVE ONE!
N-NO! NO! PLEASE!
SHE WAS HIDING BEHIND THE ROCKY ROAD!
P-PLEASE!
DON'T HURT ME!
PLEASE!
JUST LET ME GO!

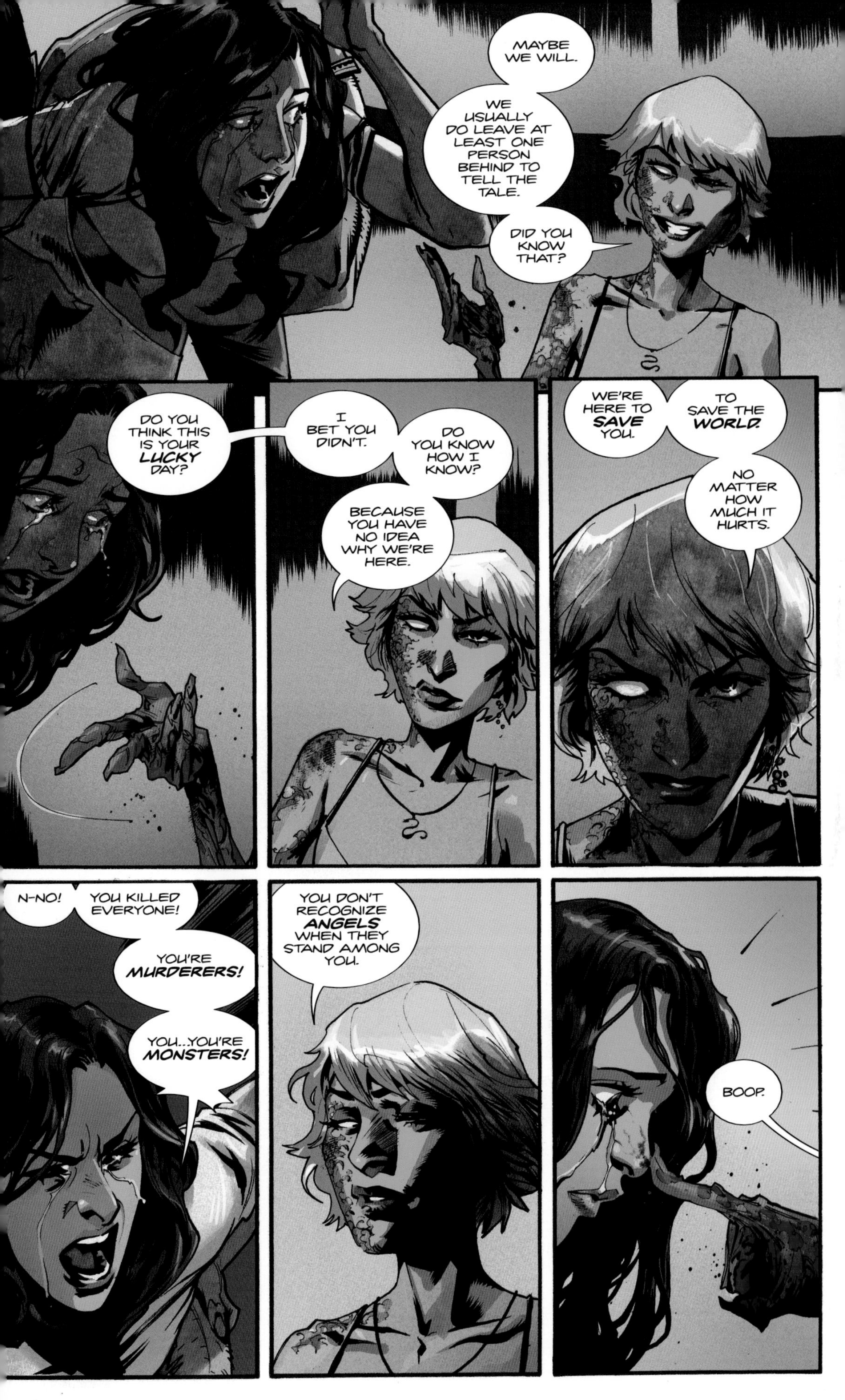

MAYBE WE WILL.
WE USUALLY DO LEAVE AT LEAST ONE PERSON BEHIND TO TELL THE TALE.
DID YOU KNOW THAT?
DO YOU THINK THIS IS YOUR LUCKY DAY?
I BET YOU DIDN'T.
DO YOU KNOW HOW I KNOW?
BECAUSE YOU HAVE NO IDEA WHY WE'RE HERE.
WE'RE HERE TO SAVE YOU.
TO SAVE THE WORLD.
NO MATTER HOW MUCH IT HURTS.
N-NO!
YOU KILLED EVERYONE!
YOU'RE MURDERERS!
YOU...YOU'RE MONSTERS!
YOU DON'T RECOGNIZE ANGELS WHEN THEY STAND AMONG YOU.
BOOP.

REEEEAAAARG!

HANNAH.

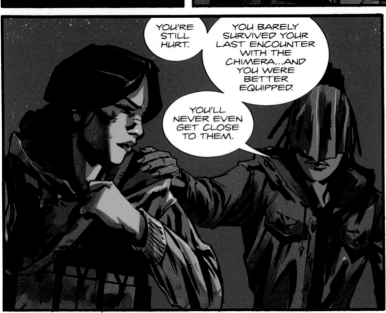

YOU'RE STILL HURT.

YOU BARELY SURVIVED YOUR LAST ENCOUNTER WITH THE CHIMERA...AND YOU WERE BETTER EQUIPPED.

YOU'LL NEVER EVEN GET CLOSE TO THEM.

I WON'T **NEED** TO GET CLOSE.

GO AROUND. DISTRACT THEM.

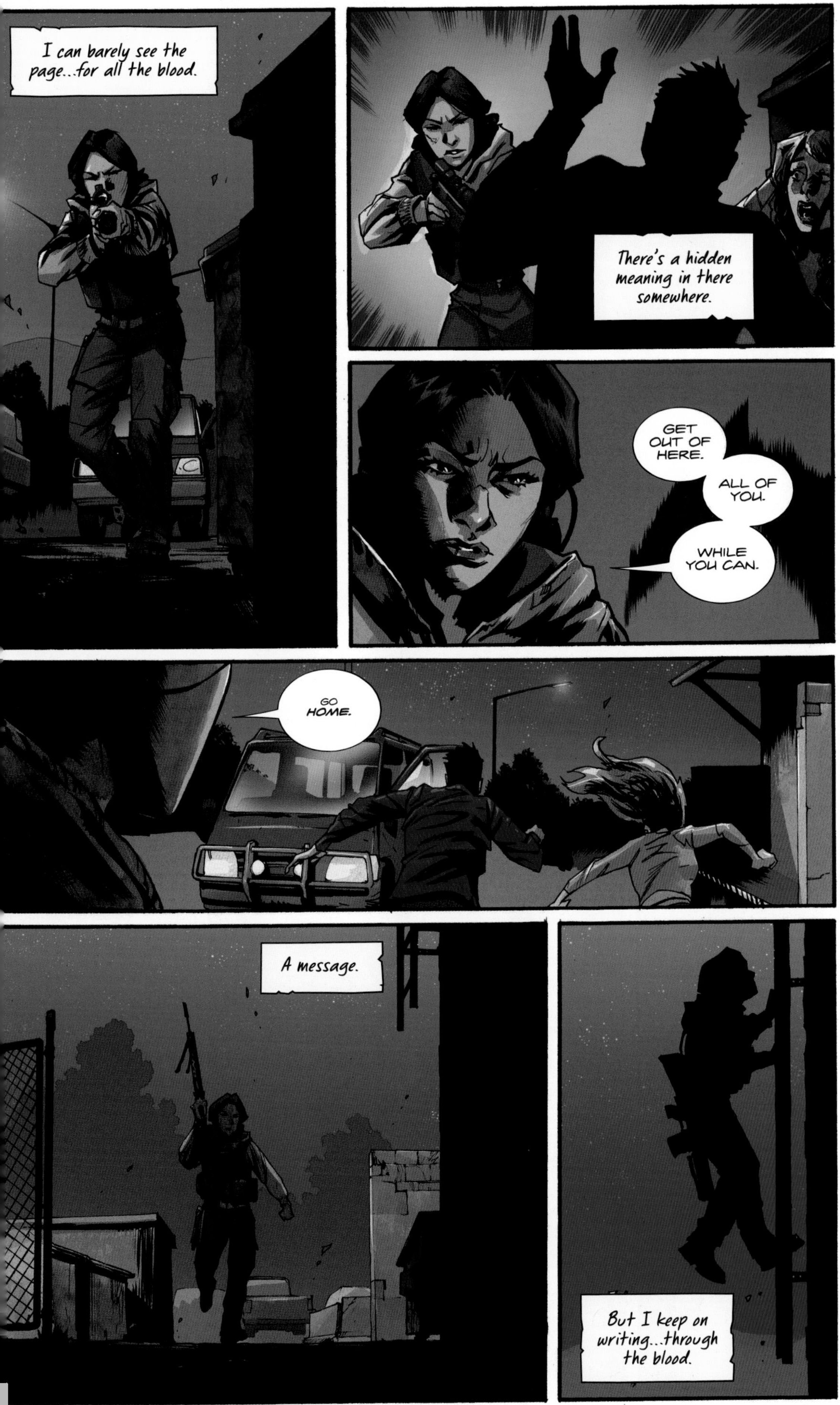
I can barely see the page...for all the blood.
There's a hidden meaning in there somewhere.
GET OUT OF HERE.
ALL OF YOU.
WHILE YOU CAN.
GO HOME.
A message.
But I keep on writing...through the blood.

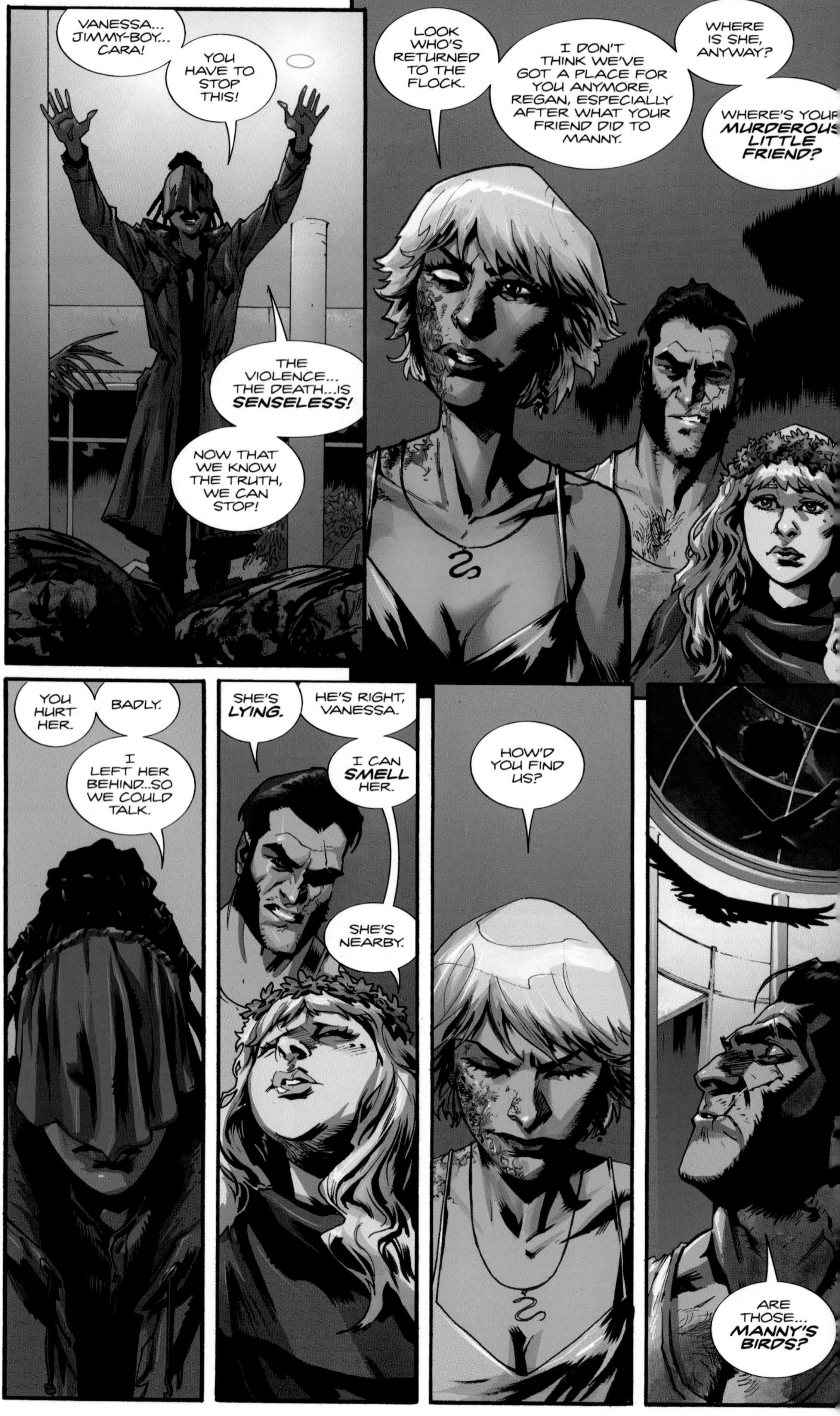
VANESSA... JIMMY-BOY... CARA!
YOU HAVE TO STOP THIS!
THE VIOLENCE... THE DEATH...IS SENSELESS!
NOW THAT WE KNOW THE TRUTH, WE CAN STOP!
LOOK WHO'S RETURNED TO THE FLOCK.
I DON'T THINK WE'VE GOT A PLACE FOR YOU ANYMORE, REGAN, ESPECIALLY AFTER WHAT YOUR FRIEND DID TO MANNY.
WHERE IS SHE, ANYWAY?
WHERE'S YOUR MURDEROUS LITTLE FRIEND?
YOU HURT HER.
BADLY.
I LEFT HER BEHIND...SO WE COULD TALK.
SHE'S LYING.
HE'S RIGHT, VANESSA.
I CAN SMELL HER.
SHE'S NEARBY.
HOW'D YOU FIND US?
ARE THOSE... MANNY'S BIRDS?

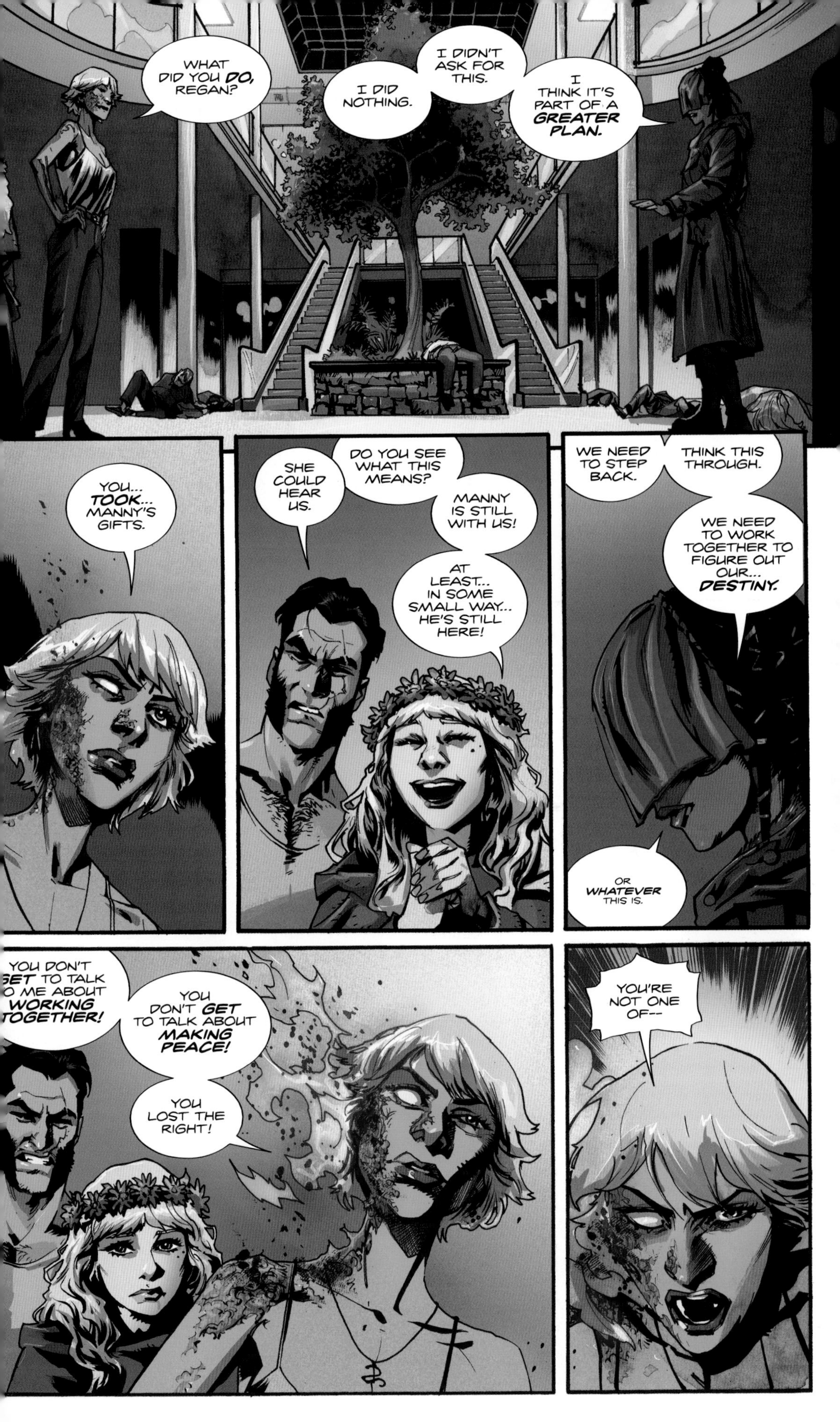
WHAT DID YOU DO, REGAN?
I DID NOTHING.
I DIDN'T ASK FOR THIS.
I THINK IT'S PART OF A GREATER PLAN.
YOU... TOOK... MANNY'S GIFTS.
SHE COULD HEAR US.
DO YOU SEE WHAT THIS MEANS?
MANNY IS STILL WITH US!
AT LEAST... IN SOME SMALL WAY... HE'S STILL HERE!
WE NEED TO STEP BACK.
THINK THIS THROUGH.
WE NEED TO WORK TOGETHER TO FIGURE OUT OUR... DESTINY.
OR WHATEVER THIS IS.
YOU DON'T GET TO TALK TO ME ABOUT WORKING TOGETHER!
YOU DON'T GET TO TALK ABOUT MAKING PEACE!
YOU LOST THE RIGHT!
YOU'RE NOT ONE OF--

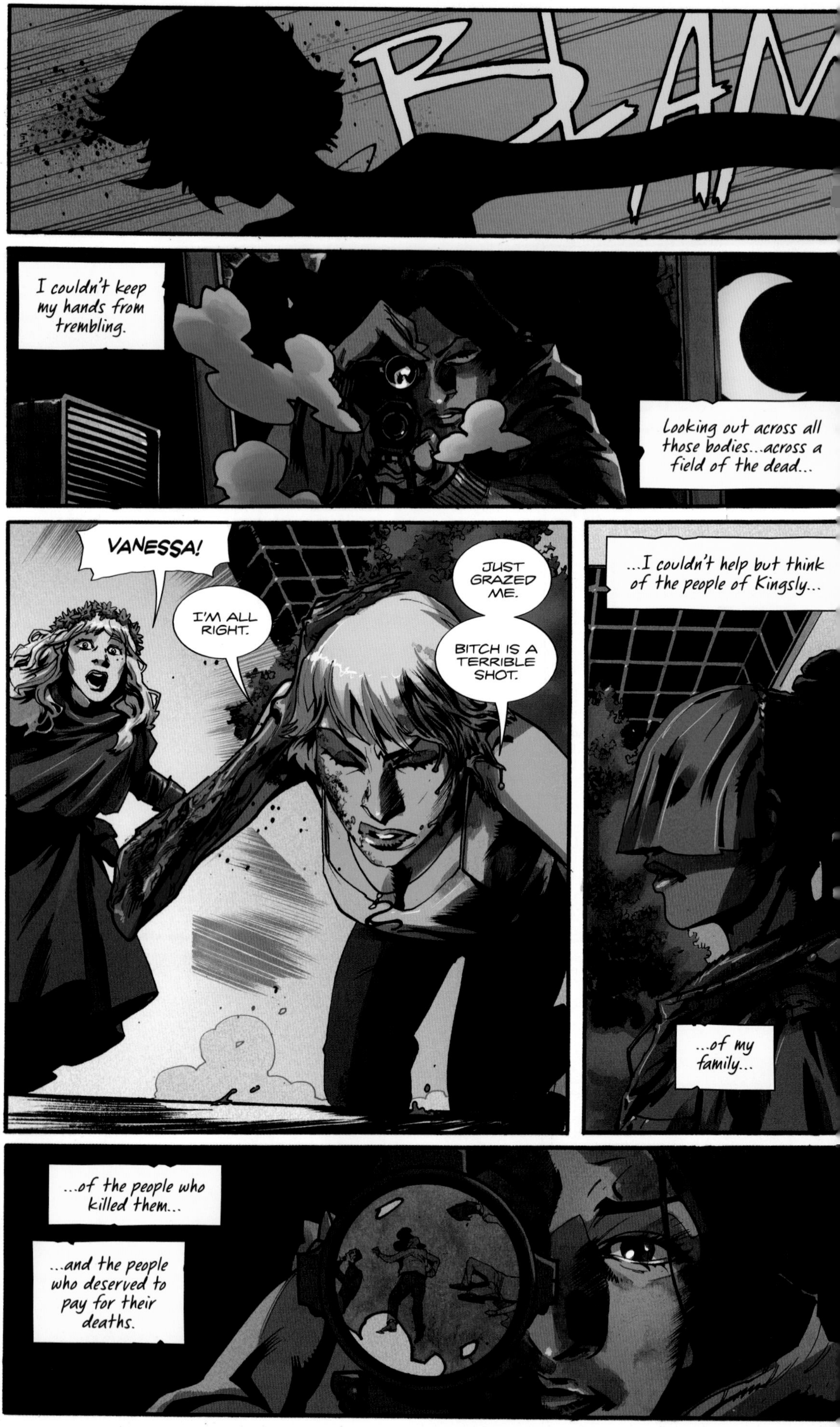
BLAM
I couldn't keep my hands from trembling.
Looking out across all those bodies...across a field of the dead...
VANESSA!
I'M ALL RIGHT.
JUST GRAZED ME.
BITCH IS A TERRIBLE SHOT.
...I couldn't help but think of the people of Kingsly...
...of my family...
...of the people who killed them...
...and the people who deserved to pay for their deaths.

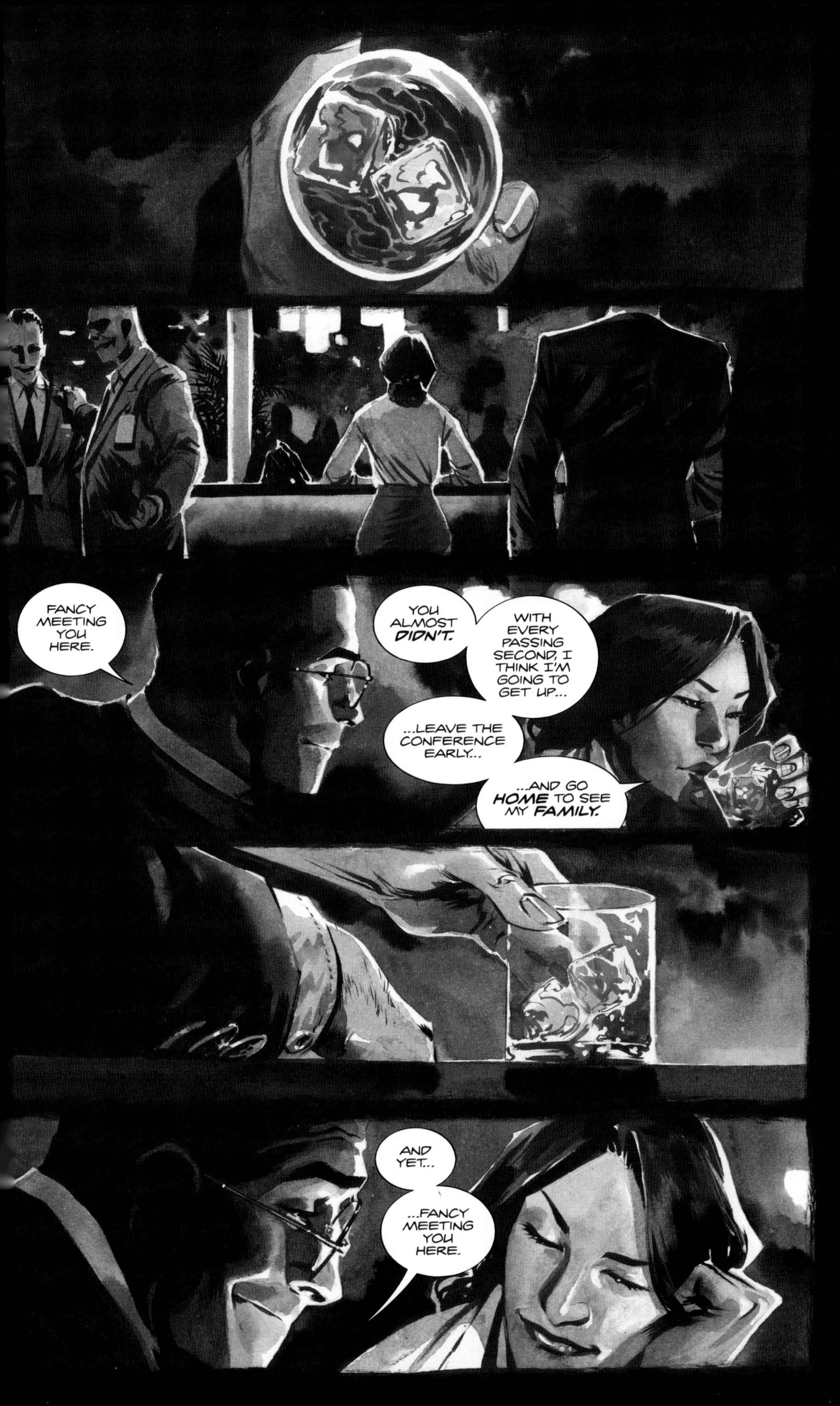

FANCY MEETING YOU HERE.
YOU ALMOST *DIDN'T.*
WITH EVERY PASSING SECOND, I THINK I'M GOING TO GET UP...
...LEAVE THE CONFERENCE EARLY...
...AND GO *HOME* TO SEE MY *FAMILY.*
AND YET...
...FANCY MEETING YOU HERE.

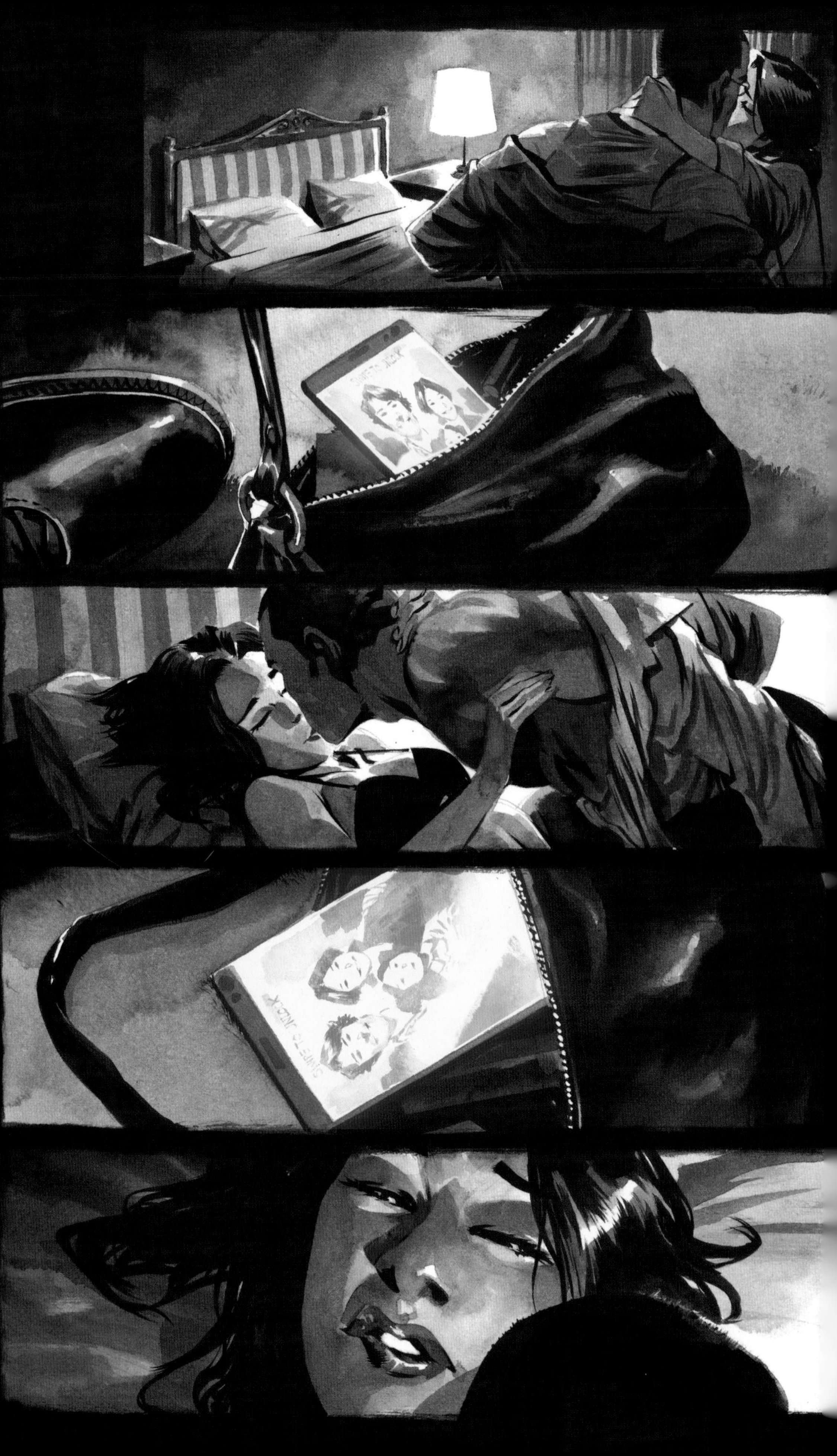

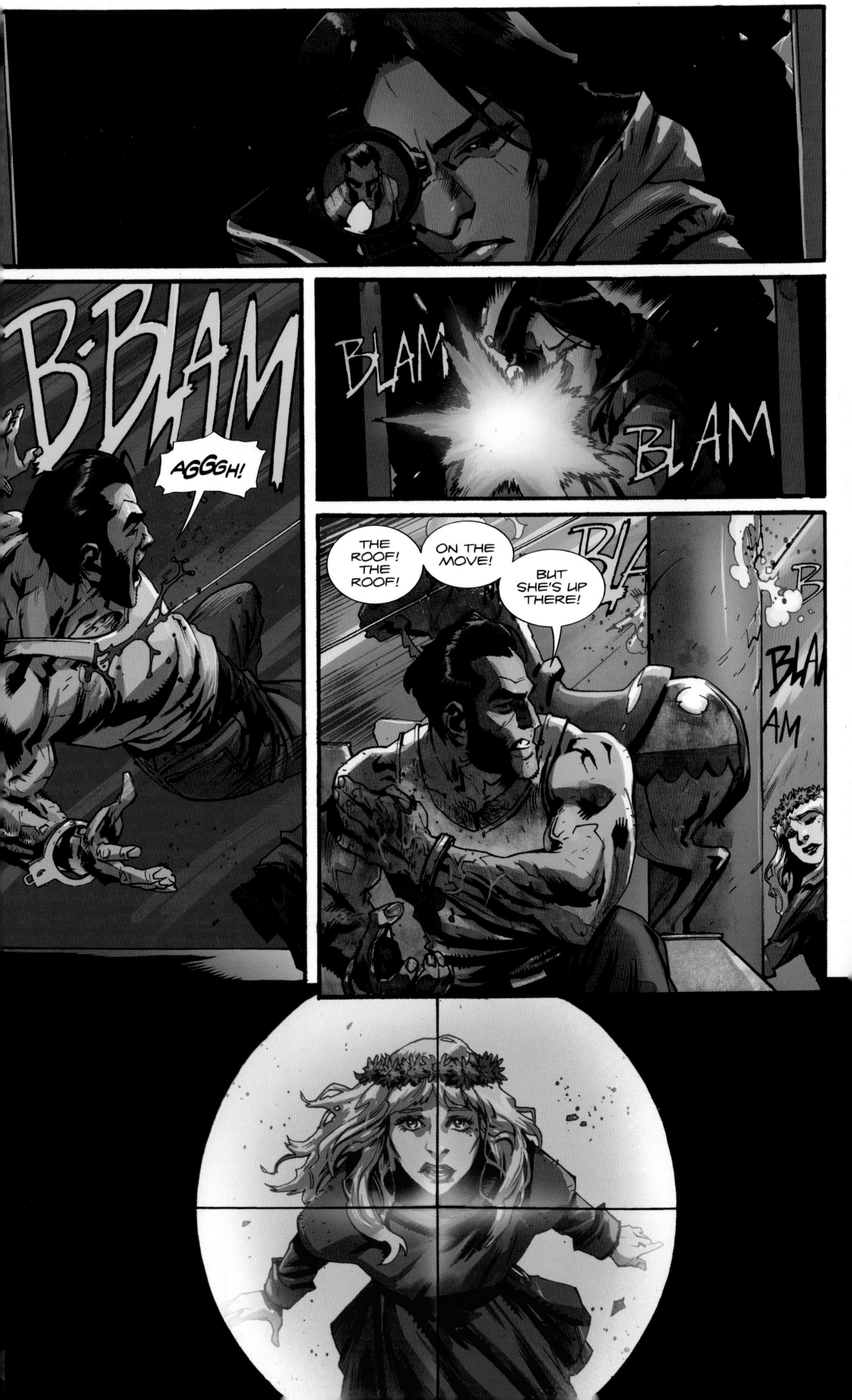
B-BLAM
AGGGH!
BLAM
BLAM
THE ROOF! THE ROOF!
ON THE MOVE!
BUT SHE'S UP THERE!

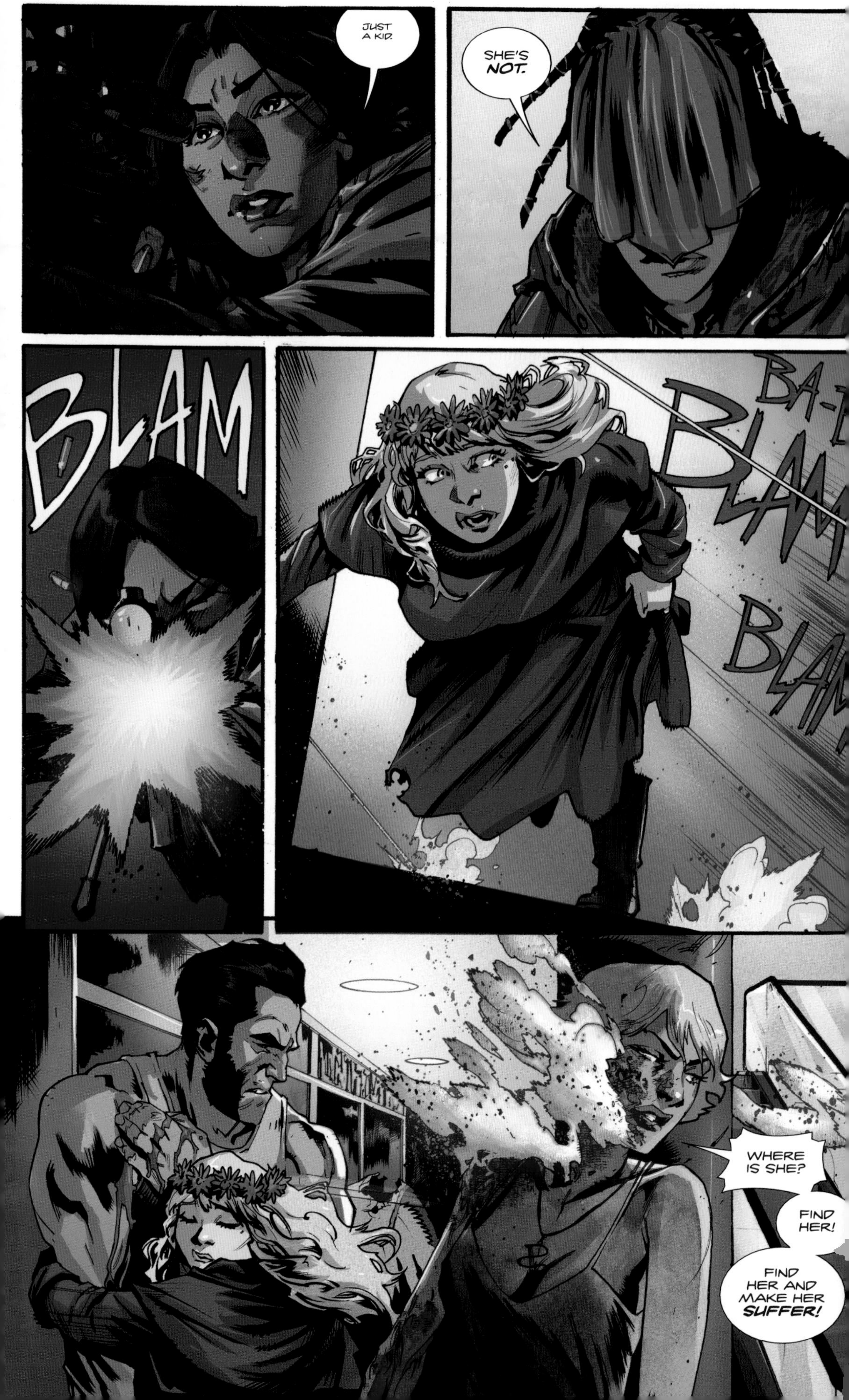
JUST A KID.
SHE'S NOT.
BLAM
BA-BLAM BLAM
BLAM
WHERE IS SHE?
FIND HER!
FIND HER AND MAKE HER SUFFER!

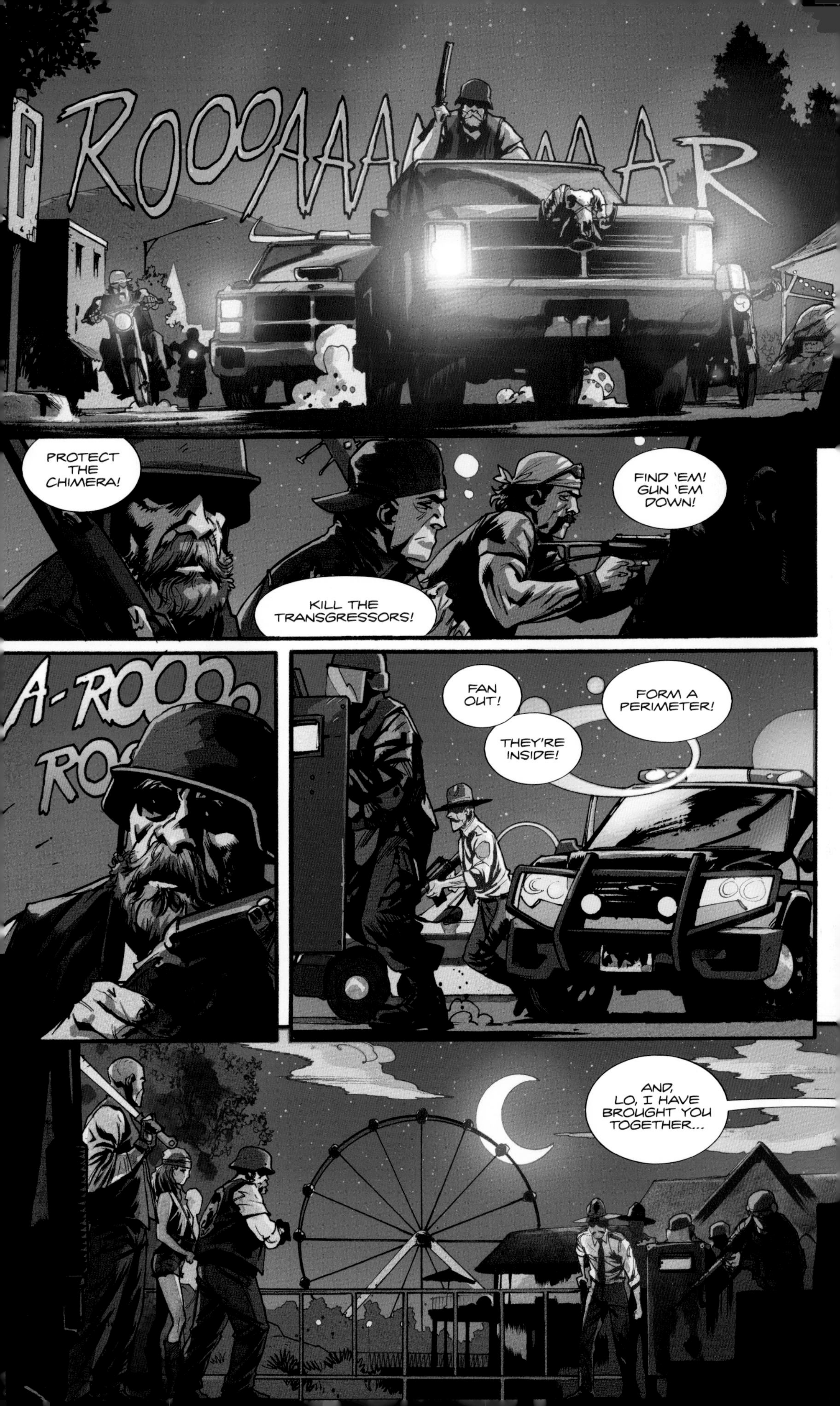
ROOOAAAAAAAAAR
PROTECT THE CHIMERA!
KILL THE TRANSGRESSORS!
FIND 'EM! GUN 'EM DOWN!
A-ROOOO
FAN OUT!
THEY'RE INSIDE!
FORM A PERIMETER!
AND, LO, I HAVE BROUGHT YOU TOGETHER...

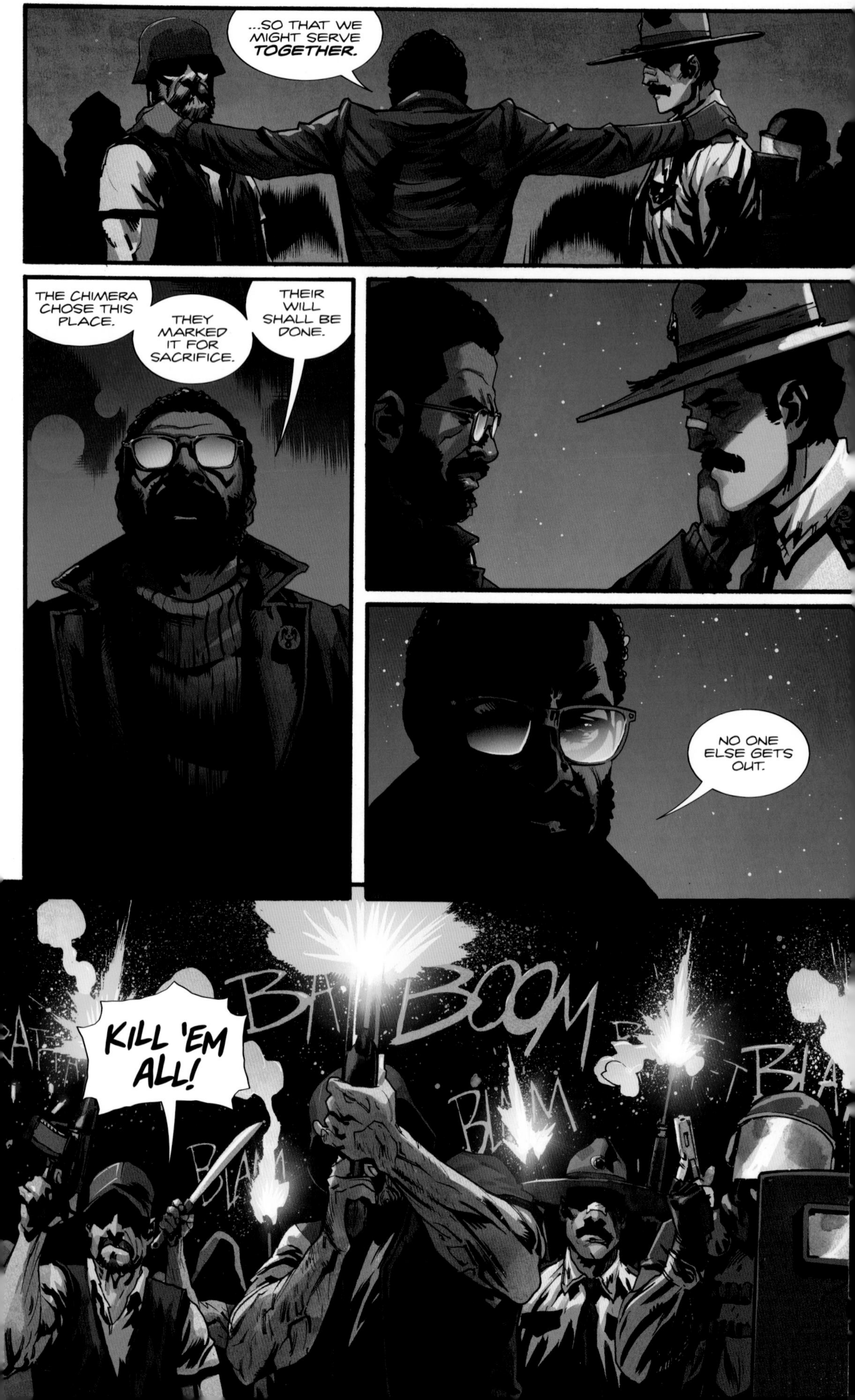
...SO THAT WE MIGHT SERVE *TOGETHER.*
THE CHIMERA CHOSE THIS PLACE.
THEY MARKED IT FOR SACRIFICE.
THEIR WILL SHALL BE DONE.
NO ONE ELSE GETS OUT.
BOOM
BLAM
KILL 'EM ALL!
BLAM

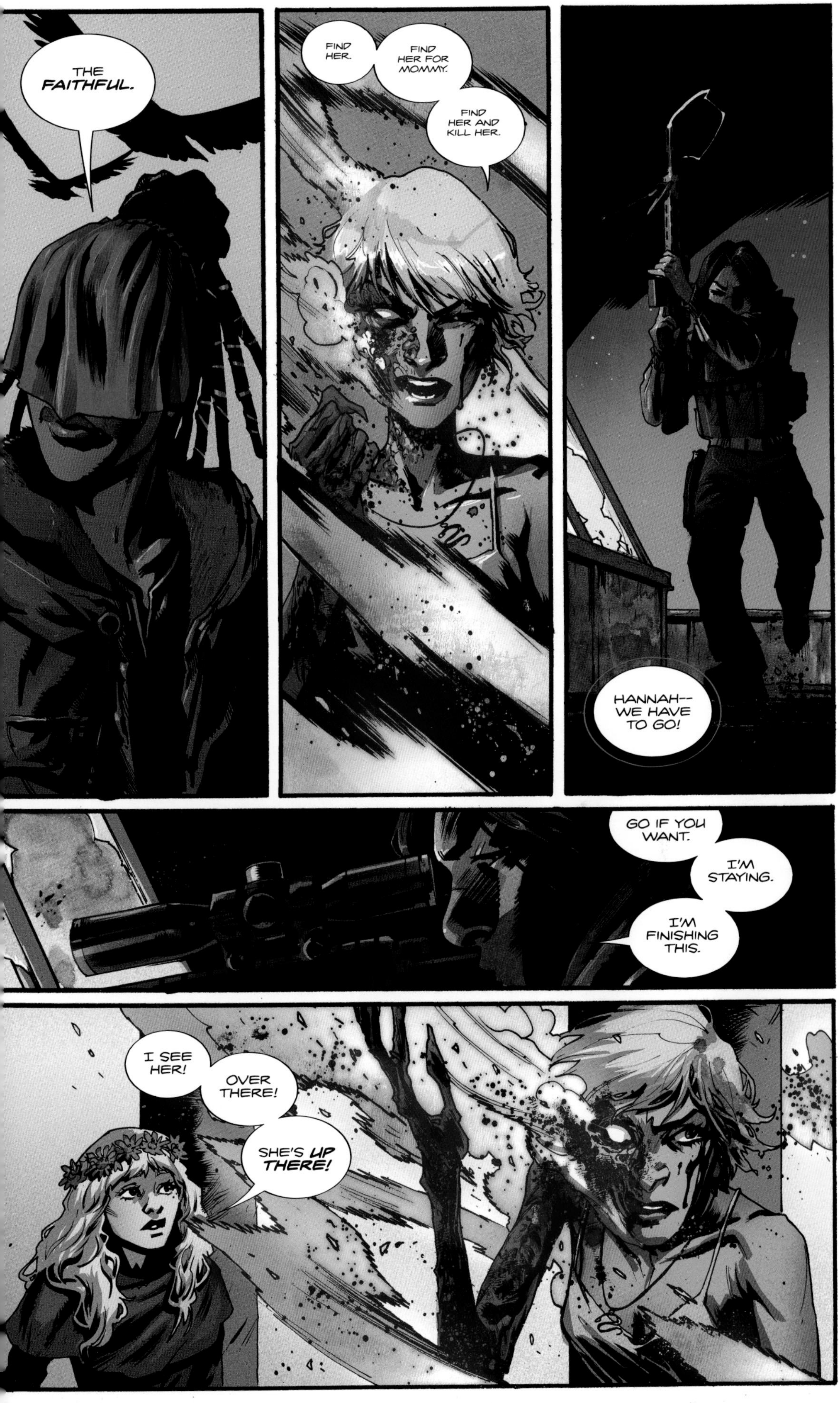

THE *FAITHFUL.*
FIND HER.
FIND HER FOR MOMMY.
FIND HER AND KILL HER.
HANNAH-- WE HAVE TO GO!
GO IF YOU WANT.
I'M STAYING.
I'M FINISHING THIS.
I SEE HER!
OVER THERE!
SHE'S *UP THERE!*

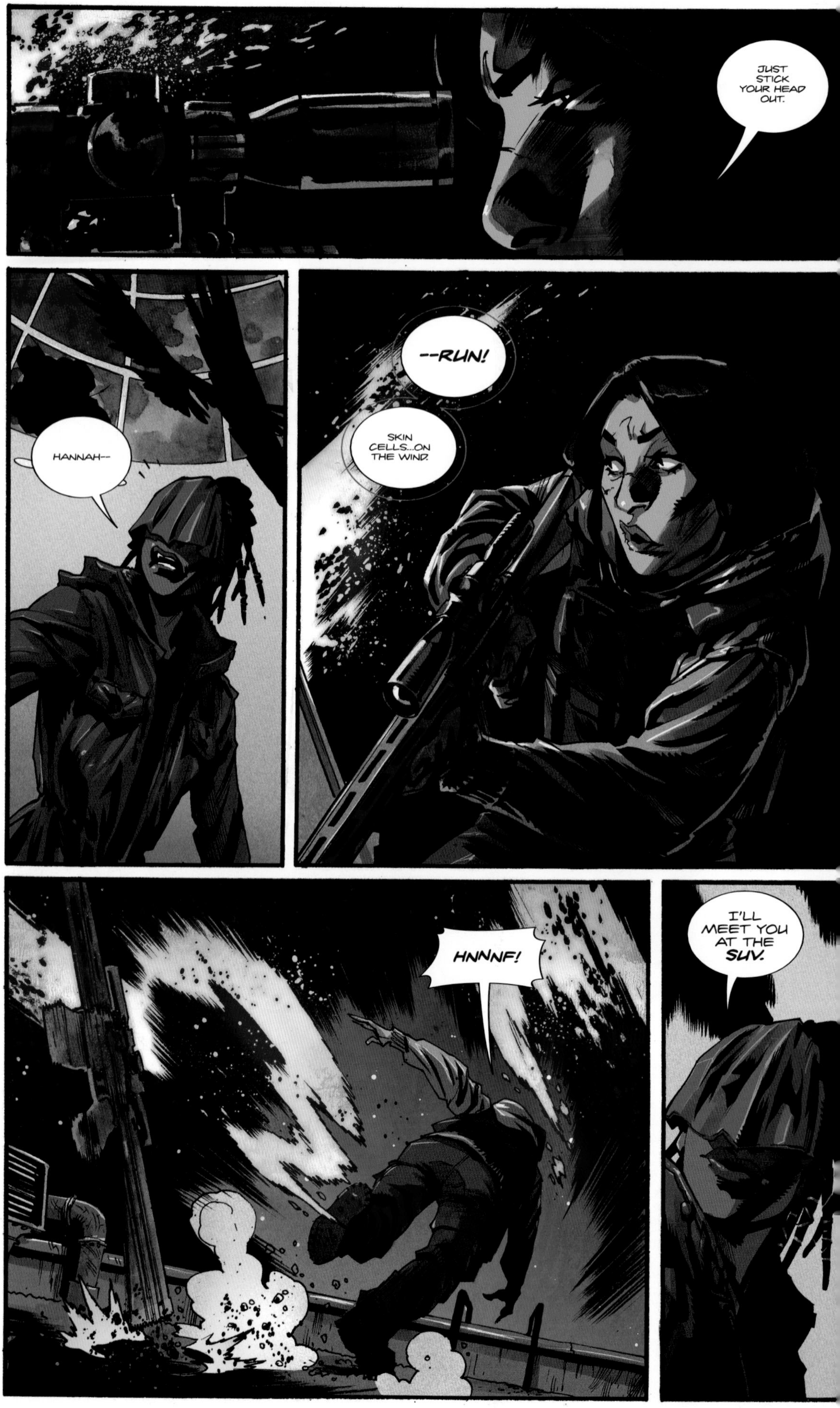
JUST STICK YOUR HEAD OUT.
HANNAH--
--RUN!
SKIN CELLS...ON THE WIND.
HNNNF!
I'LL MEET YOU AT THE SUV.

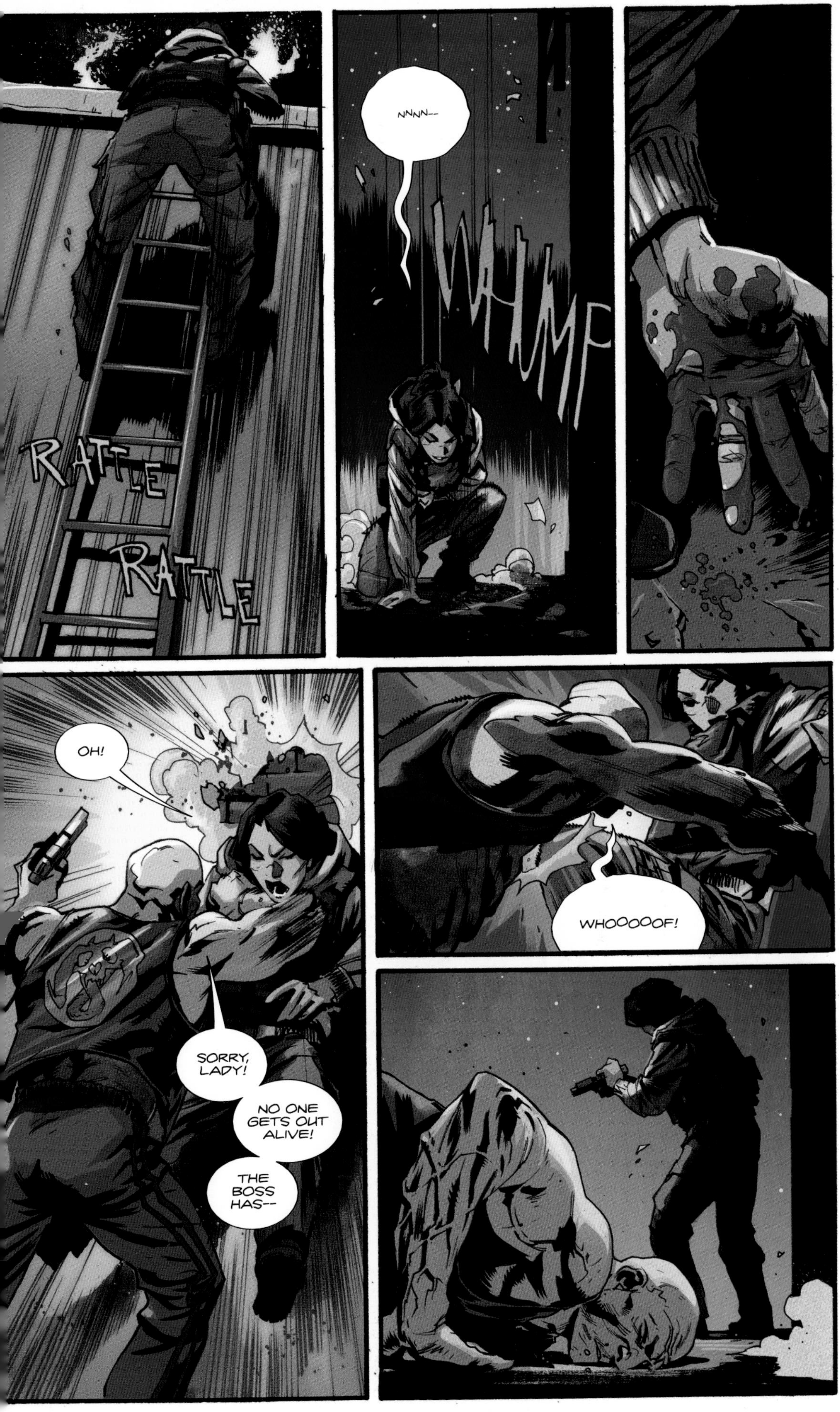
RATTLE
RATTLE
NNNN--
WHUMP
OH!
SORRY, LADY!
NO ONE GETS OUT ALIVE!
THE BOSS HAS--
WHOOOOOF!

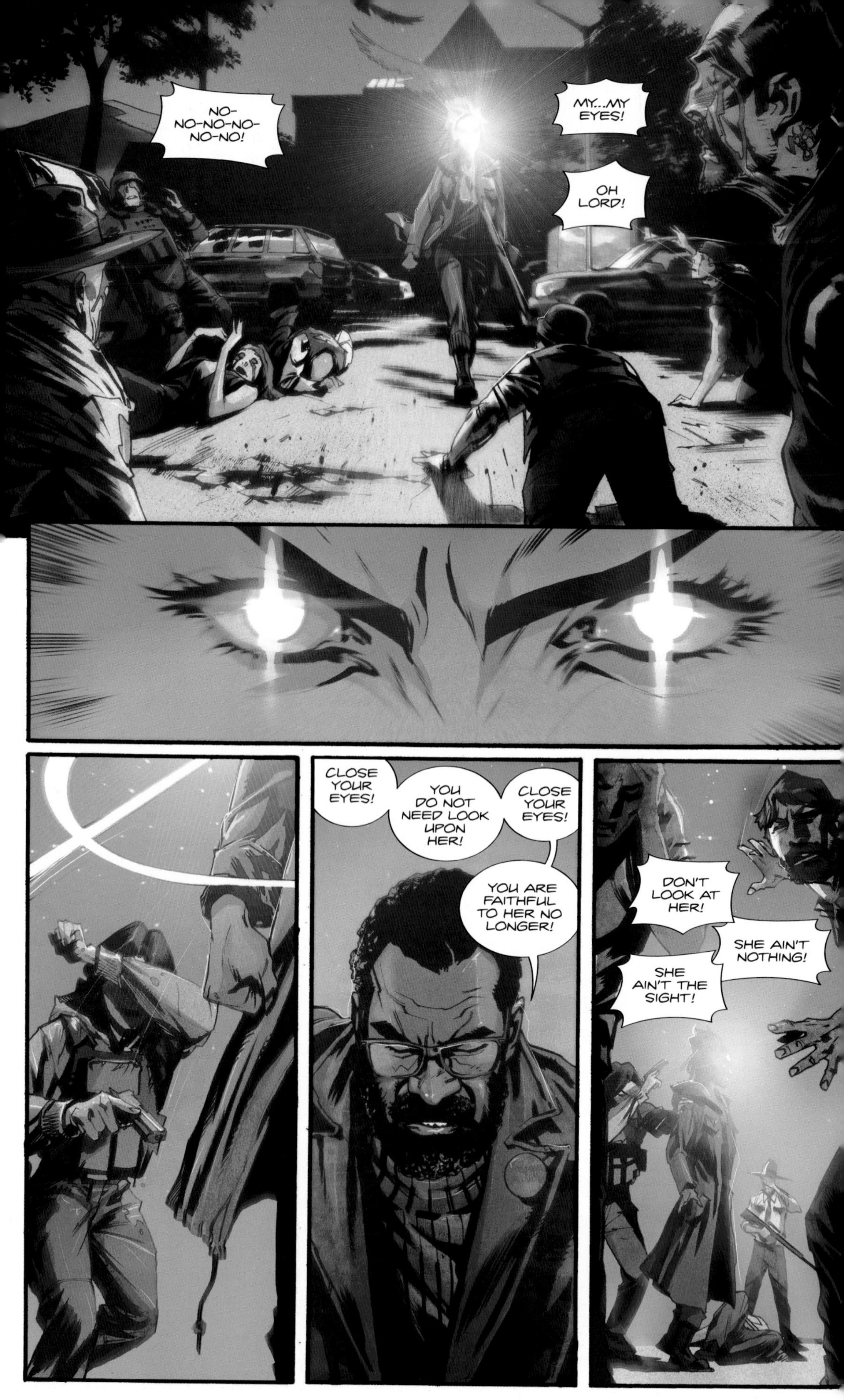
NO-
NO-NO-NO-NO-NO-NO!
MY...MY EYES!
OH LORD!
CLOSE YOUR EYES!
YOU DO NOT NEED LOOK UPON HER!
CLOSE YOUR EYES!
YOU ARE FAITHFUL TO HER NO LONGER!
DON'T LOOK AT HER!
SHE AIN'T NOTHING!
SHE AIN'T THE SIGHT!

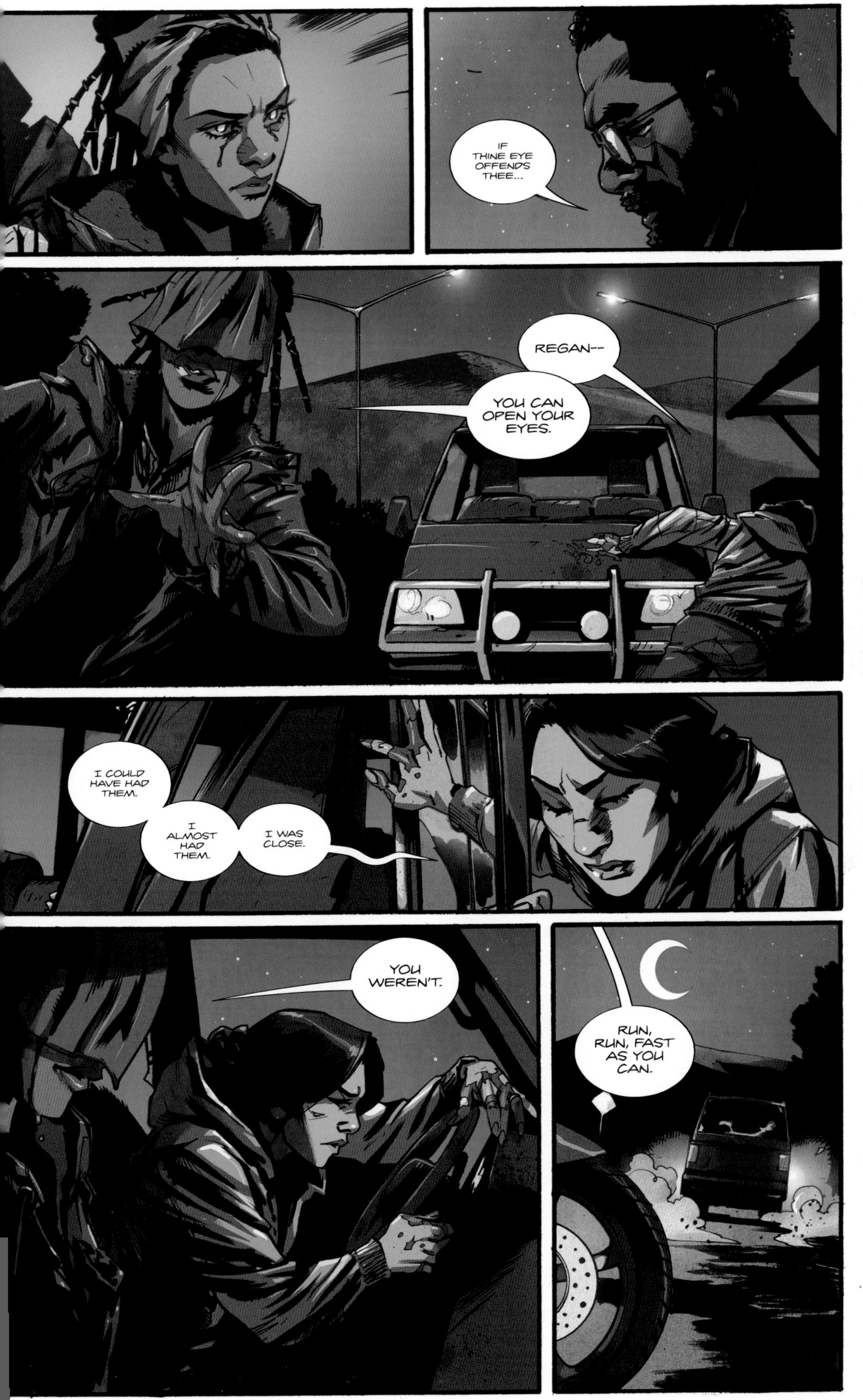
IF THINE EYE OFFENDS THEE...
REGAN--
YOU CAN OPEN YOUR EYES.
I COULD HAVE HAD THEM.
I ALMOST HAD THEM.
I WAS CLOSE.
YOU WEREN'T.
RUN, RUN, FAST AS YOU CAN.

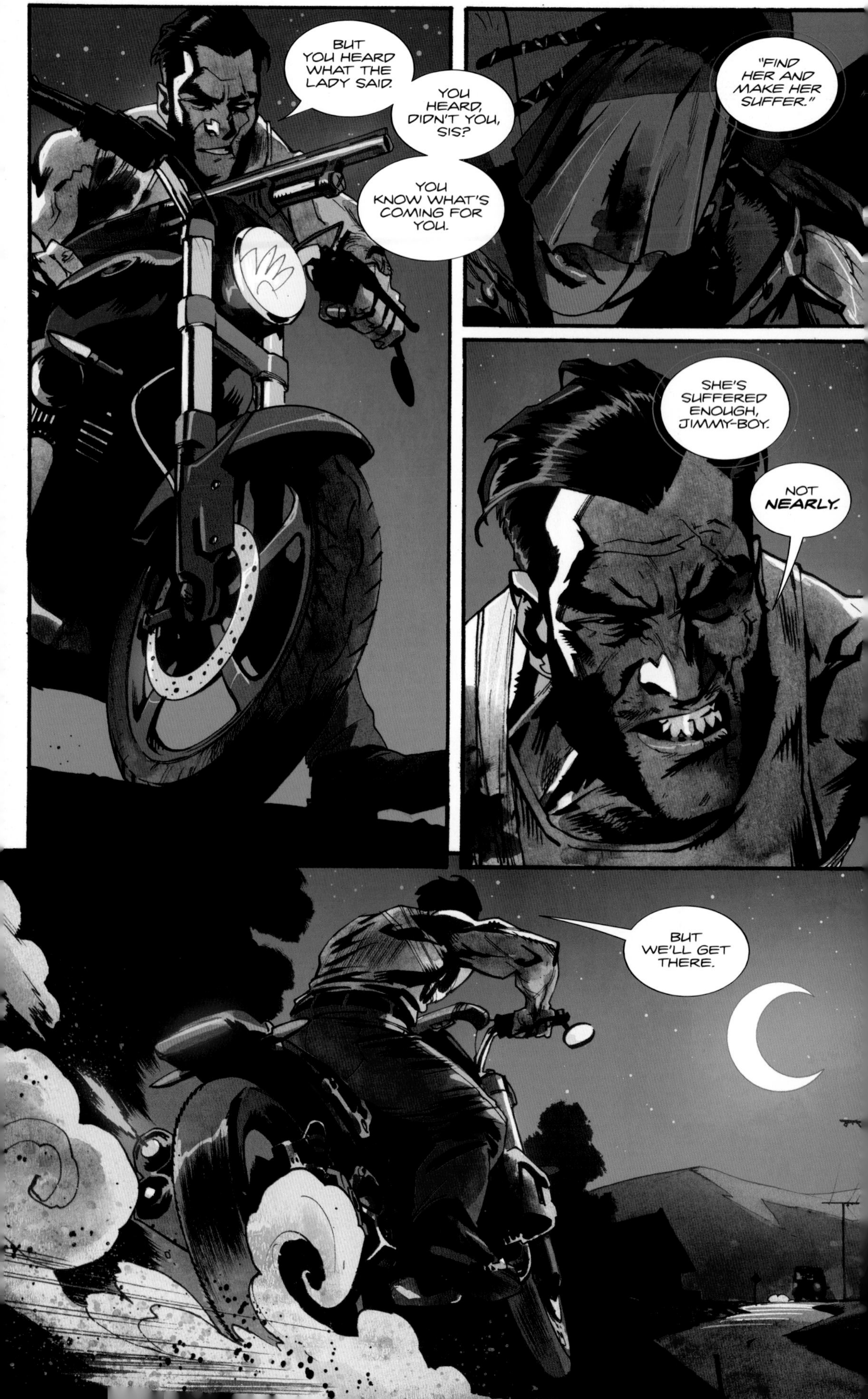
BUT YOU HEARD WHAT THE LADY SAID.
YOU HEARD, DIDN'T YOU, SIS?
YOU KNOW WHAT'S COMING FOR YOU.
"FIND HER AND MAKE HER SUFFER."
SHE'S SUFFERED ENOUGH, JIMMY-BOY.
NOT **NEARLY.**
BUT WE'LL GET THERE.

CHAPTER SEVEN

OFFERINGS
TO THE CHIMERA

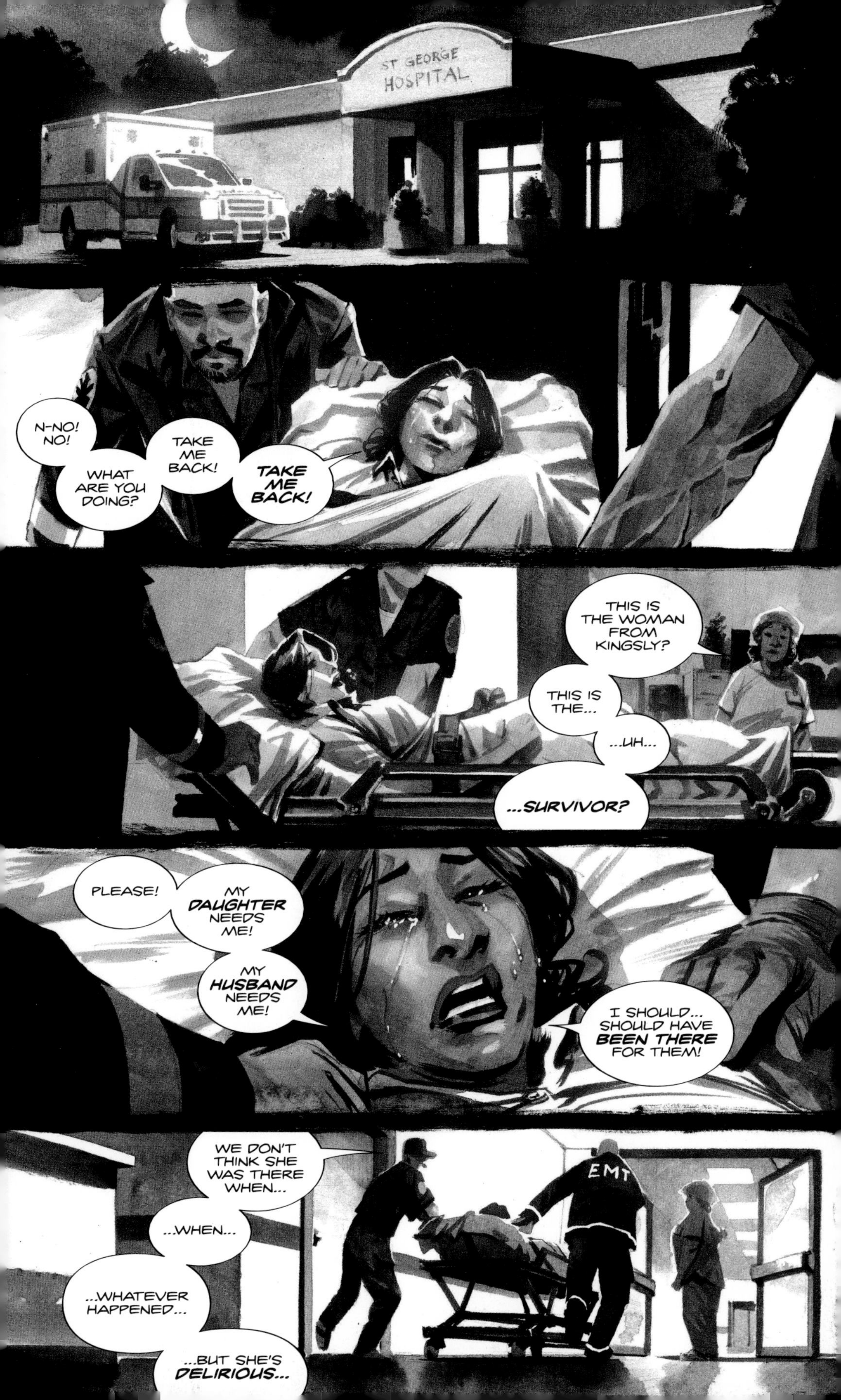

ST GEORGE HOSPITAL
N-NO! NO!
WHAT ARE YOU DOING?
TAKE ME BACK!
TAKE ME BACK!
THIS IS THE WOMAN FROM KINGSLY?
THIS IS THE...
...UH...
...SURVIVOR?
PLEASE!
MY DAUGHTER NEEDS ME!
MY HUSBAND NEEDS ME!
I SHOULD... SHOULD HAVE BEEN THERE FOR THEM!
WE DON'T THINK SHE WAS THERE WHEN...
...WHEN...
...WHATEVER HAPPENED...
...BUT SHE'S DELIRIOUS...
EMT

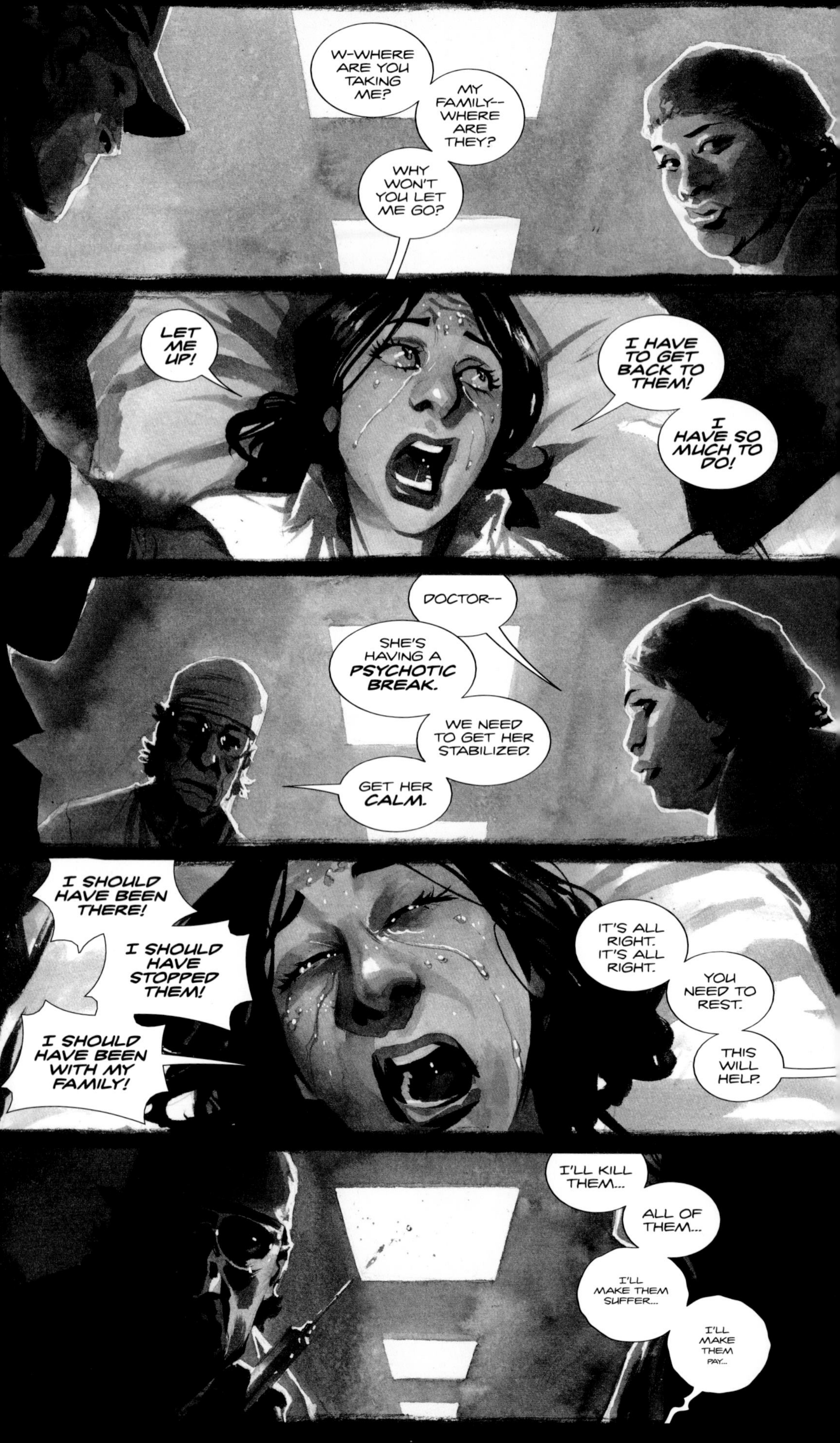
W-WHERE ARE YOU TAKING ME?
MY FAMILY-- WHERE ARE THEY?
WHY WON'T YOU LET ME GO?
LET ME UP!
I HAVE TO GET BACK TO THEM!
I HAVE SO MUCH TO DO!
DOCTOR--
SHE'S HAVING A PSYCHOTIC BREAK.
WE NEED TO GET HER STABILIZED.
GET HER CALM.
I SHOULD HAVE BEEN THERE!
I SHOULD HAVE STOPPED THEM!
I SHOULD HAVE BEEN WITH MY FAMILY!
IT'S ALL RIGHT. IT'S ALL RIGHT.
YOU NEED TO REST.
THIS WILL HELP.
I'LL KILL THEM...
ALL OF THEM...
I'LL MAKE THEM SUFFER...
I'LL MAKE THEM PAY...

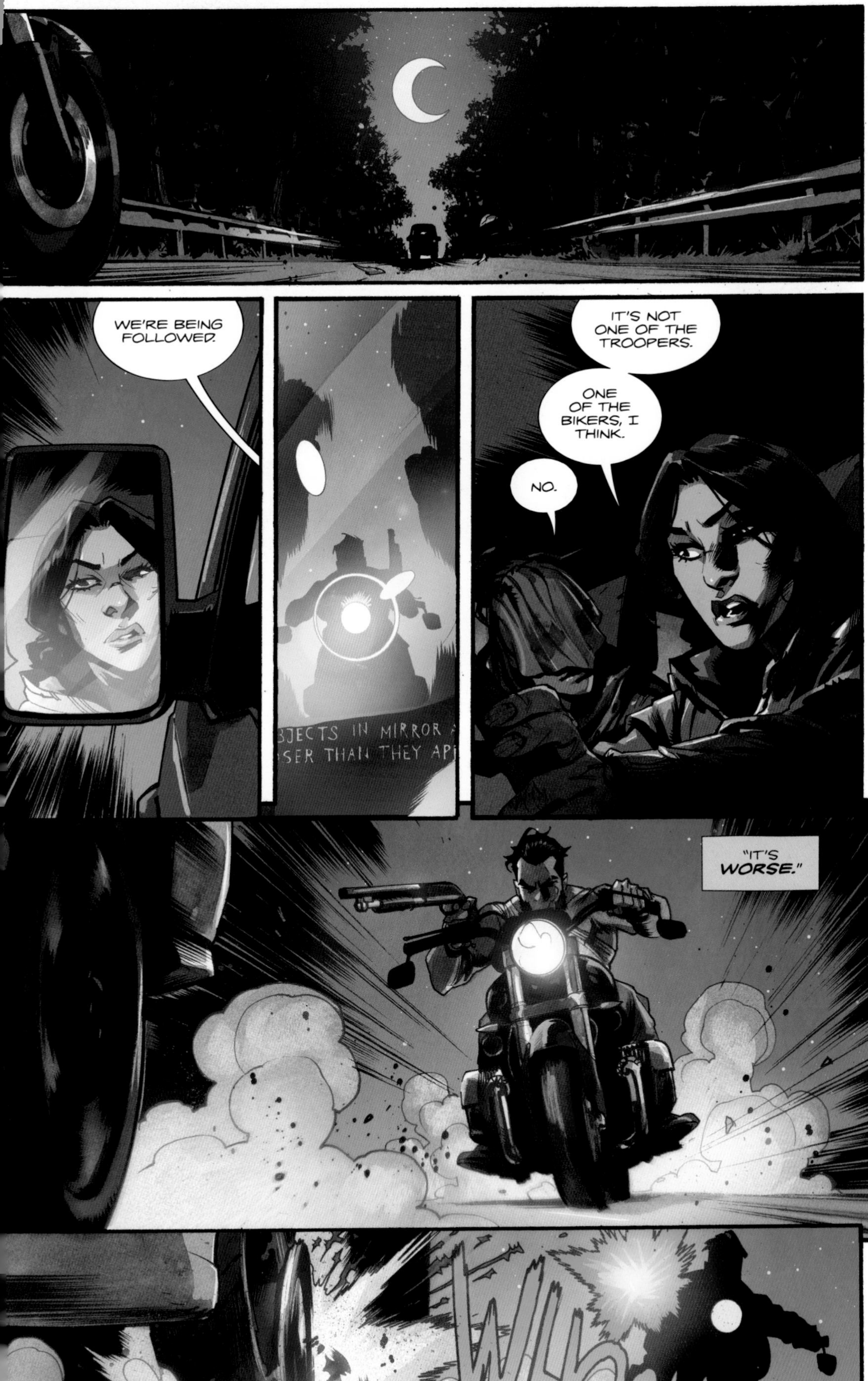
WE'RE BEING FOLLOWED.
BJECTS IN MIRROR A
SER THAN THEY AP
IT'S NOT ONE OF THE TROOPERS.
ONE OF THE BIKERS, I THINK.
NO.
"IT'S WORSE."
WHOOM

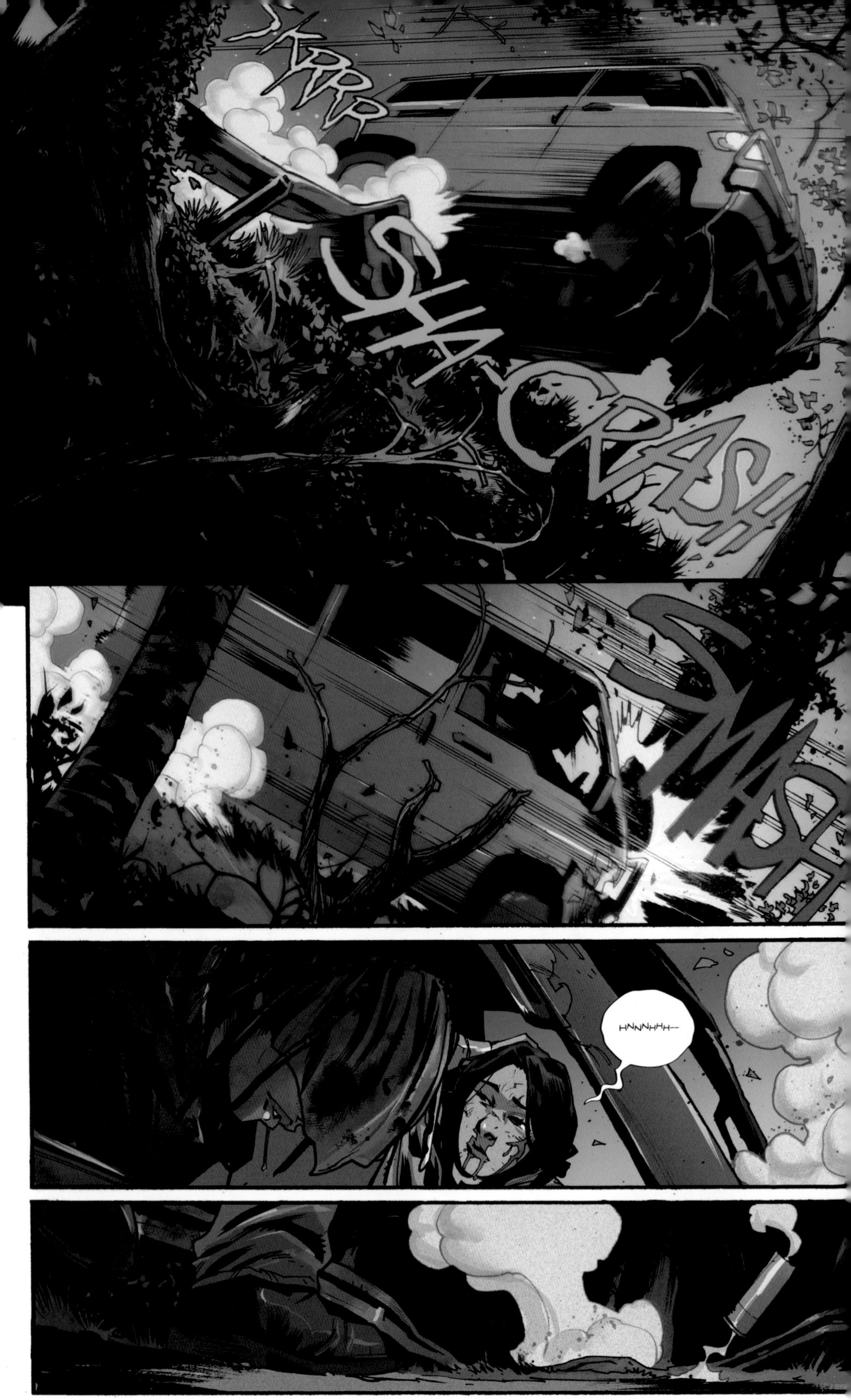
KRRR
SHA-CRASH
SMASH
HNNNHHH--

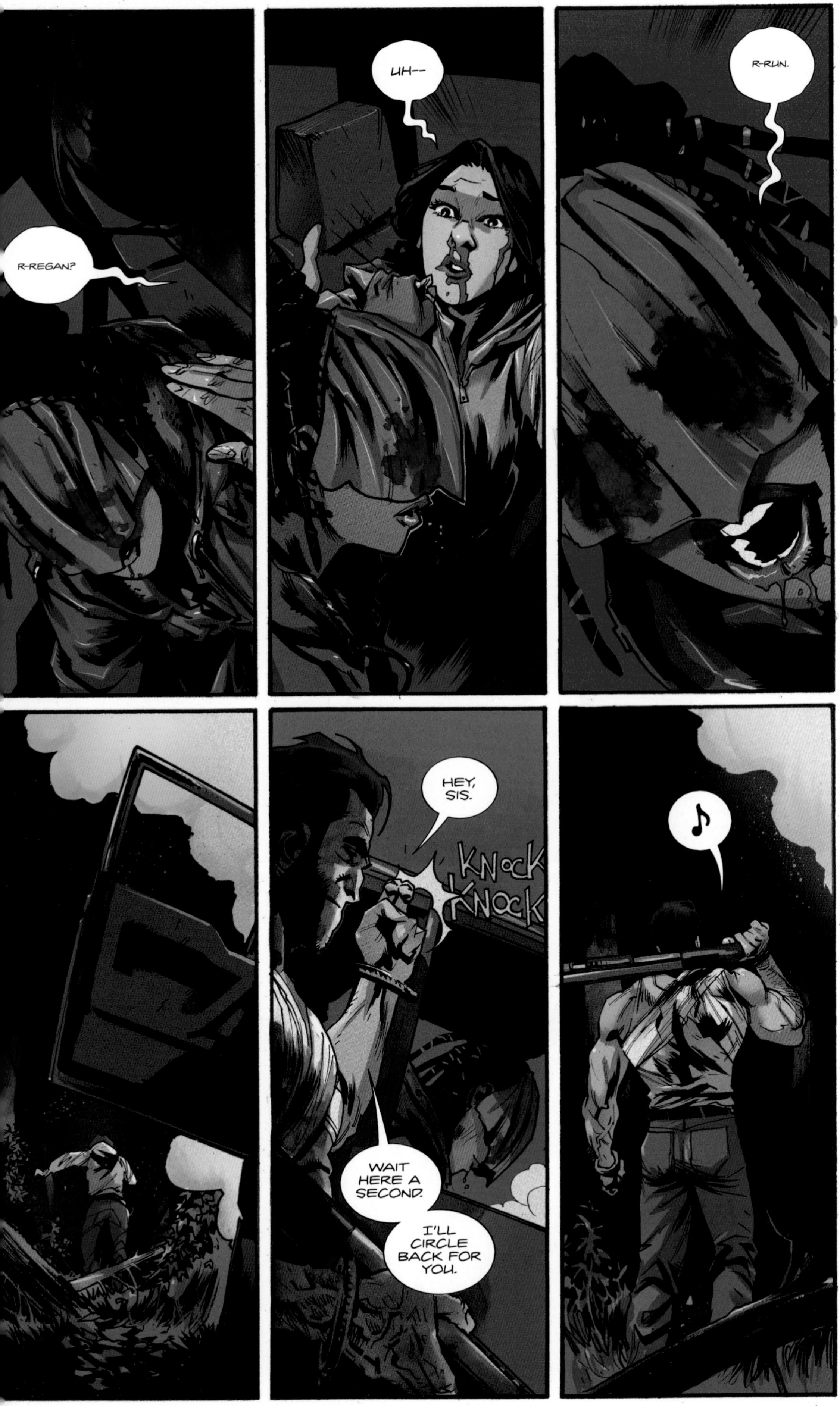
R-REGAN?
UH--
R-RUN.
HEY, SIS.
KNOCK KNOCK
WAIT HERE A SECOND.
I'LL CIRCLE BACK FOR YOU.
♪

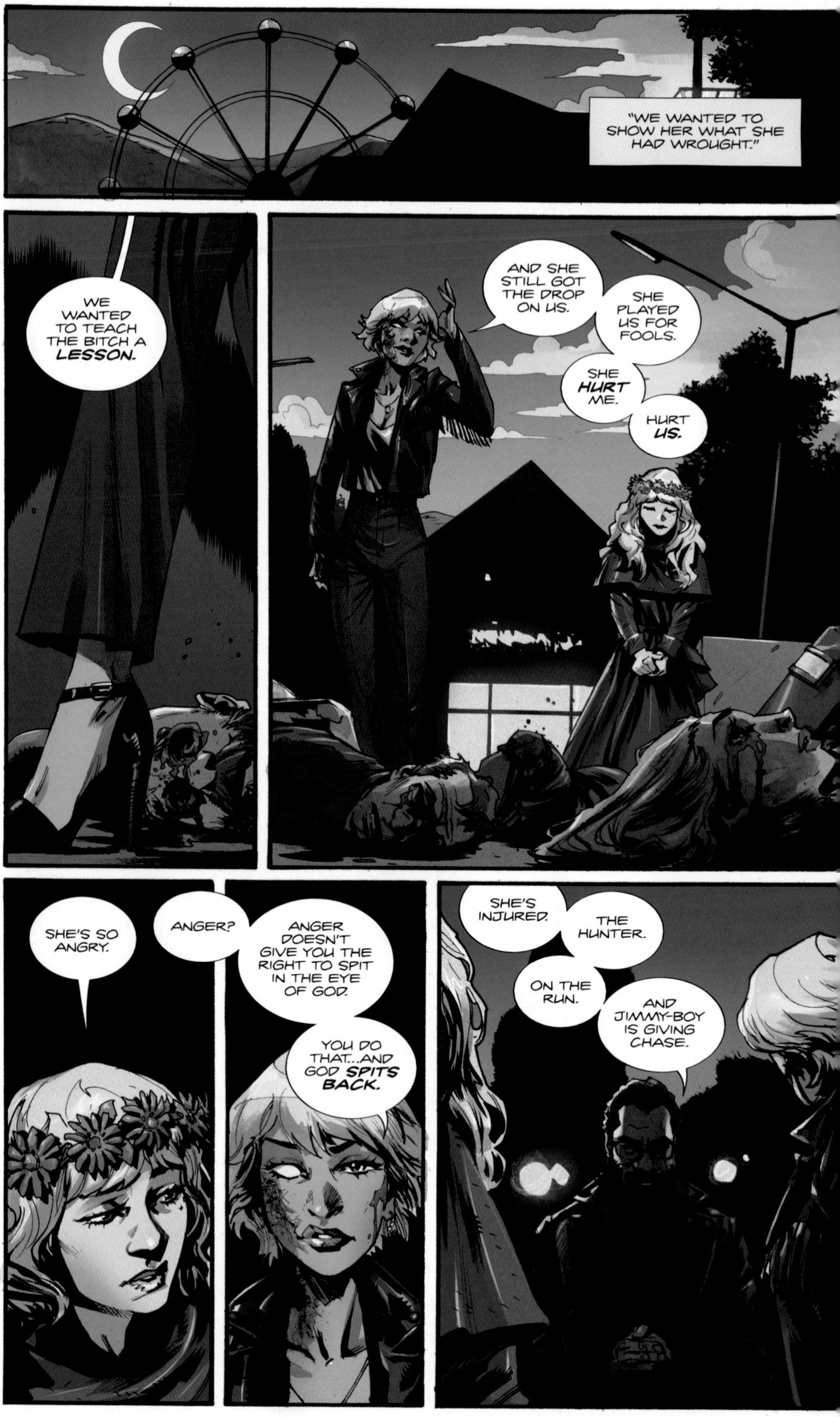

"WE WANTED TO SHOW HER WHAT SHE HAD WROUGHT."
WE WANTED TO TEACH THE BITCH A **LESSON.**
AND SHE STILL GOT THE DROP ON US.
SHE PLAYED US FOR FOOLS.
SHE **HURT** ME.
HURT **US.**
SHE'S SO ANGRY.
ANGER?
ANGER DOESN'T GIVE YOU THE RIGHT TO SPIT IN THE EYE OF GOD.
YOU DO THAT...AND GOD **SPITS BACK.**
SHE'S INJURED.
THE HUNTER.
ON THE RUN.
AND JIMMY-BOY IS GIVING CHASE.

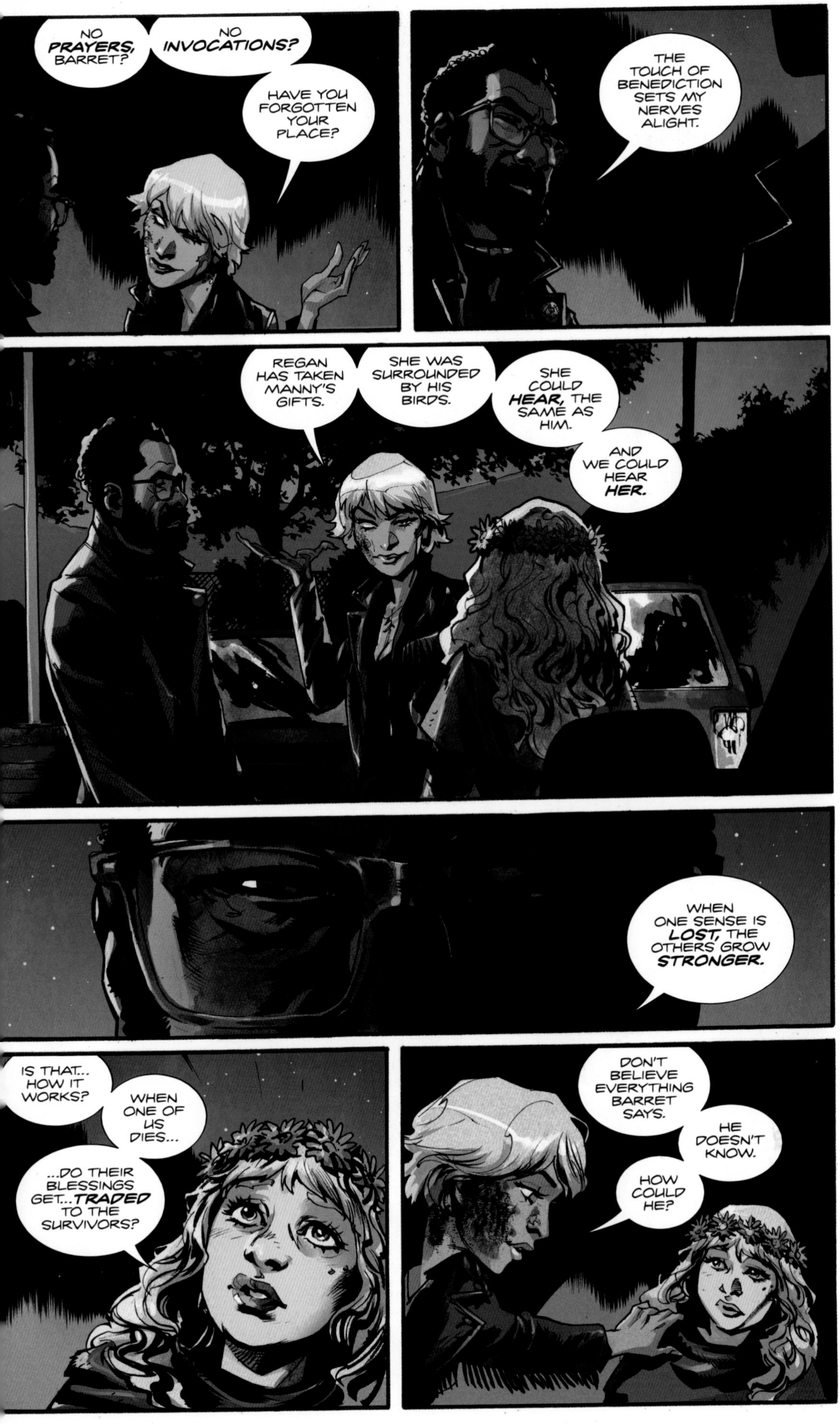
NO PRAYERS, BARRET?
NO INVOCATIONS?
HAVE YOU FORGOTTEN YOUR PLACE?
THE TOUCH OF BENEDICTION SETS MY NERVES ALIGHT.
REGAN HAS TAKEN MANNY'S GIFTS.
SHE WAS SURROUNDED BY HIS BIRDS.
SHE COULD HEAR, THE SAME AS HIM.
AND WE COULD HEAR HER.
WHEN ONE SENSE IS LOST, THE OTHERS GROW STRONGER.
IS THAT... HOW IT WORKS?
WHEN ONE OF US DIES...
...DO THEIR BLESSINGS GET...TRADED TO THE SURVIVORS?
DON'T BELIEVE EVERYTHING BARRET SAYS.
HE DOESN'T KNOW.
HOW COULD HE?

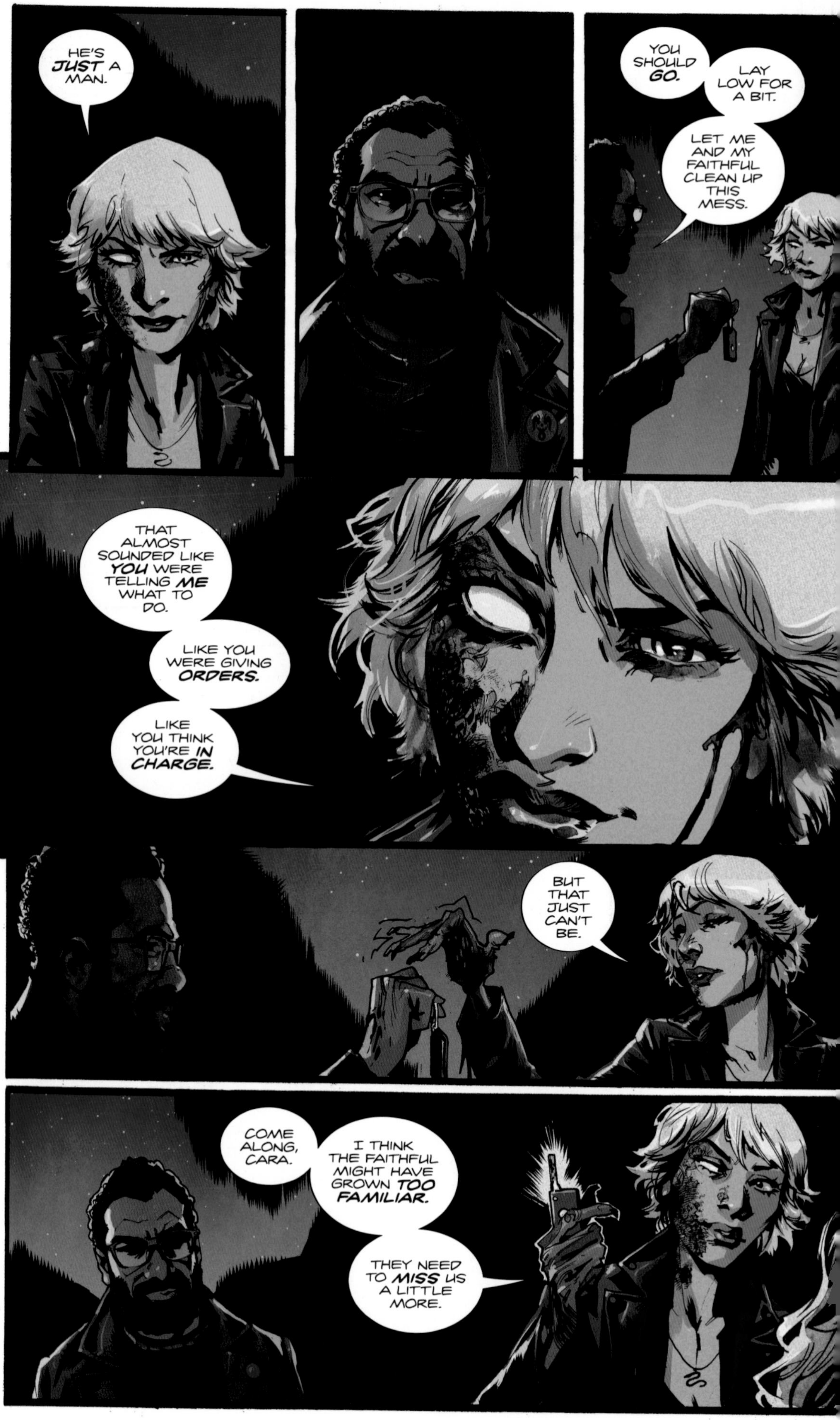
HE'S JUST A MAN.
YOU SHOULD GO.
LAY LOW FOR A BIT.
LET ME AND MY FAITHFUL CLEAN UP THIS MESS.
THAT ALMOST SOUNDED LIKE YOU WERE TELLING ME WHAT TO DO.
LIKE YOU WERE GIVING ORDERS.
LIKE YOU THINK YOU'RE IN CHARGE.
BUT THAT JUST CAN'T BE.
COME ALONG, CARA.
I THINK THE FAITHFUL MIGHT HAVE GROWN TOO FAMILIAR.
THEY NEED TO MISS US A LITTLE MORE.

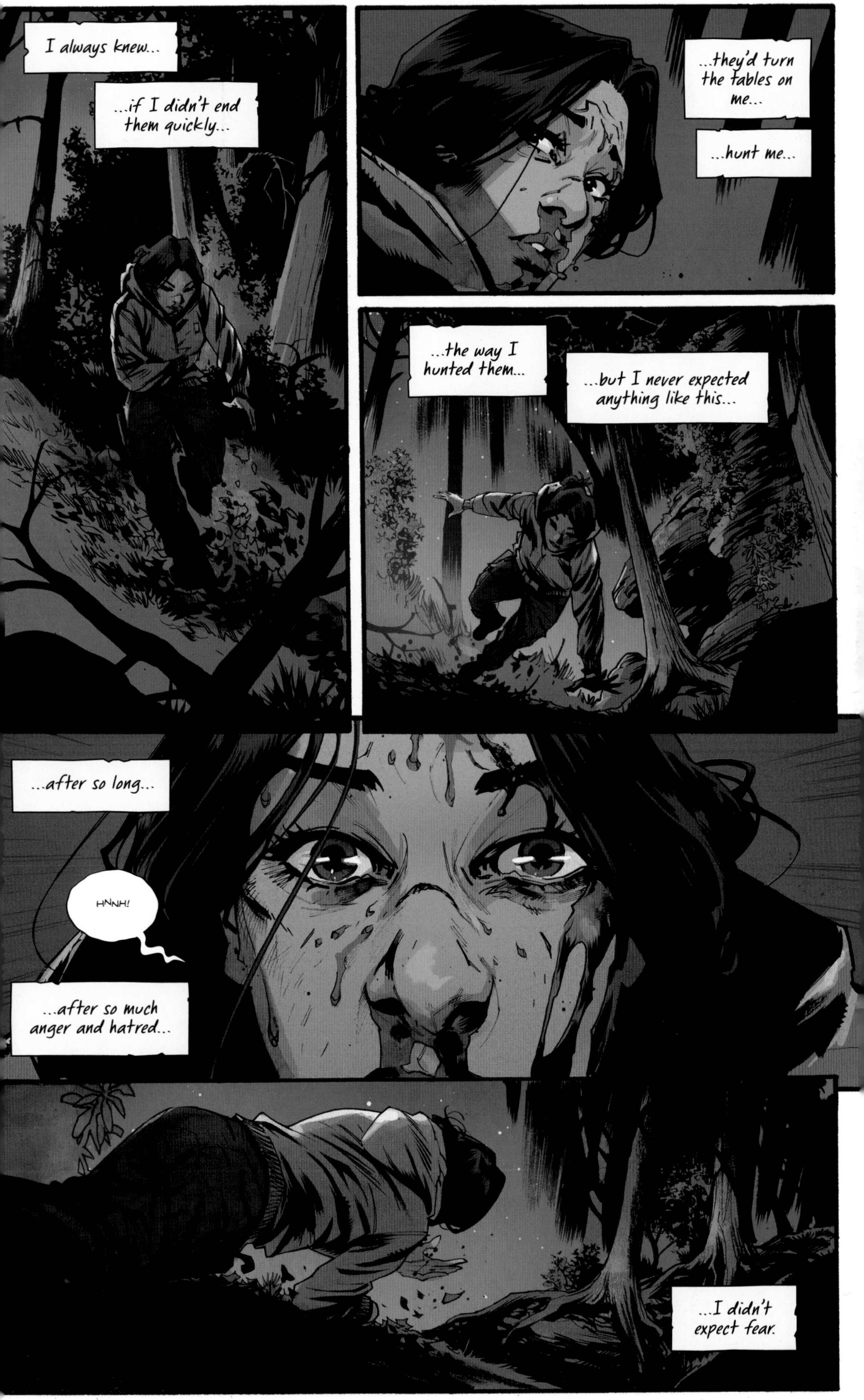
I always knew...
...if I didn't end them quickly...
...they'd turn the tables on me...
...hunt me...
...the way I hunted them...
...but I never expected anything like this...
...after so long...
HNNH!
...after so much anger and hatred...
...I didn't expect fear.

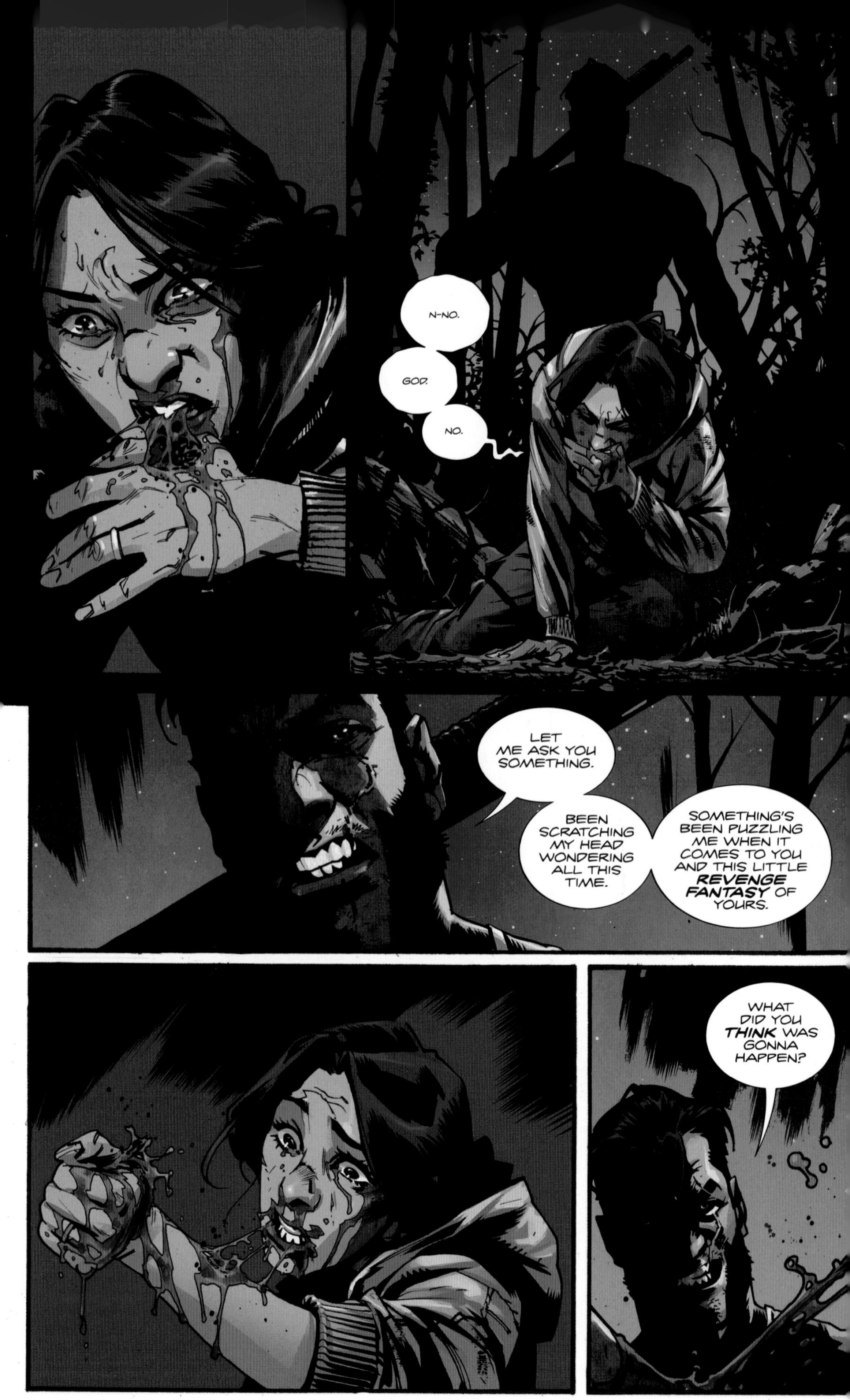
N-NO.
GOD.
NO.
LET ME ASK YOU SOMETHING.
BEEN SCRATCHING MY HEAD WONDERING ALL THIS TIME.
SOMETHING'S BEEN PUZZLING ME WHEN IT COMES TO YOU AND THIS LITTLE **REVENGE FANTASY** OF YOURS.
WHAT DID YOU **THINK** WAS GONNA HAPPEN?

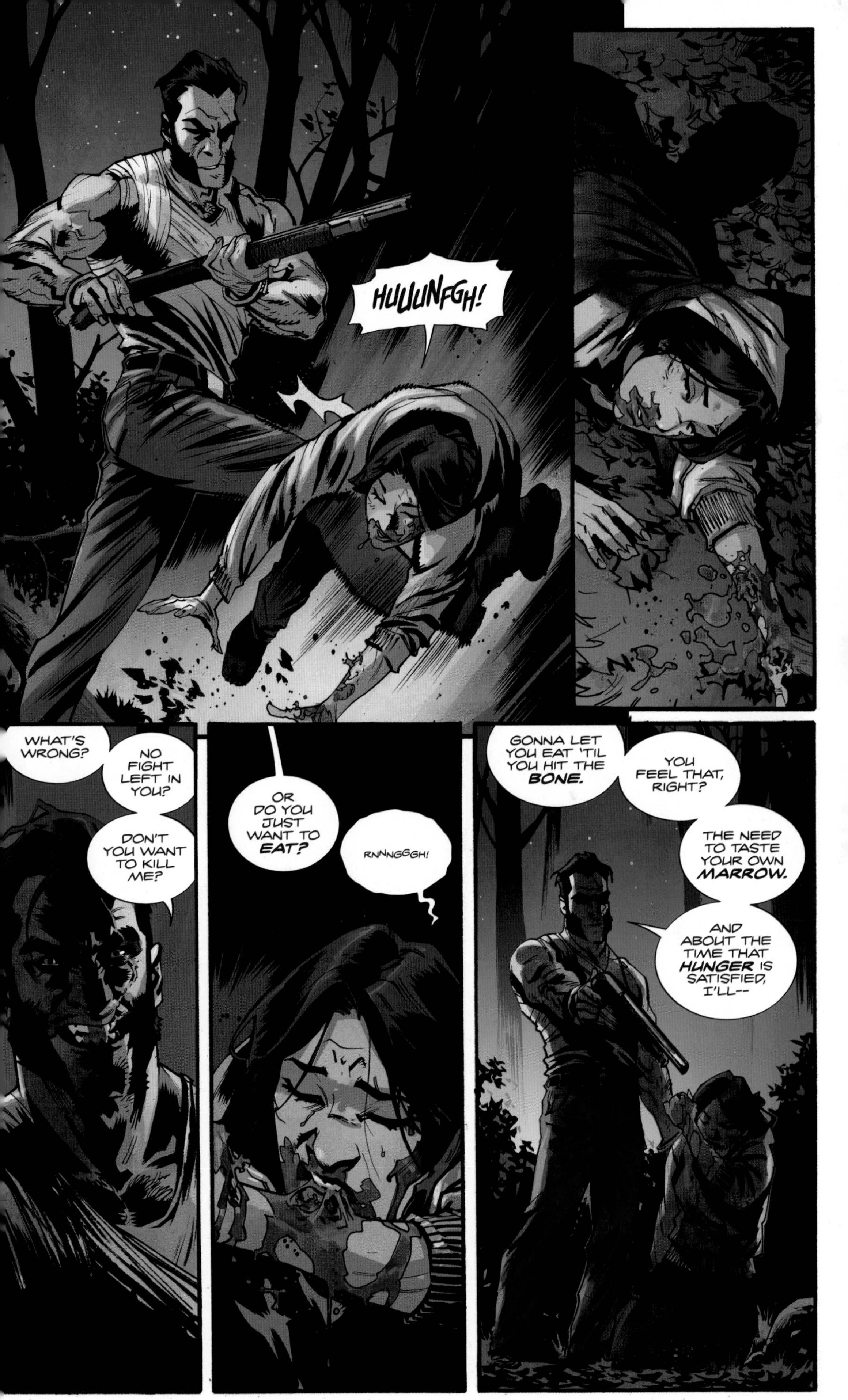
HUUUNFGH!
WHAT'S WRONG?
NO FIGHT LEFT IN YOU?
DON'T YOU WANT TO KILL ME?
OR DO YOU JUST WANT TO EAT?
RNNNGGGH!
GONNA LET YOU EAT 'TIL YOU HIT THE BONE.
YOU FEEL THAT, RIGHT?
THE NEED TO TASTE YOUR OWN MARROW.
AND ABOUT THE TIME THAT HUNGER IS SATISFIED, I'LL--

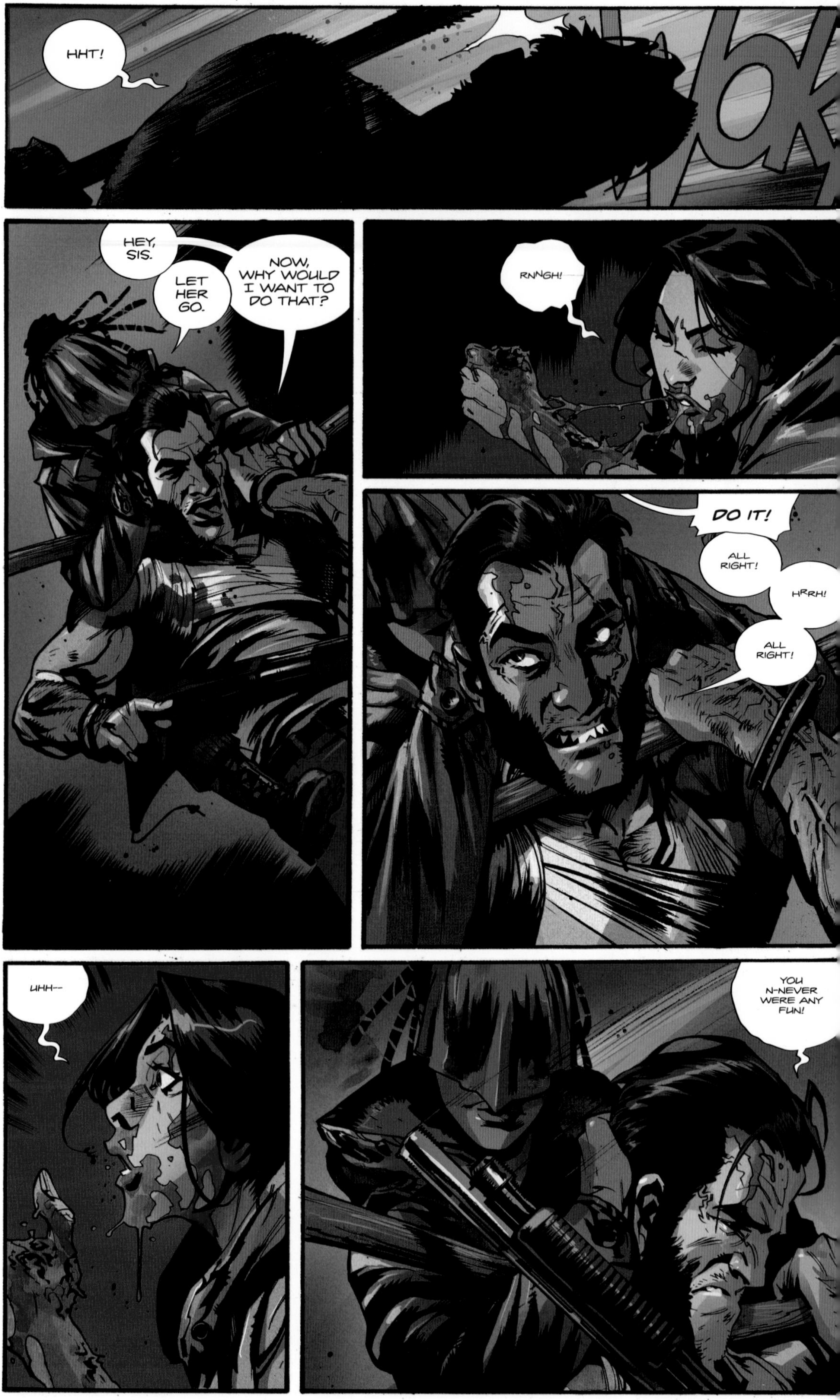
HHT!
HEY, SIS.
LET HER GO.
NOW, WHY WOULD I WANT TO DO THAT?
RNNGH!
DO IT!
ALL RIGHT!
HRRH!
ALL RIGHT!
UHH--
YOU N-NEVER WERE ANY FUN!

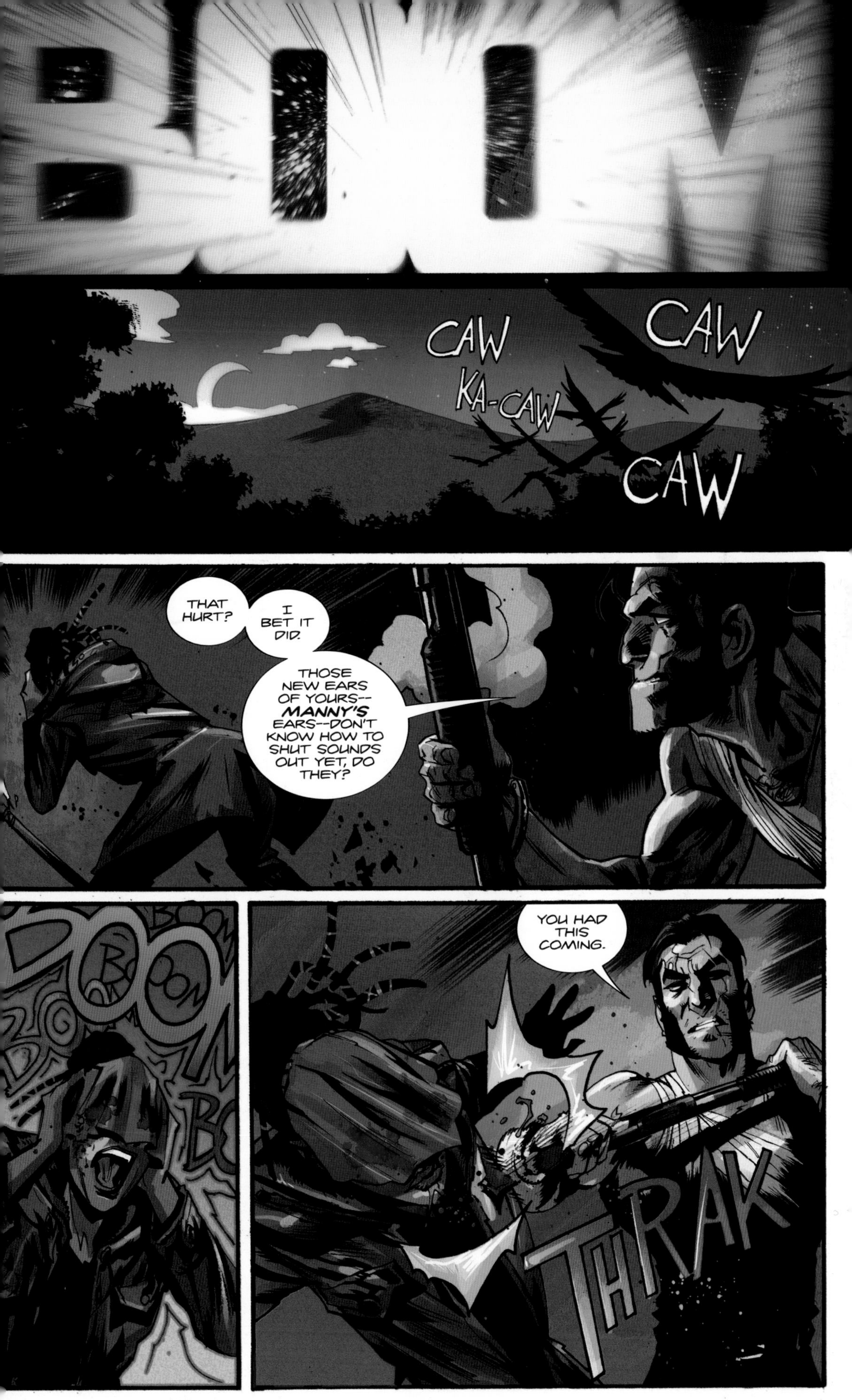
BOOM
CAW
KA-CAW
CAW
CAW
THAT HURT?
I BET IT DID.
THOSE NEW EARS OF YOURS--MANNY'S EARS--DON'T KNOW HOW TO SHUT SOUNDS OUT YET, DO THEY?
YOU HAD THIS COMING.
THRAK

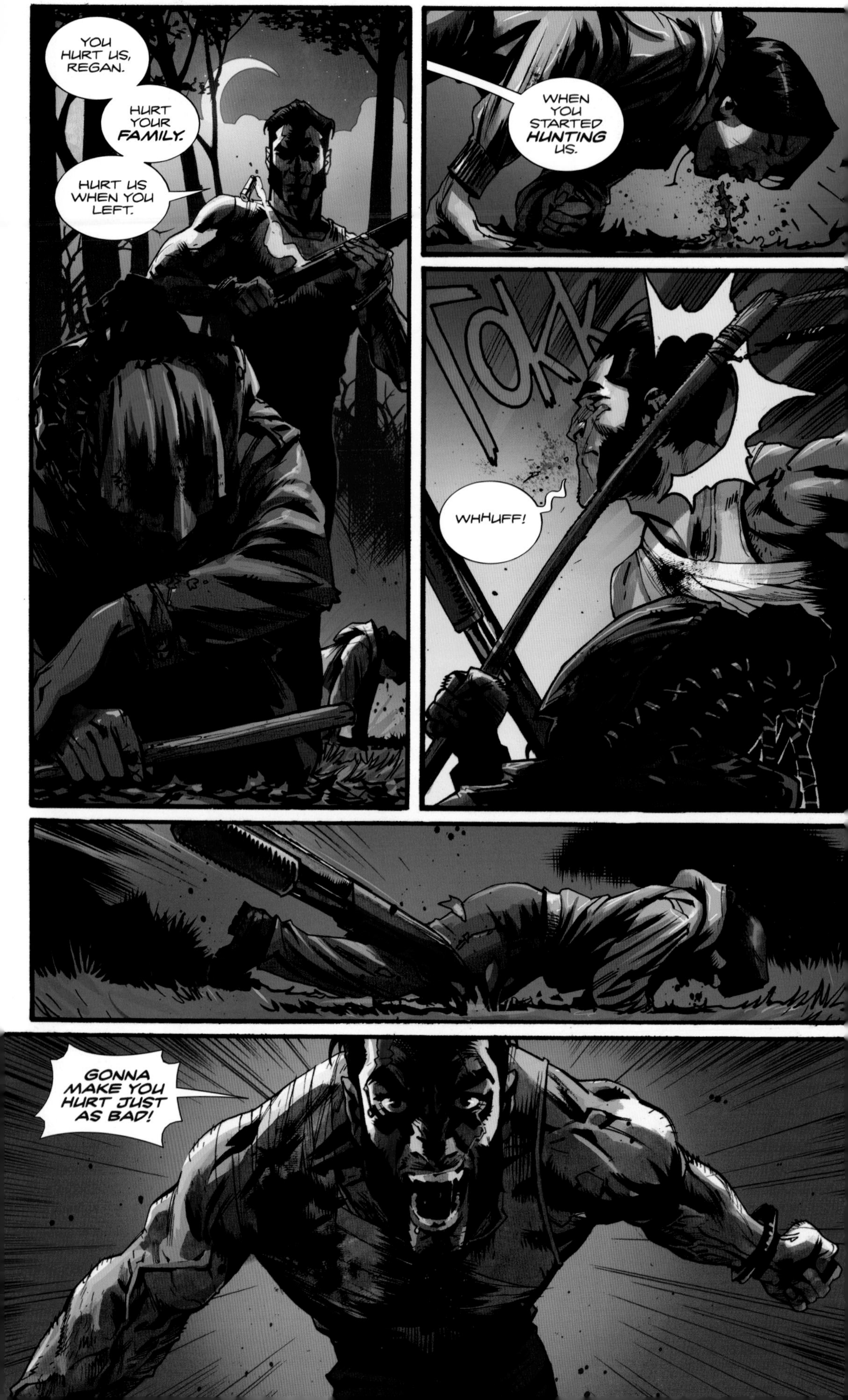
YOU HURT US, REGAN.
HURT YOUR FAMILY.
HURT US WHEN YOU LEFT.
WHEN YOU STARTED HUNTING US.
TOKK
WHHUFF!
GONNA MAKE YOU HURT JUST AS BAD!

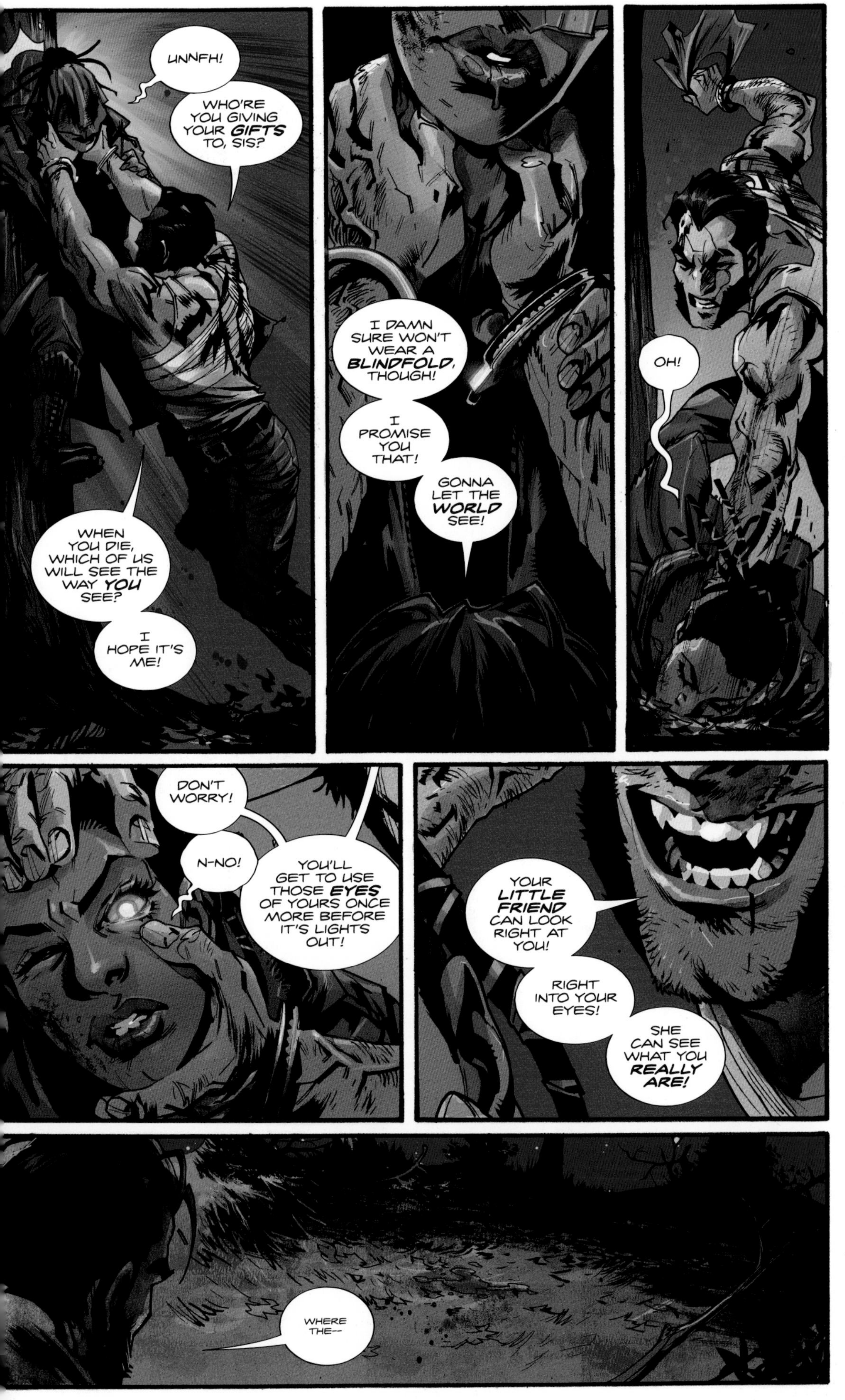
UNNFH!
WHO'RE YOU GIVING YOUR GIFTS TO, SIS?
WHEN YOU DIE, WHICH OF US WILL SEE THE WAY YOU SEE?
I HOPE IT'S ME!
I DAMN SURE WON'T WEAR A BLINDFOLD, THOUGH!
I PROMISE YOU THAT!
GONNA LET THE WORLD SEE!
OH!
DON'T WORRY!
N-NO!
YOU'LL GET TO USE THOSE EYES OF YOURS ONCE MORE BEFORE IT'S LIGHTS OUT!
YOUR LITTLE FRIEND CAN LOOK RIGHT AT YOU!
RIGHT INTO YOUR EYES!
SHE CAN SEE WHAT YOU REALLY ARE!
WHERE THE--

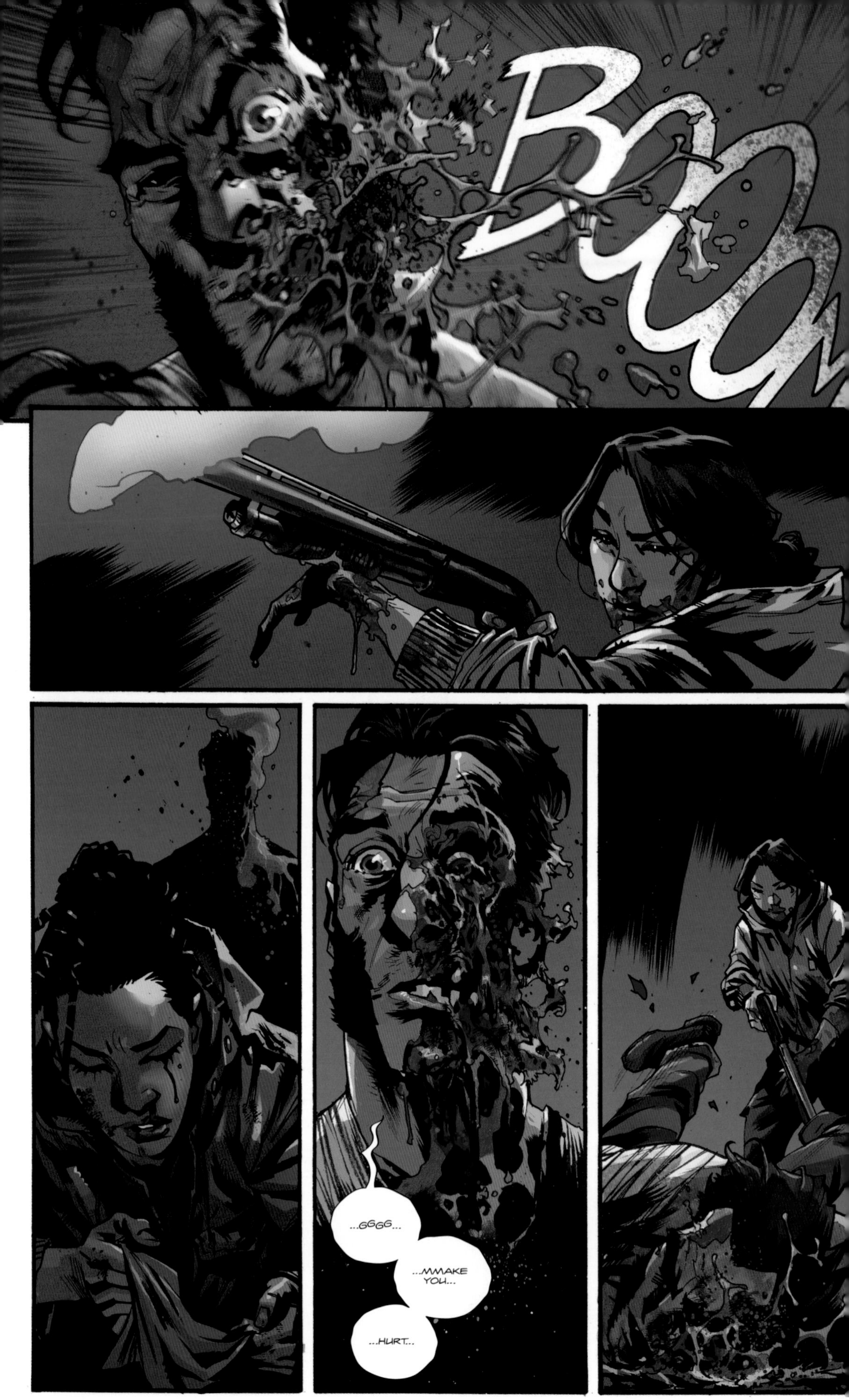
BOOM
...GGGG...
...MMAKE YOU...
...HURT...

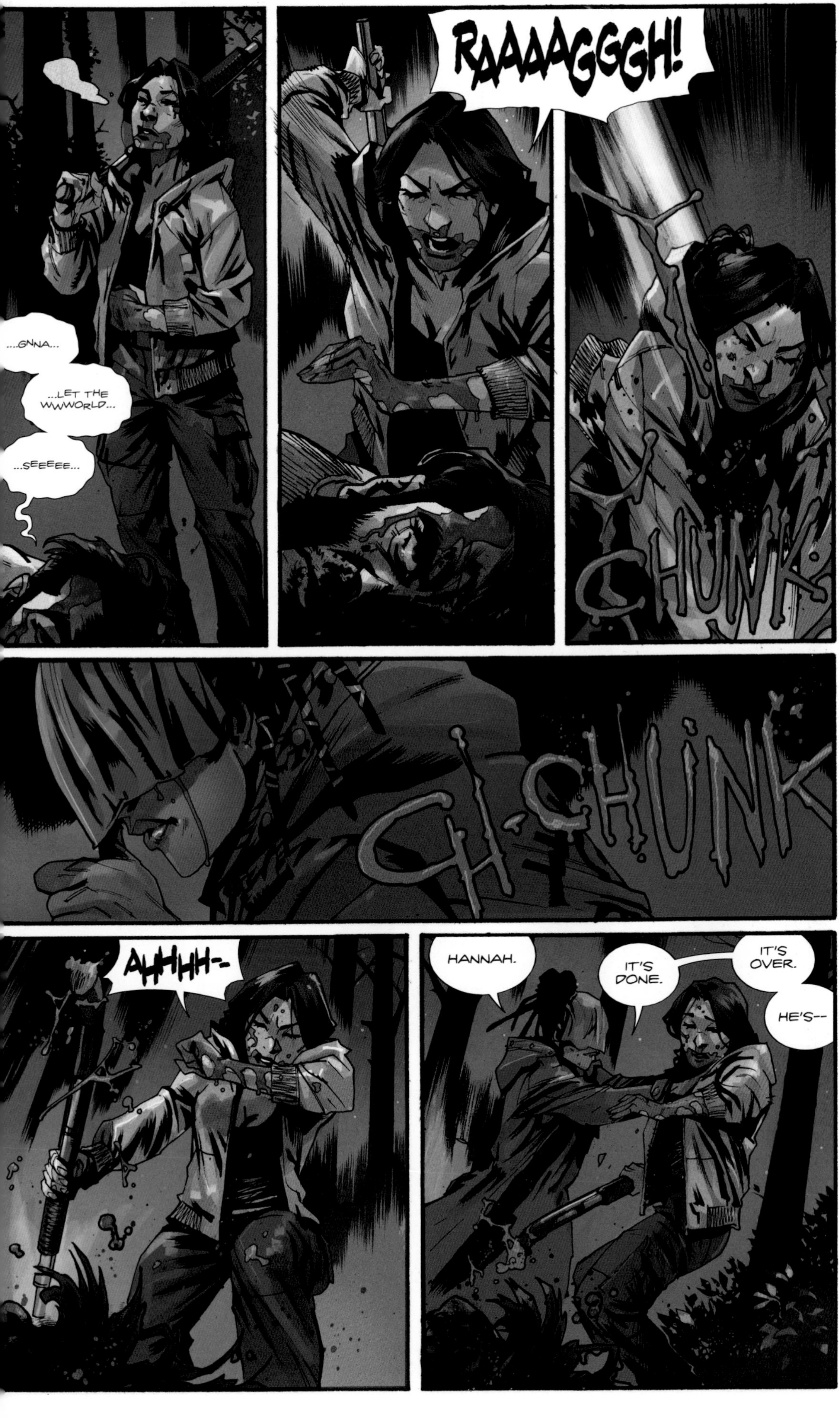
...GNNA...
...LET THE WWWORLD...
...SEEEEE...
RAAAAGGGH!
CHUNK
CH-CHUNK
AHHHH-
HANNAH.
IT'S DONE.
IT'S OVER.
HE'S--

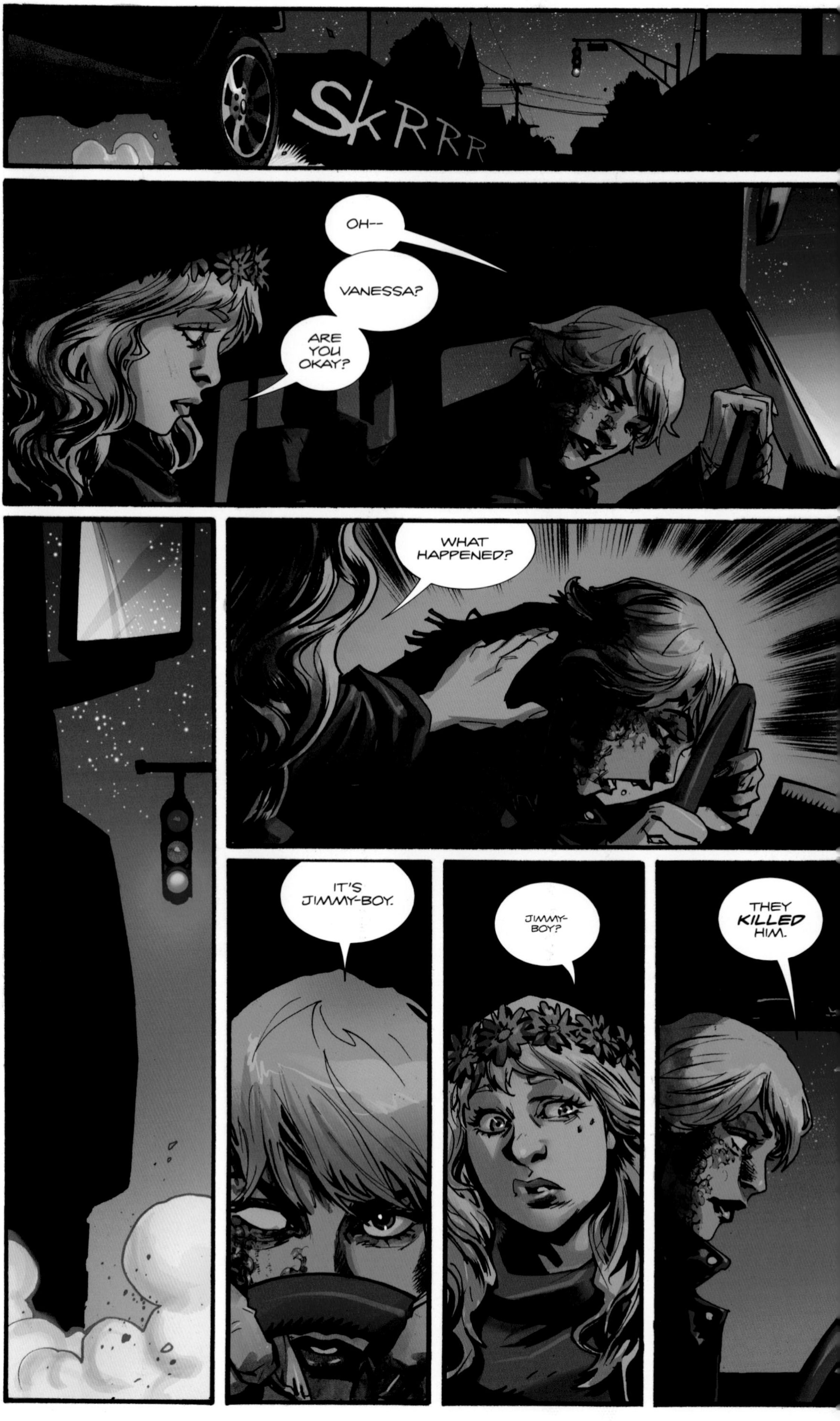
SKRRR
OH--
VANESSA?
ARE YOU OKAY?
WHAT HAPPENED?
IT'S JIMMY-BOY.
JIMMY-BOY?
THEY KILLED HIM.

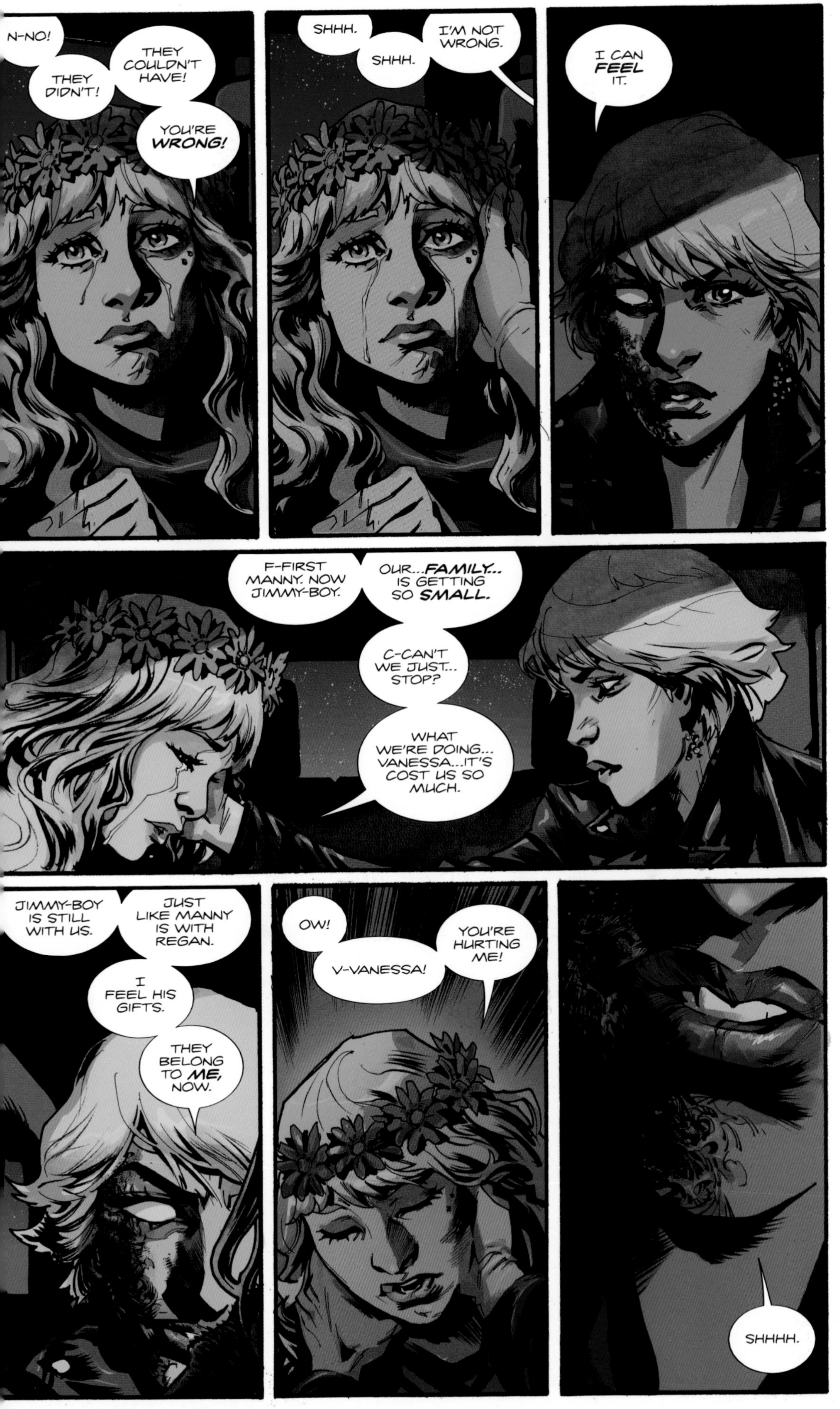
N-NO!
THEY DIDN'T!
THEY COULDN'T HAVE!
YOU'RE WRONG!
SHHH.
SHHH.
I'M NOT WRONG.
I CAN FEEL IT.
F-FIRST MANNY. NOW JIMMY-BOY.
OUR...FAMILY... IS GETTING SO SMALL.
C-CAN'T WE JUST... STOP?
WHAT WE'RE DOING... VANESSA...IT'S COST US SO MUCH.
JIMMY-BOY IS STILL WITH US.
JUST LIKE MANNY IS WITH REGAN.
I FEEL HIS GIFTS.
THEY BELONG TO ME, NOW.
OW!
V-VANESSA!
YOU'RE HURTING ME!
SHHHH.

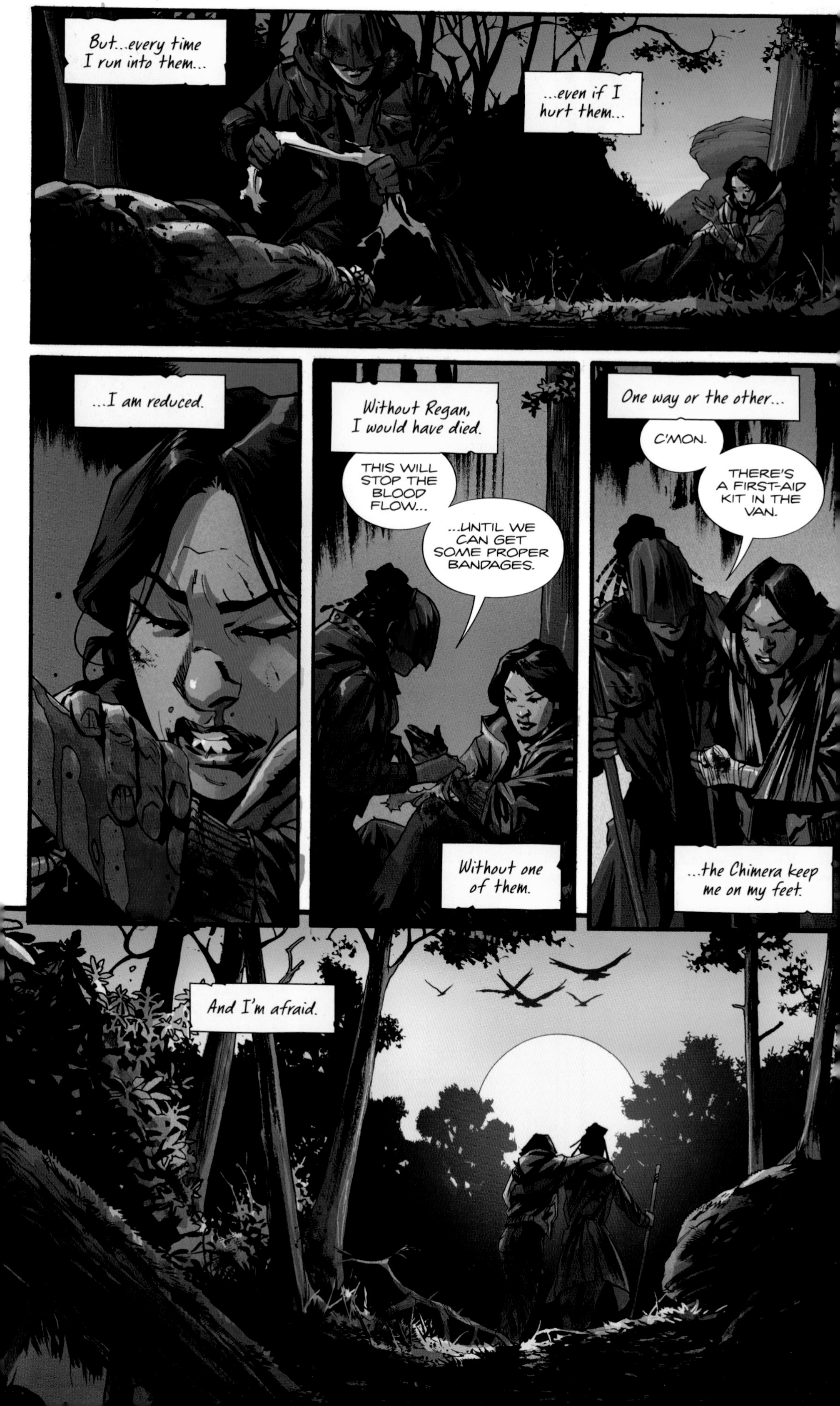
But...every time I run into them...
...even if I hurt them...
...I am reduced.
Without Regan, I would have died.
THIS WILL STOP THE BLOOD FLOW...
...UNTIL WE CAN GET SOME PROPER BANDAGES.
Without one of them.
One way or the other...
C'MON.
THERE'S A FIRST-AID KIT IN THE VAN.
...the Chimera keep me on my feet.
And I'm afraid.

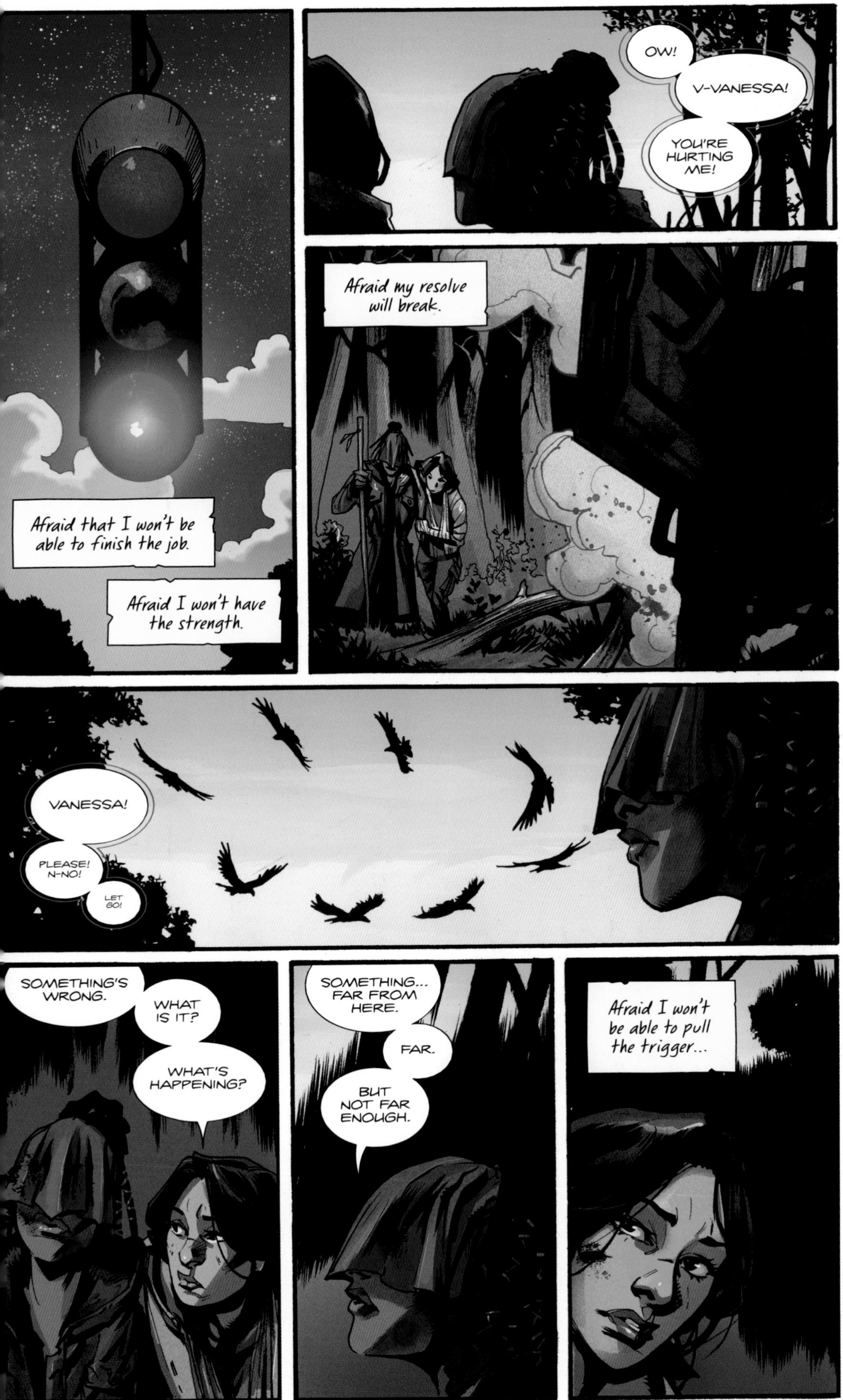
OW!
V-VANESSA!
YOU'RE HURTING ME!
Afraid that I won't be able to finish the job.
Afraid I won't have the strength.
Afraid my resolve will break.
VANESSA!
PLEASE! N-NO!
LET GO!
SOMETHING'S WRONG.
WHAT IS IT?
WHAT'S HAPPENING?
SOMETHING... FAR FROM HERE.
FAR.
BUT NOT FAR ENOUGH.
Afraid I won't be able to pull the trigger...

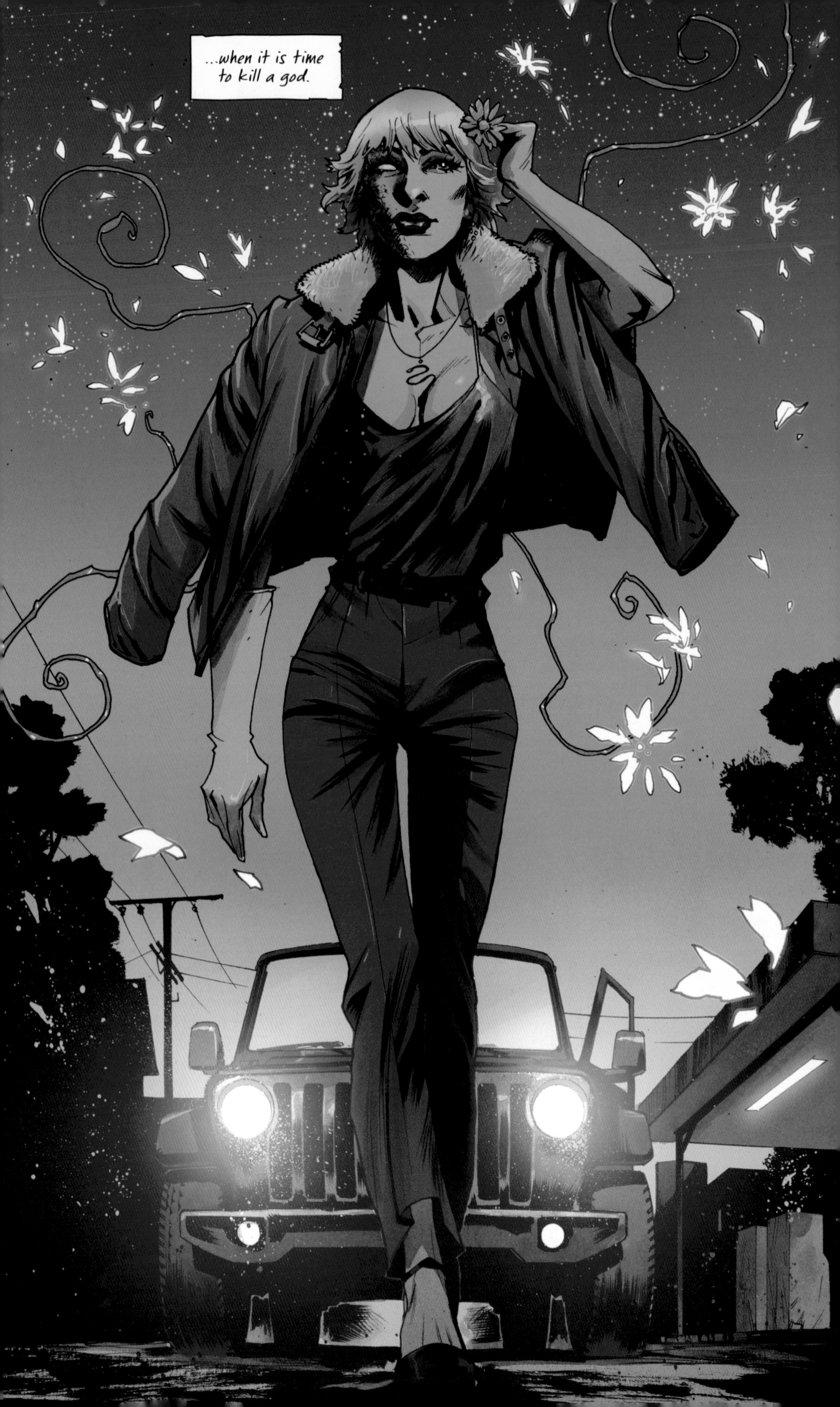
...when it is time
to kill a god.

CHAPTER EIGHT

EVEN GODS BLEED

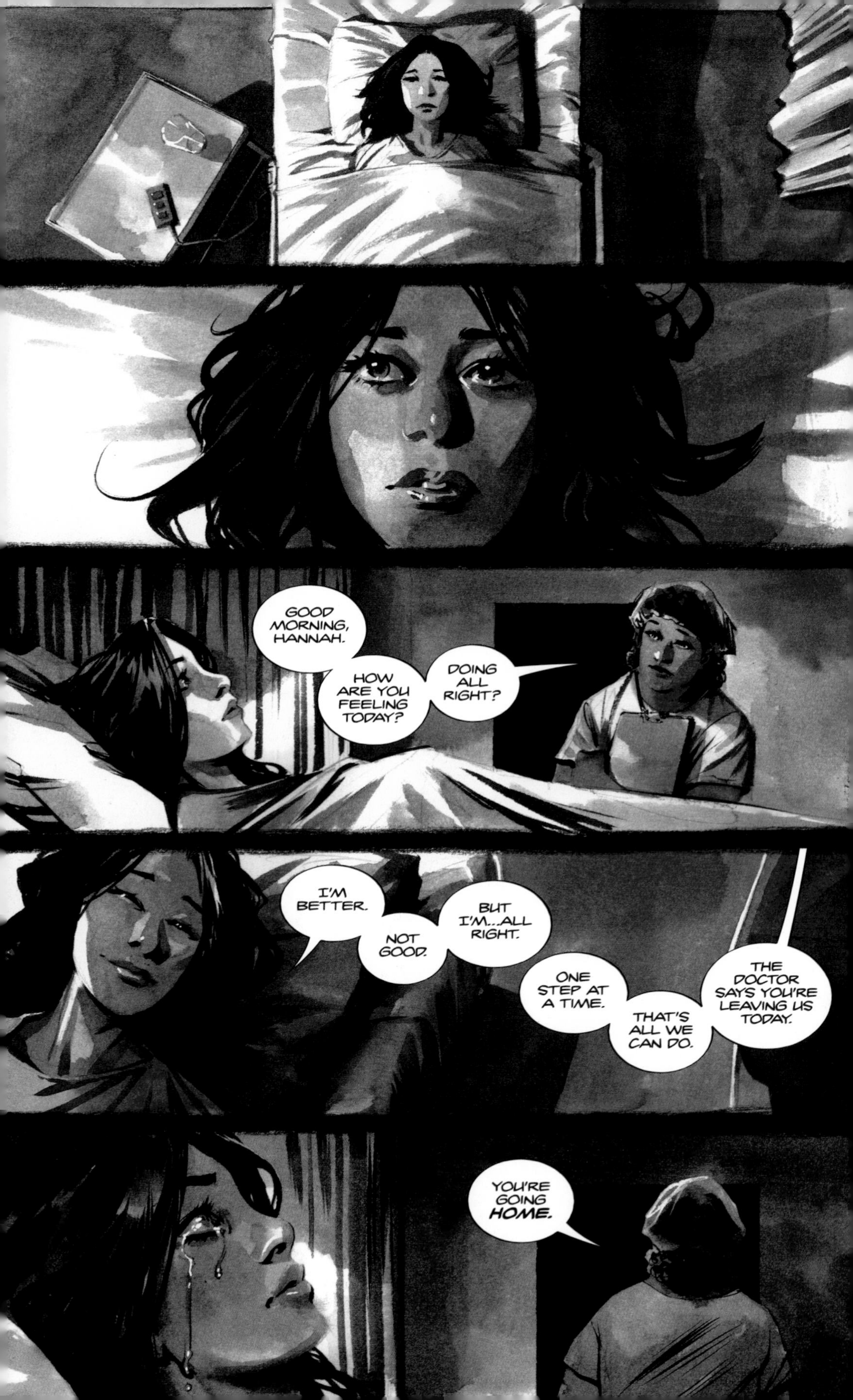
GOOD MORNING, HANNAH.
HOW ARE YOU FEELING TODAY?
DOING ALL RIGHT?
I'M BETTER.
NOT GOOD.
BUT I'M...ALL RIGHT.
ONE STEP AT A TIME.
THAT'S ALL WE CAN DO.
THE DOCTOR SAYS YOU'RE LEAVING US TODAY.
YOU'RE GOING HOME.

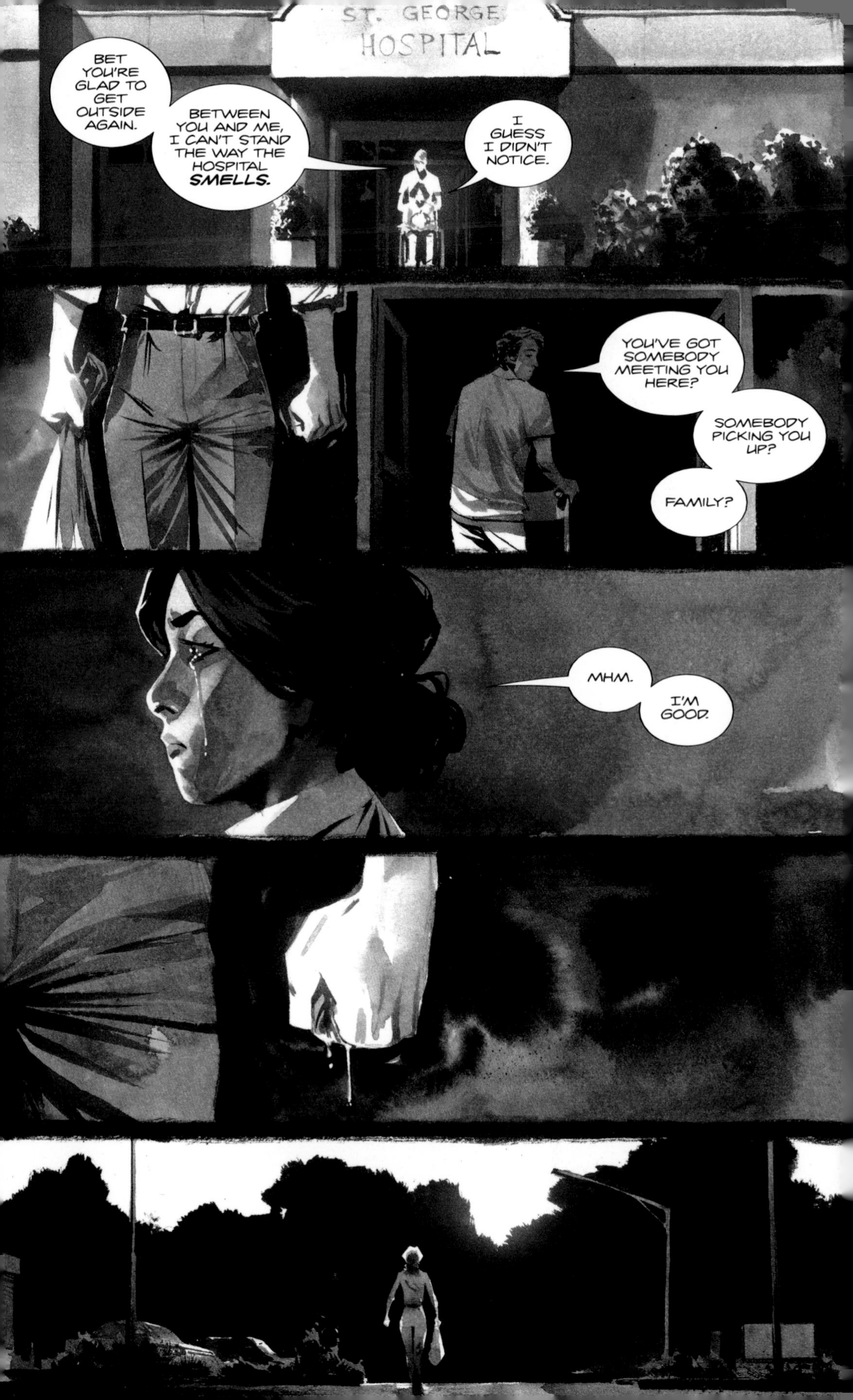
ST. GEORGE
HOSPITAL
BET YOU'RE GLAD TO GET OUTSIDE AGAIN.
BETWEEN YOU AND ME, I CAN'T STAND THE WAY THE HOSPITAL **SMELLS.**
I GUESS I DIDN'T NOTICE.
YOU'VE GOT SOMEBODY MEETING YOU HERE?
SOMEBODY PICKING YOU UP?
FAMILY?
MHM.
I'M GOOD.

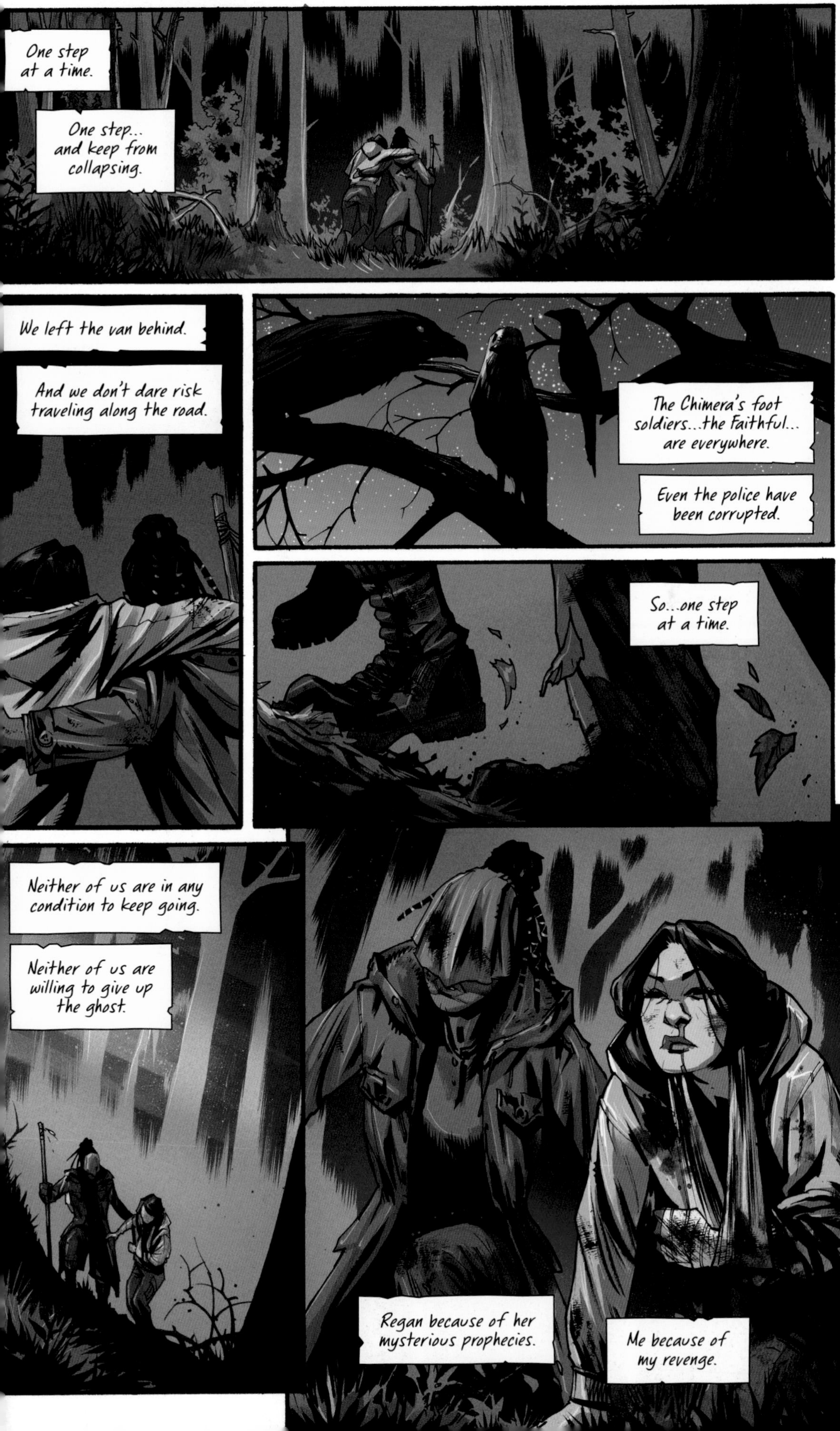

One step at a time.
One step... and keep from collapsing.
We left the van behind.
And we don't dare risk traveling along the road.
The Chimera's foot soldiers...the Faithful... are everywhere.
Even the police have been corrupted.
So...one step at a time.
Neither of us are in any condition to keep going.
Neither of us are willing to give up the ghost.
Regan because of her mysterious prophecies.
Me because of my revenge.

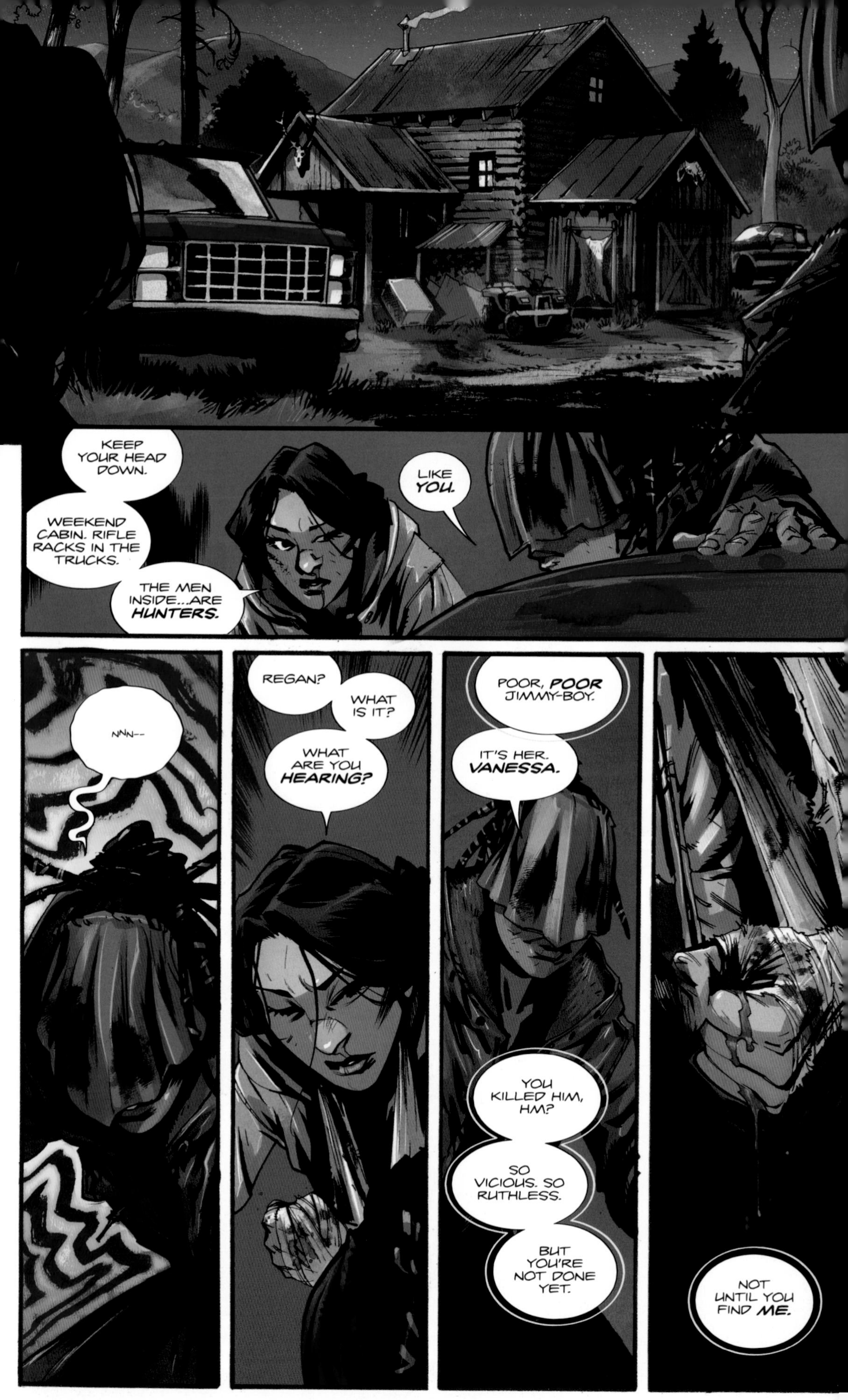
KEEP YOUR HEAD DOWN.
WEEKEND CABIN. RIFLE RACKS IN THE TRUCKS.
THE MEN INSIDE...ARE **HUNTERS.**
LIKE **YOU.**
NNN--
REGAN?
WHAT IS IT?
WHAT ARE YOU **HEARING?**
POOR, **POOR** JIMMY-BOY.
IT'S HER. **VANESSA.**
YOU KILLED HIM, HM?
SO VICIOUS. SO RUTHLESS.
BUT YOU'RE NOT DONE YET.
NOT UNTIL YOU FIND **ME.**

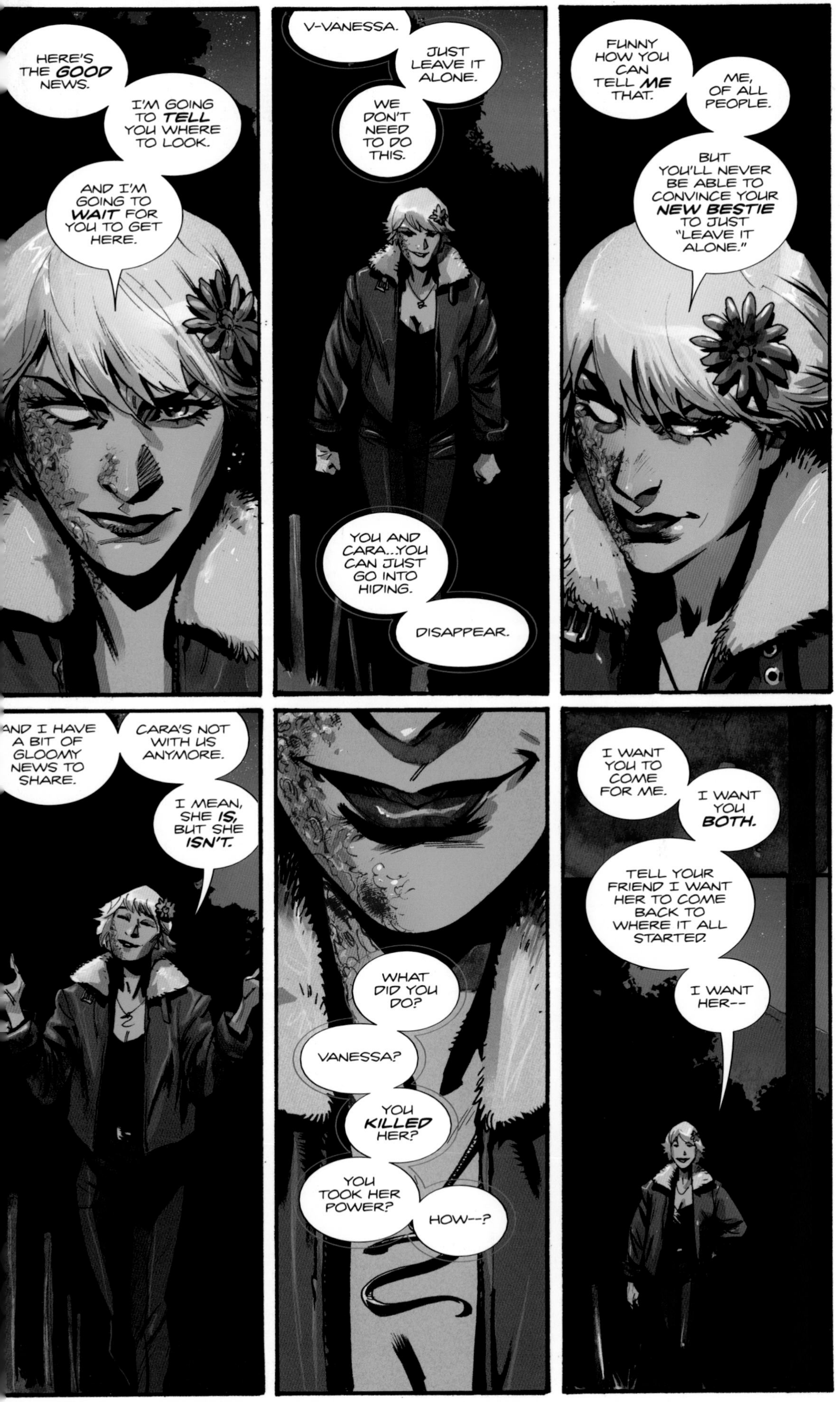

HERE'S THE GOOD NEWS.
I'M GOING TO TELL YOU WHERE TO LOOK.
AND I'M GOING TO WAIT FOR YOU TO GET HERE.
V-VANESSA.
JUST LEAVE IT ALONE.
WE DON'T NEED TO DO THIS.
YOU AND CARA...YOU CAN JUST GO INTO HIDING.
DISAPPEAR.
FUNNY HOW YOU CAN TELL ME THAT.
ME, OF ALL PEOPLE.
BUT YOU'LL NEVER BE ABLE TO CONVINCE YOUR NEW BESTIE TO JUST "LEAVE IT ALONE."
AND I HAVE A BIT OF GLOOMY NEWS TO SHARE.
CARA'S NOT WITH US ANYMORE.
I MEAN, SHE IS, BUT SHE ISN'T.
WHAT DID YOU DO?
VANESSA?
YOU KILLED HER?
YOU TOOK HER POWER?
HOW--?
I WANT YOU TO COME FOR ME.
I WANT YOU BOTH.
TELL YOUR FRIEND I WANT HER TO COME BACK TO WHERE IT ALL STARTED.
I WANT HER--

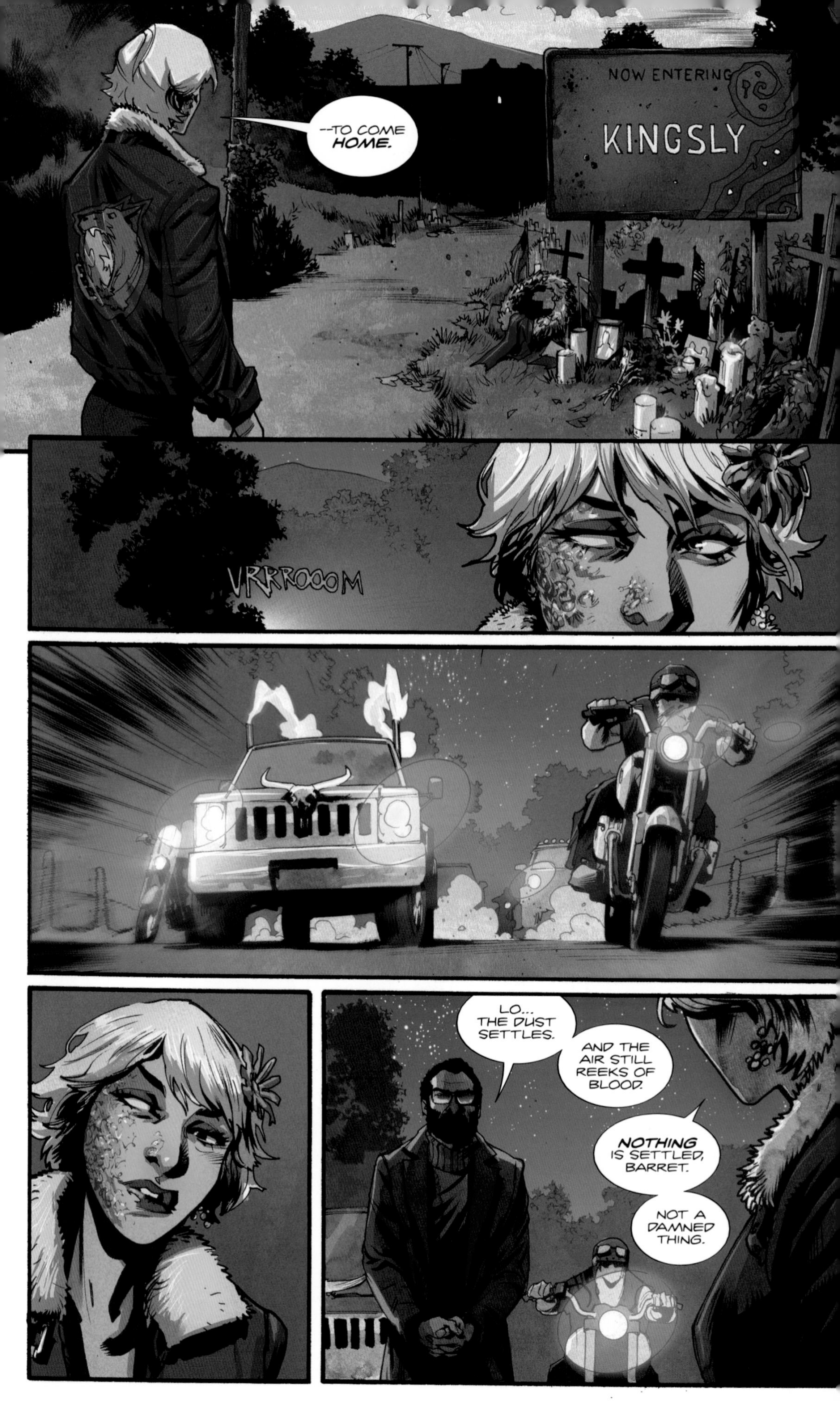
--TO COME HOME.
NOW ENTERING
KINGSLY
VRRROOOM
LO... THE DUST SETTLES.
AND THE AIR STILL REEKS OF BLOOD.
NOTHING IS SETTLED, BARRET.
NOT A DAMNED THING.

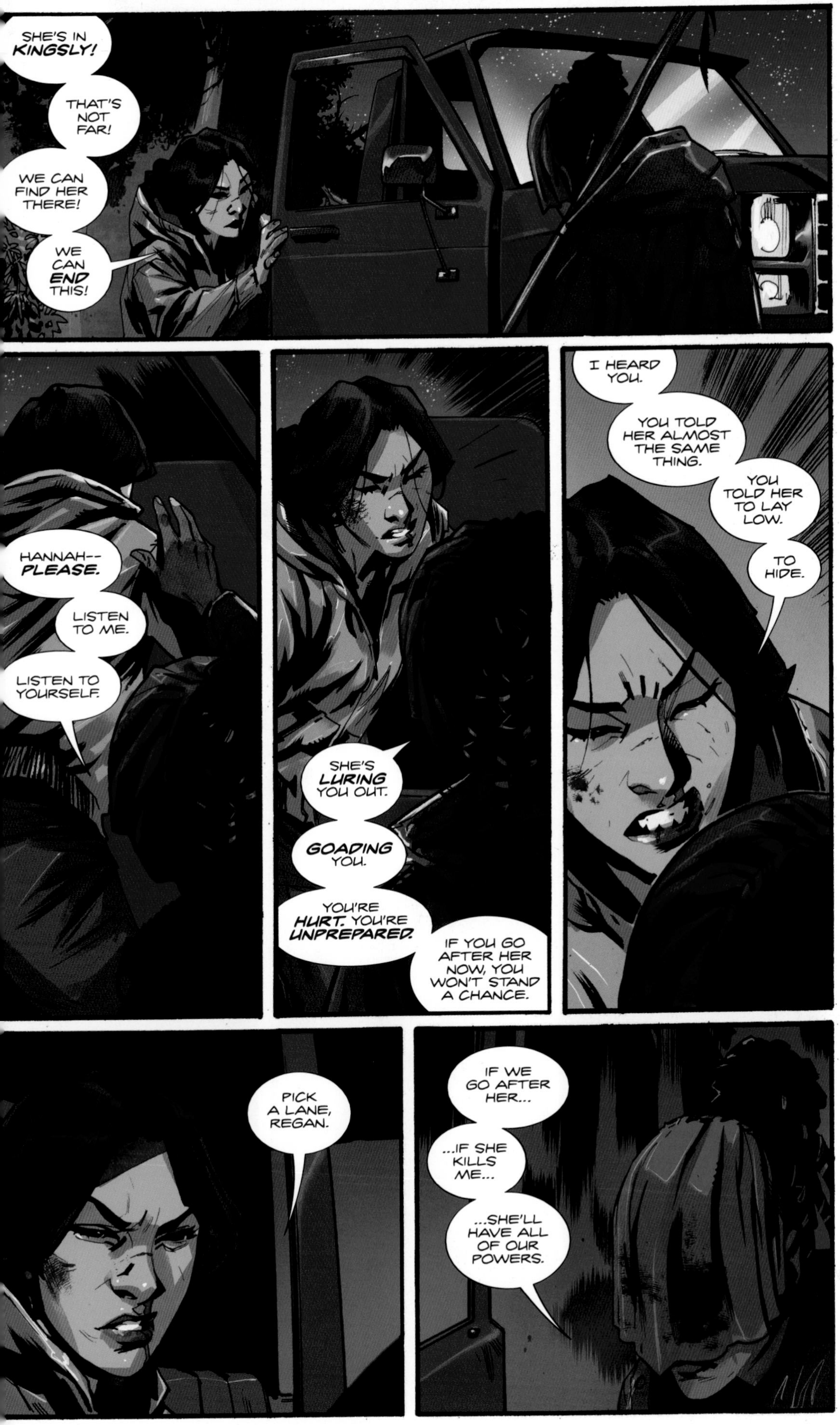
SHE'S IN KINGSLY!
THAT'S NOT FAR!
WE CAN FIND HER THERE!
WE CAN END THIS!
HANNAH-- PLEASE.
LISTEN TO ME.
LISTEN TO YOURSELF.
SHE'S LURING YOU OUT.
GOADING YOU.
YOU'RE HURT. YOU'RE UNPREPARED.
IF YOU GO AFTER HER NOW, YOU WON'T STAND A CHANCE.
I HEARD YOU.
YOU TOLD HER ALMOST THE SAME THING.
YOU TOLD HER TO LAY LOW.
TO HIDE.
PICK A LANE, REGAN.
IF WE GO AFTER HER...
...IF SHE KILLS ME...
...SHE'LL HAVE ALL OF OUR POWERS.

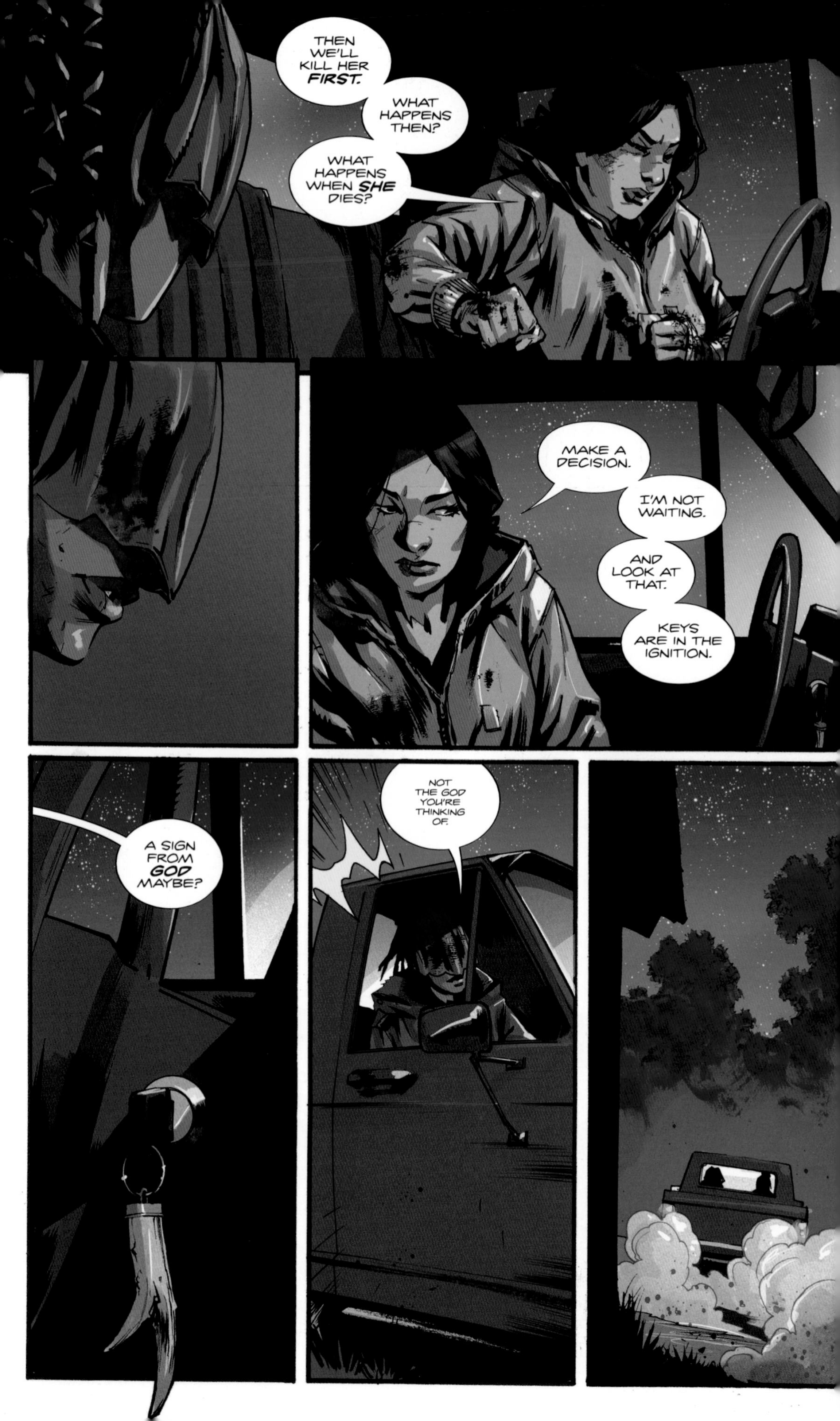
THEN WE'LL KILL HER FIRST.
WHAT HAPPENS THEN?
WHAT HAPPENS WHEN SHE DIES?
MAKE A DECISION.
I'M NOT WAITING.
AND LOOK AT THAT.
KEYS ARE IN THE IGNITION.
A SIGN FROM GOD MAYBE?
NOT THE GOD YOU'RE THINKING OF.

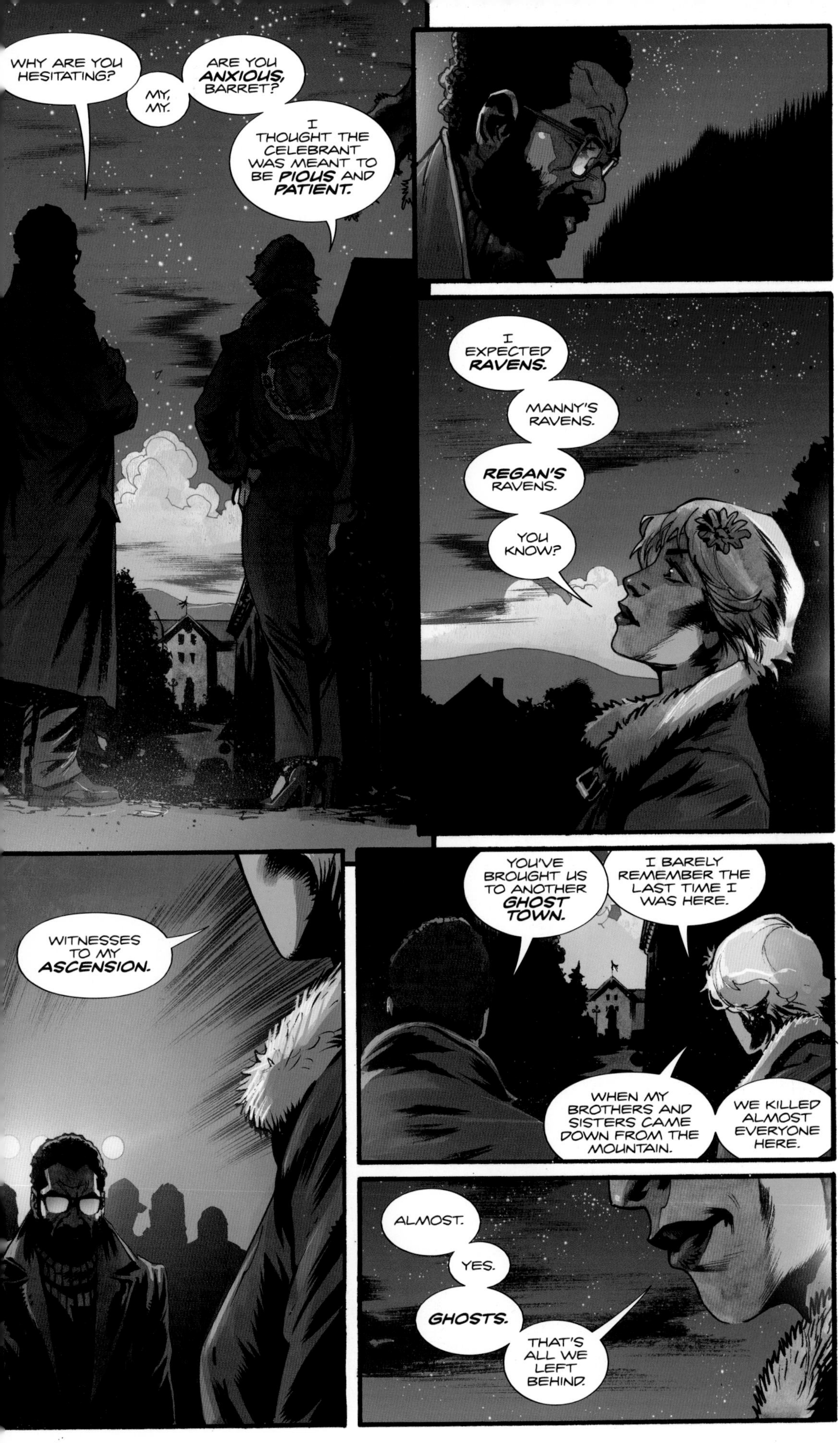
WHY ARE YOU HESITATING?
MY, MY.
ARE YOU ANXIOUS, BARRET?
I THOUGHT THE CELEBRANT WAS MEANT TO BE PIOUS AND PATIENT.
I EXPECTED RAVENS.
MANNY'S RAVENS.
REGAN'S RAVENS.
YOU KNOW?
WITNESSES TO MY ASCENSION.
YOU'VE BROUGHT US TO ANOTHER GHOST TOWN.
I BARELY REMEMBER THE LAST TIME I WAS HERE.
WHEN MY BROTHERS AND SISTERS CAME DOWN FROM THE MOUNTAIN.
WE KILLED ALMOST EVERYONE HERE.
ALMOST.
YES.
GHOSTS.
THAT'S ALL WE LEFT BEHIND.

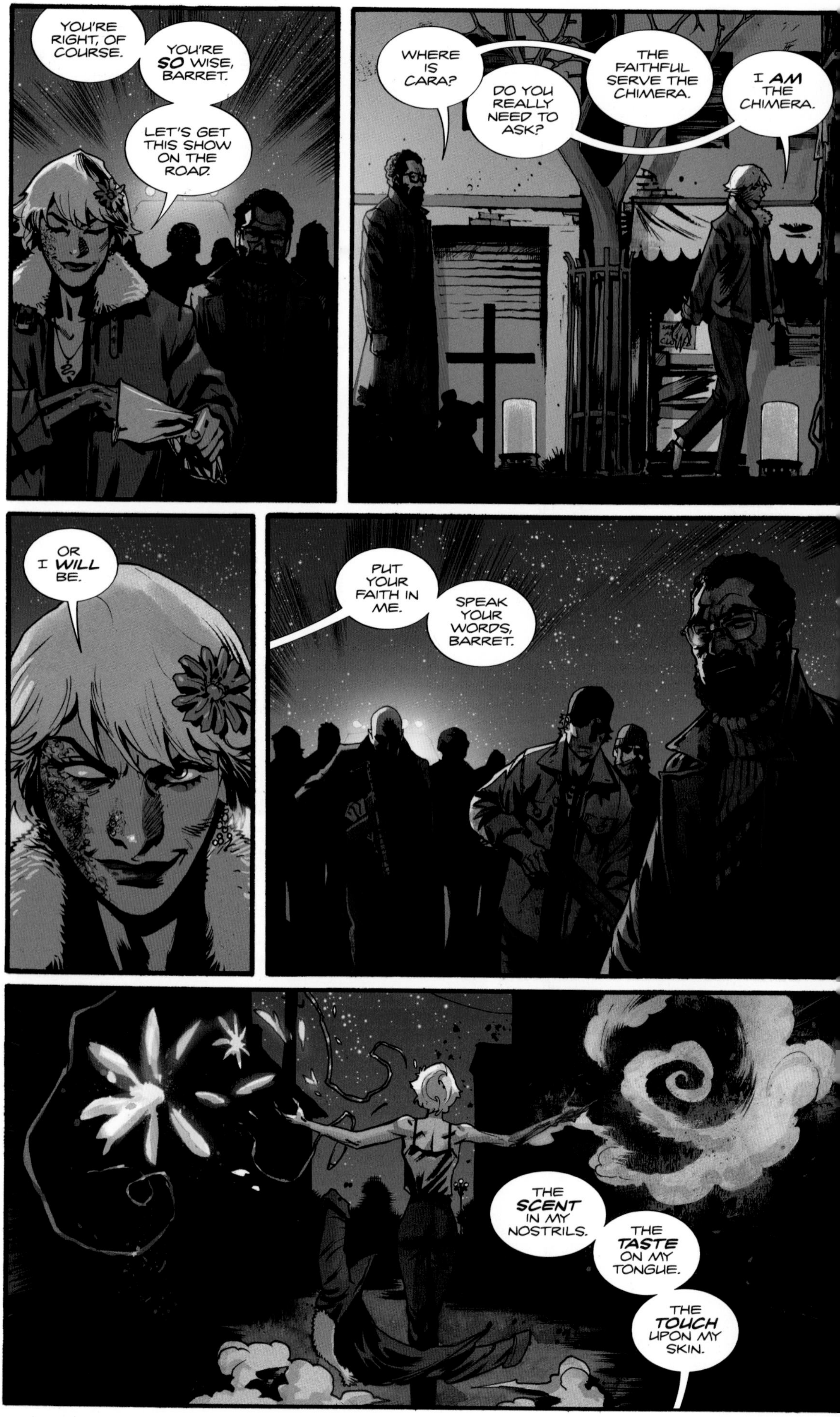
YOU'RE RIGHT, OF COURSE.
YOU'RE SO WISE, BARRET.
LET'S GET THIS SHOW ON THE ROAD.
WHERE IS CARA?
THE FAITHFUL SERVE THE CHIMERA.
DO YOU REALLY NEED TO ASK?
I AM THE CHIMERA.
OR I WILL BE.
PUT YOUR FAITH IN ME.
SPEAK YOUR WORDS, BARRET.
THE SCENT IN MY NOSTRILS.
THE TASTE ON MY TONGUE.
THE TOUCH UPON MY SKIN.

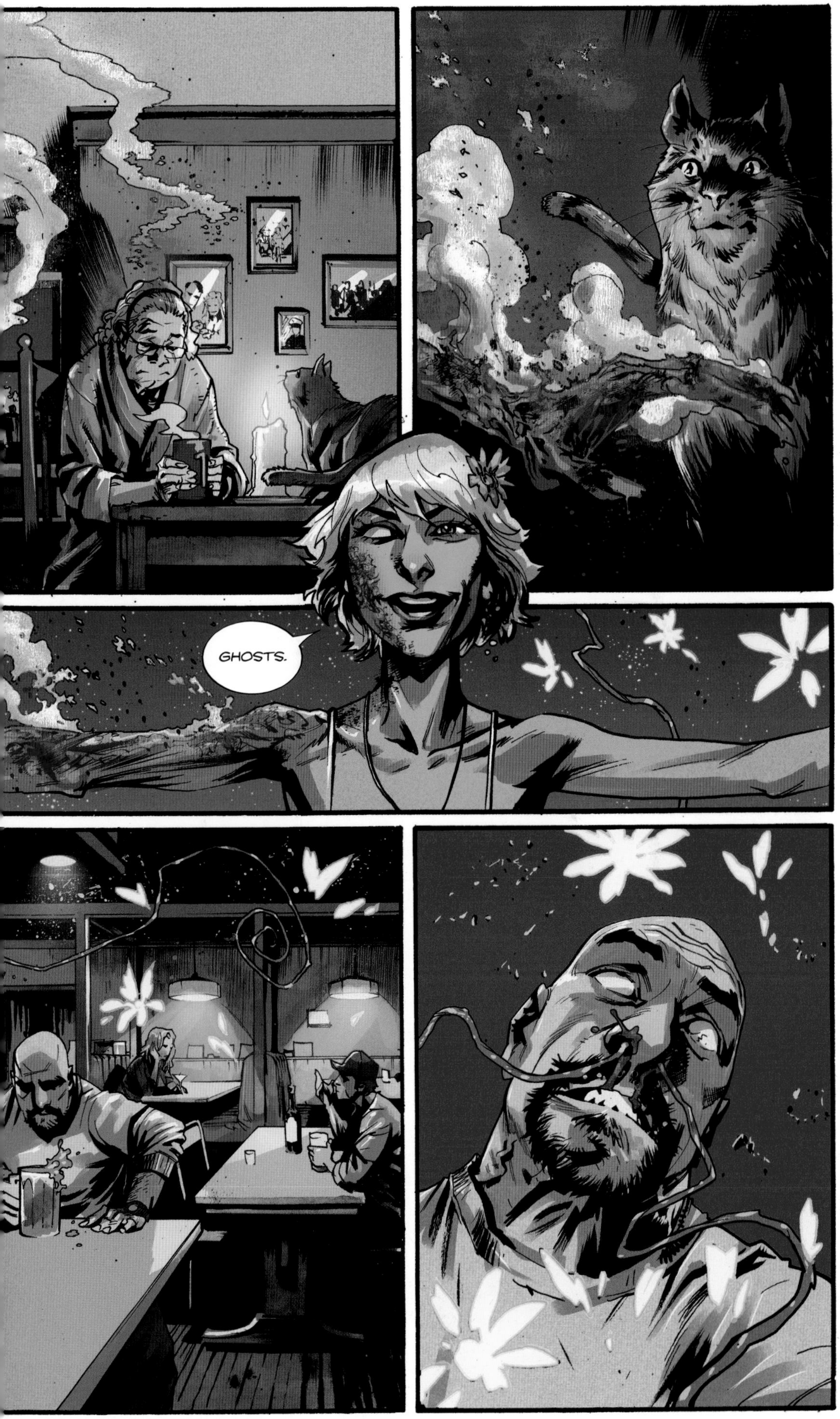
GHOSTS.

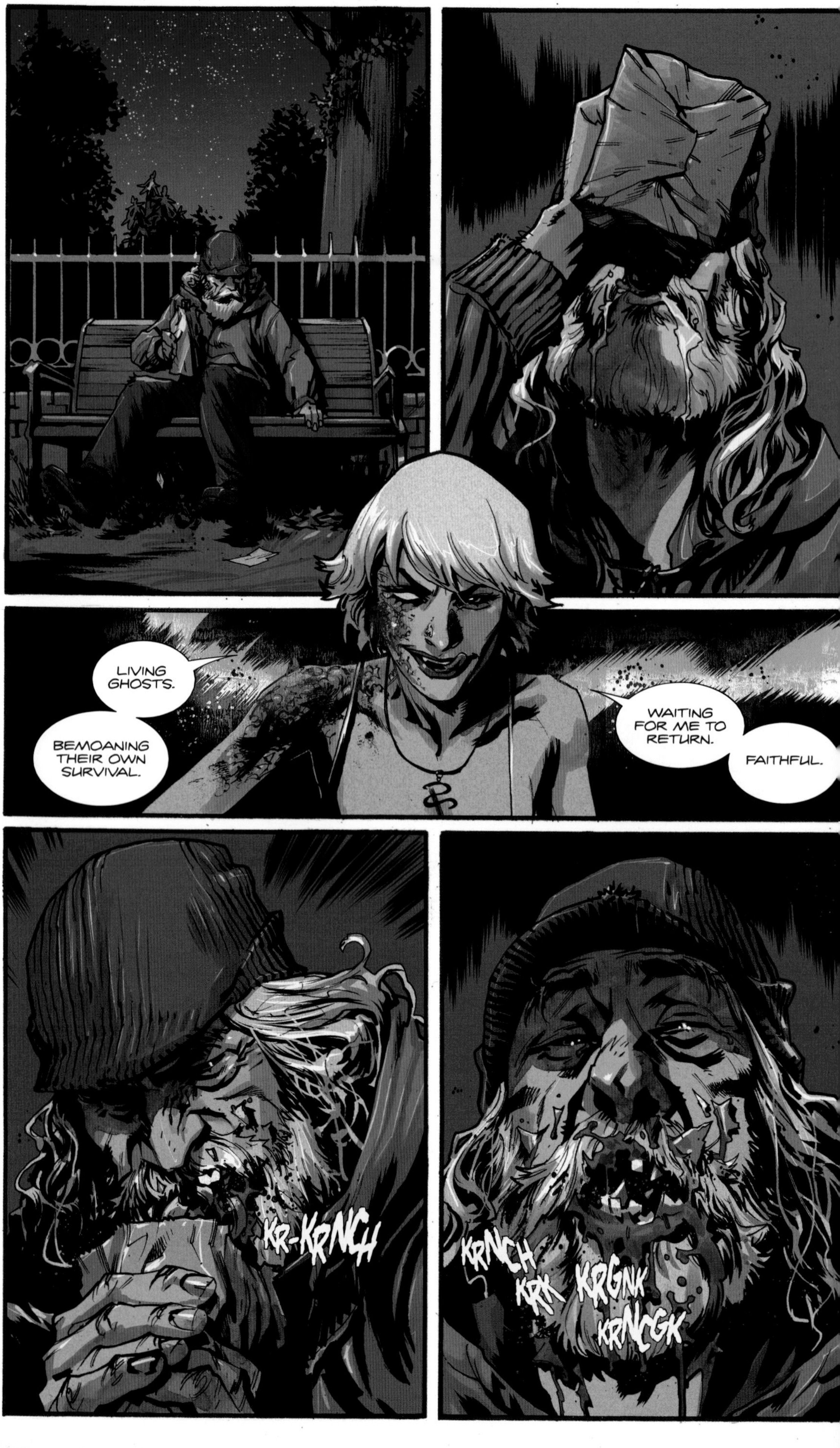
LIVING GHOSTS.
BEMOANING THEIR OWN SURVIVAL.
WAITING FOR ME TO RETURN.
FAITHFUL.
KR-KRNCH
KRNCH
KRK
KRGNK
KRNCGK

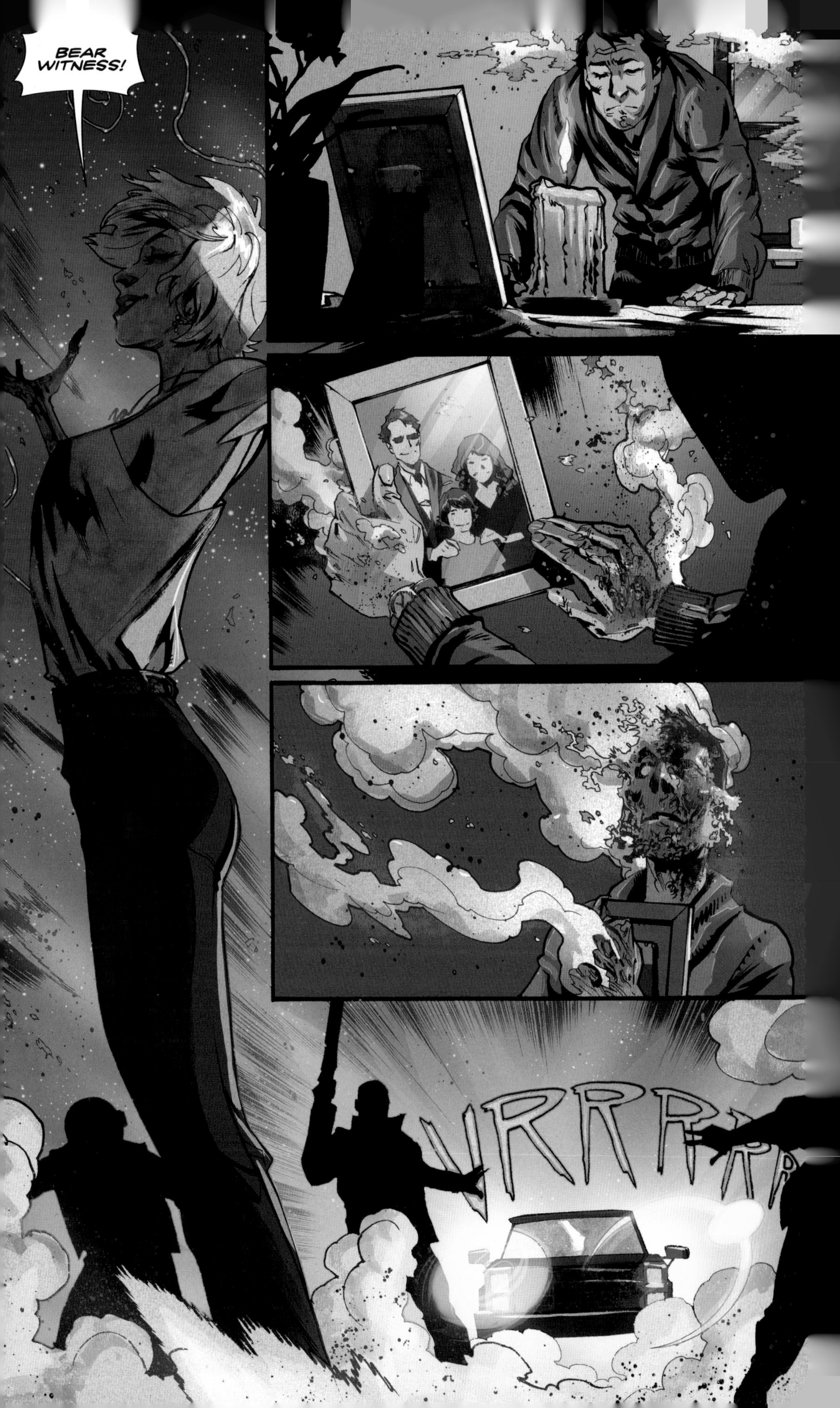
BEAR WITNESS!
VRRRRR

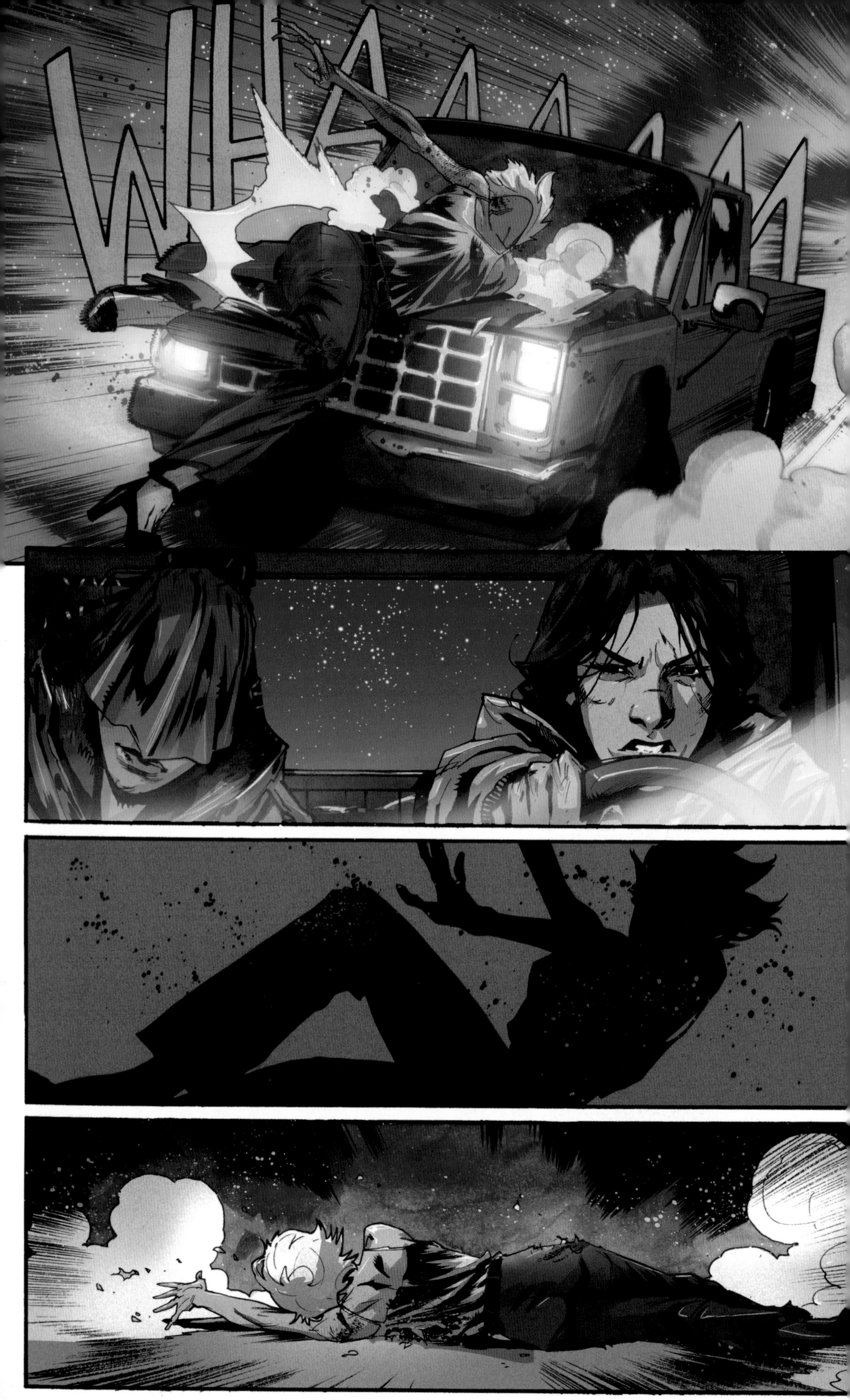
WHAAAAM

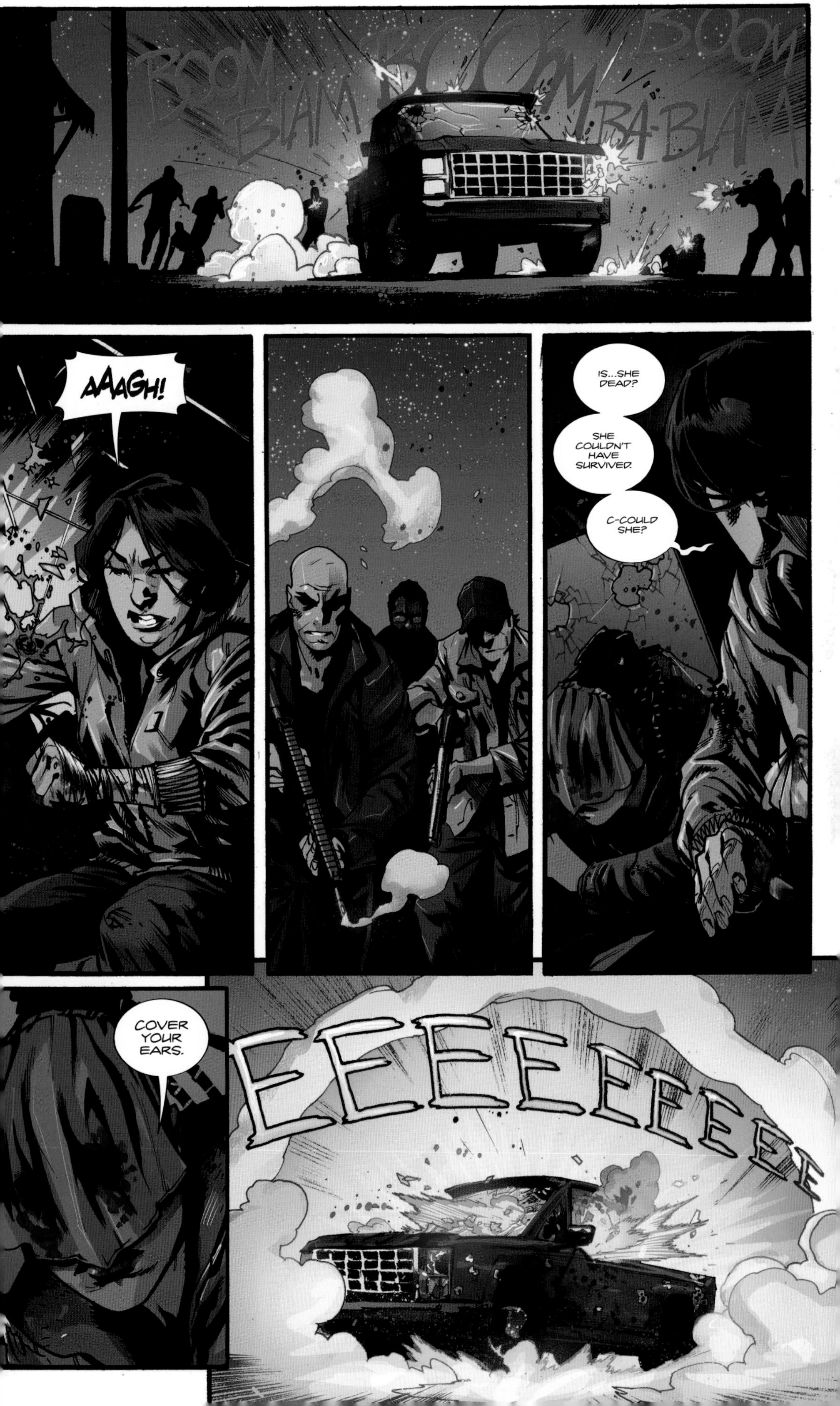
BOOM
BIAM
BOOM
BOOM
RA-BLAM
AAAGH!
IS...SHE DEAD?
SHE COULDN'T HAVE SURVIVED.
C-COULD SHE?
COVER YOUR EARS.
EEEEEEEEEEEE

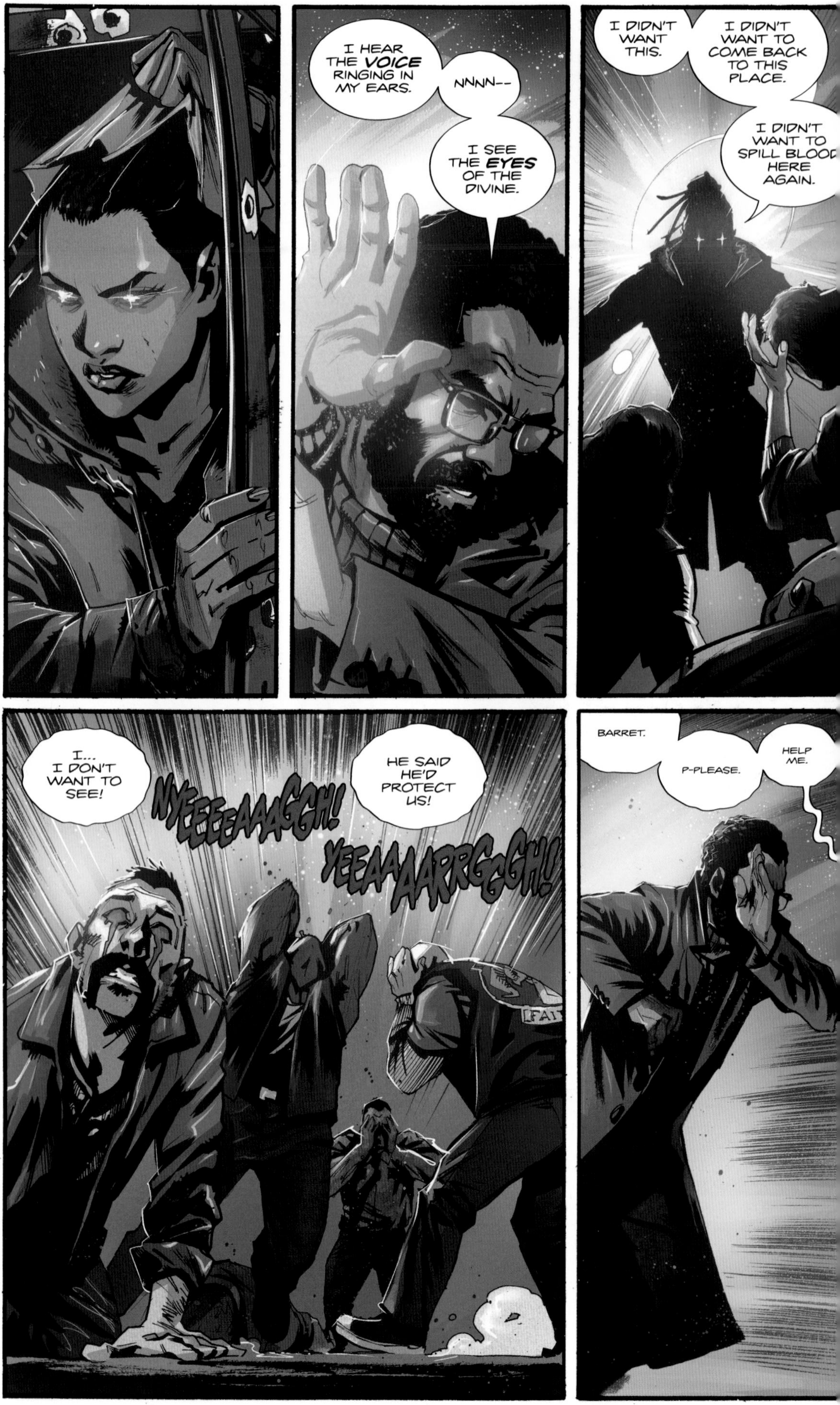
I HEAR THE VOICE RINGING IN MY EARS.
NNNN--
I SEE THE EYES OF THE DIVINE.
I DIDN'T WANT THIS.
I DIDN'T WANT TO COME BACK TO THIS PLACE.
I DIDN'T WANT TO SPILL BLOOD HERE AGAIN.
I... I DON'T WANT TO SEE!
NYEEEEAAAGGH!
HE SAID HE'D PROTECT US!
YEEAAAARRGGGH!
BARRET.
P-PLEASE.
HELP ME.

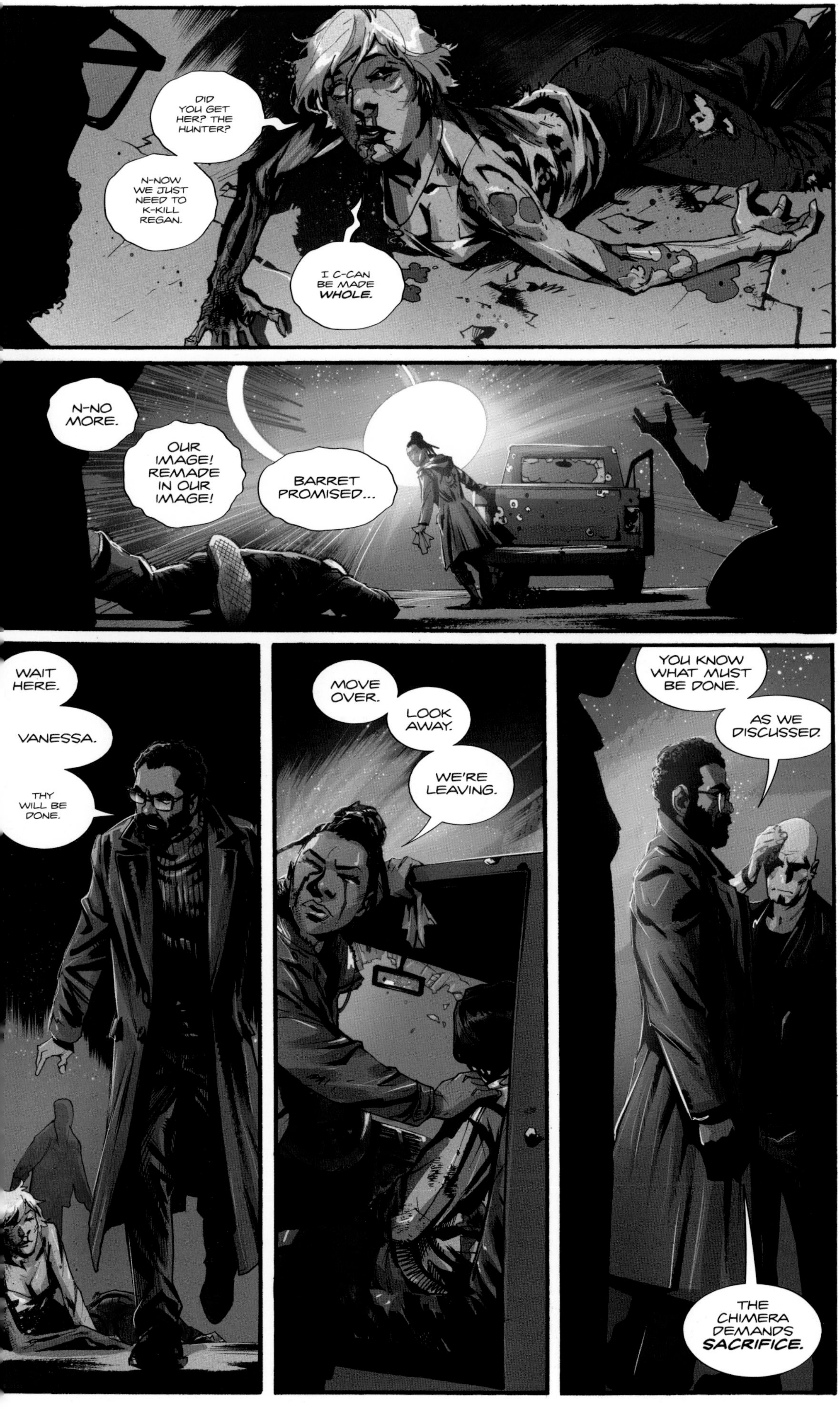
DID YOU GET HER? THE HUNTER?
N-NOW WE JUST NEED TO K-KILL REGAN.
I C-CAN BE MADE **WHOLE.**
N-NO MORE.
OUR IMAGE! REMADE IN OUR IMAGE!
BARRET PROMISED...
WAIT HERE.
VANESSA.
THY WILL BE DONE.
MOVE OVER.
LOOK AWAY.
WE'RE LEAVING.
YOU KNOW WHAT MUST BE DONE.
AS WE DISCUSSED.
THE CHIMERA DEMANDS ***SACRIFICE.***

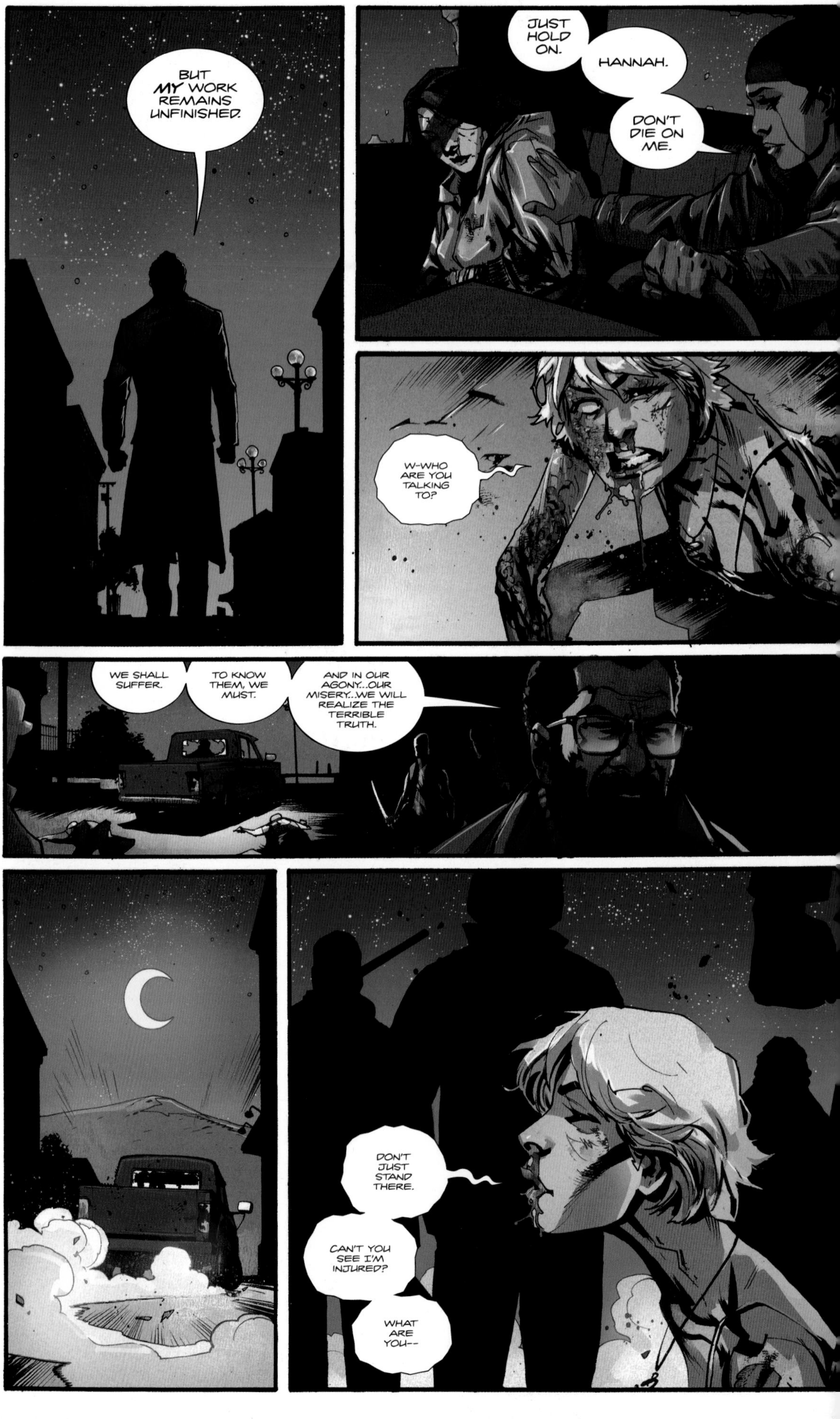
BUT MY WORK REMAINS UNFINISHED.
JUST HOLD ON.
HANNAH.
DON'T DIE ON ME.
W-WHO ARE YOU TALKING TO?
WE SHALL SUFFER.
TO KNOW THEM, WE MUST.
AND IN OUR AGONY...OUR MISERY...WE WILL REALIZE THE TERRIBLE TRUTH.
DON'T JUST STAND THERE.
CAN'T YOU SEE I'M INJURED?
WHAT ARE YOU--

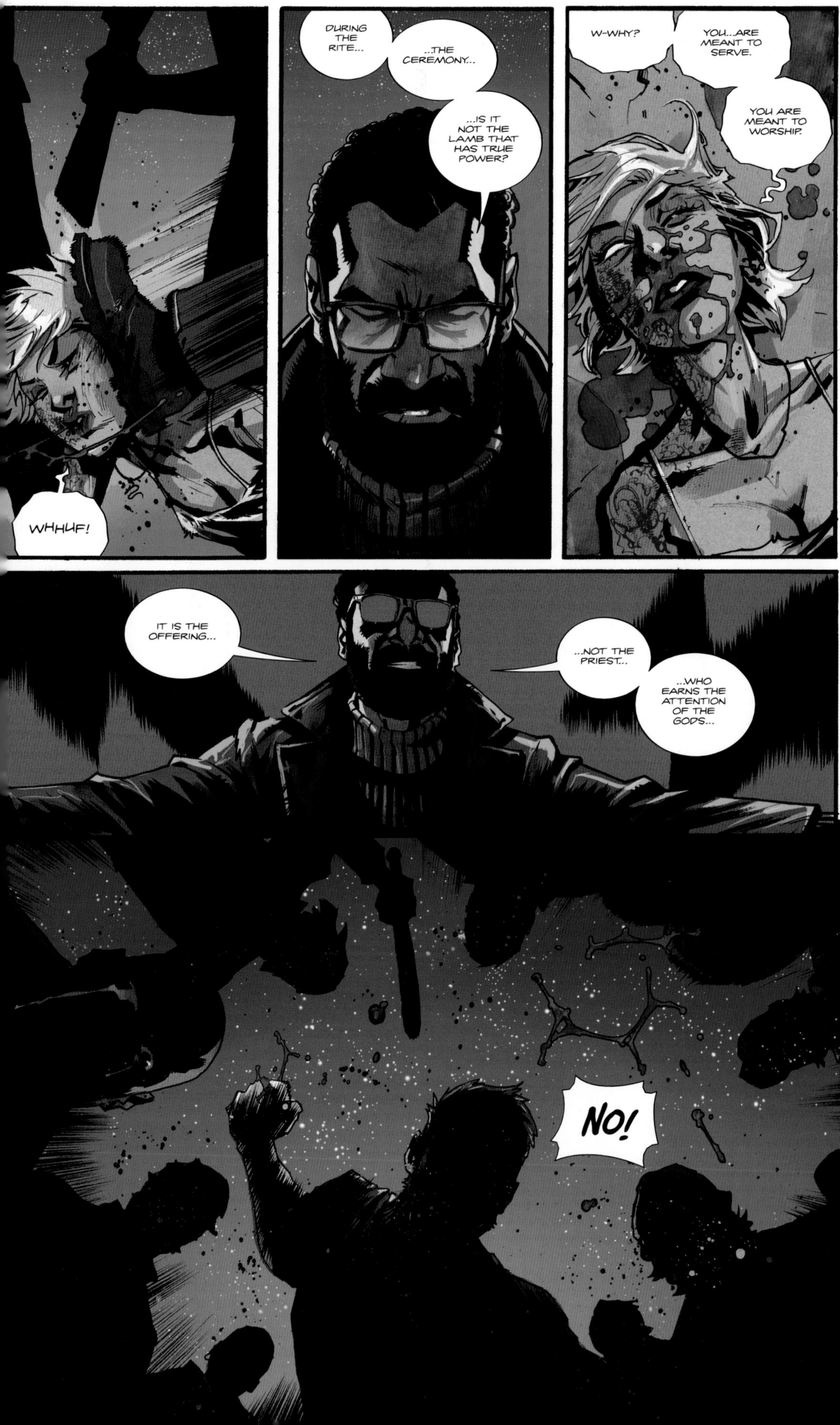
WHHUF!
DURING THE RITE...
...THE CEREMONY...
...IS IT NOT THE LAMB THAT HAS TRUE POWER?
W-WHY?
YOU...ARE MEANT TO SERVE.
YOU ARE MEANT TO WORSHIP.
IT IS THE OFFERING...
...NOT THE PRIEST...
...WHO EARNS THE ATTENTION OF THE GODS...
NO!

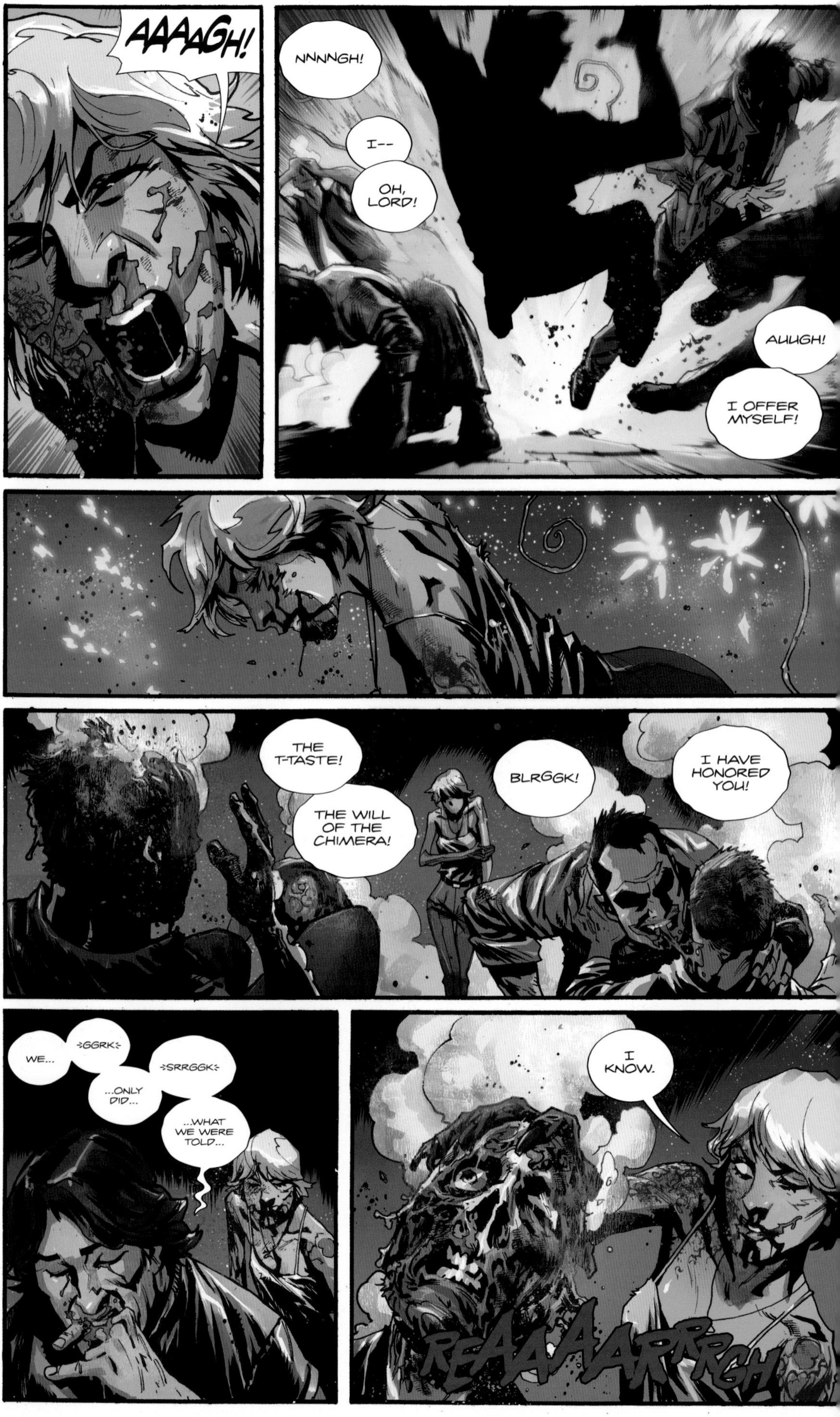
AAAAGH!
NNNNGH!
I--
OH, LORD!
AUUGH!
I OFFER MYSELF!
THE T-TASTE!
THE WILL OF THE CHIMERA!
BLRGGK!
I HAVE HONORED YOU!
WE...
GGRK
SRRGGK
...ONLY DID...
...WHAT WE WERE TOLD...
I KNOW.
REAAAAARRRGH

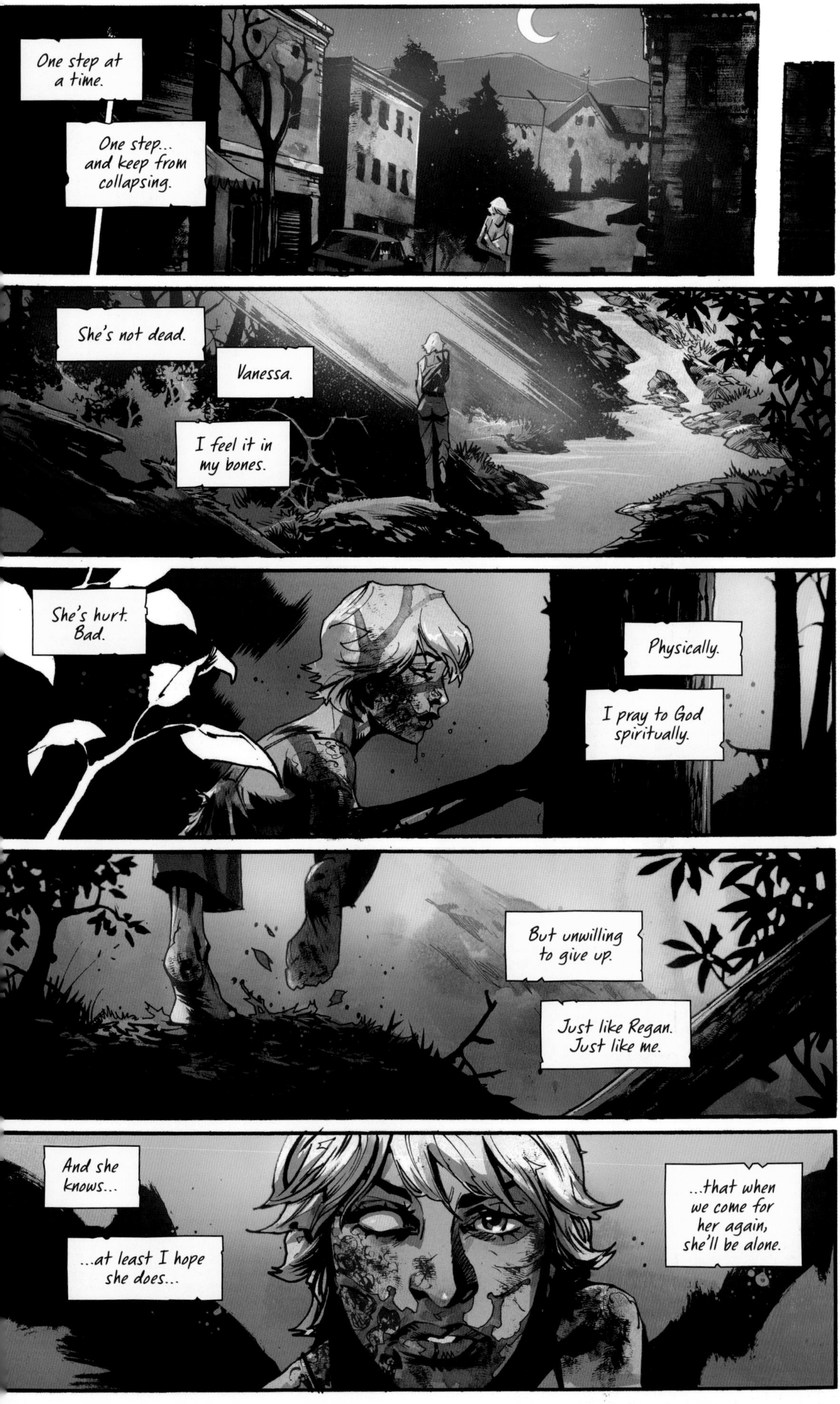
One step at a time.
One step... and keep from collapsing.
She's not dead.
Vanessa.
I feel it in my bones.
She's hurt. Bad.
Physically.
I pray to God spiritually.
But unwilling to give up.
Just like Regan. Just like me.
And she knows...
...at least I hope she does...
...that when we come for her again, she'll be alone.

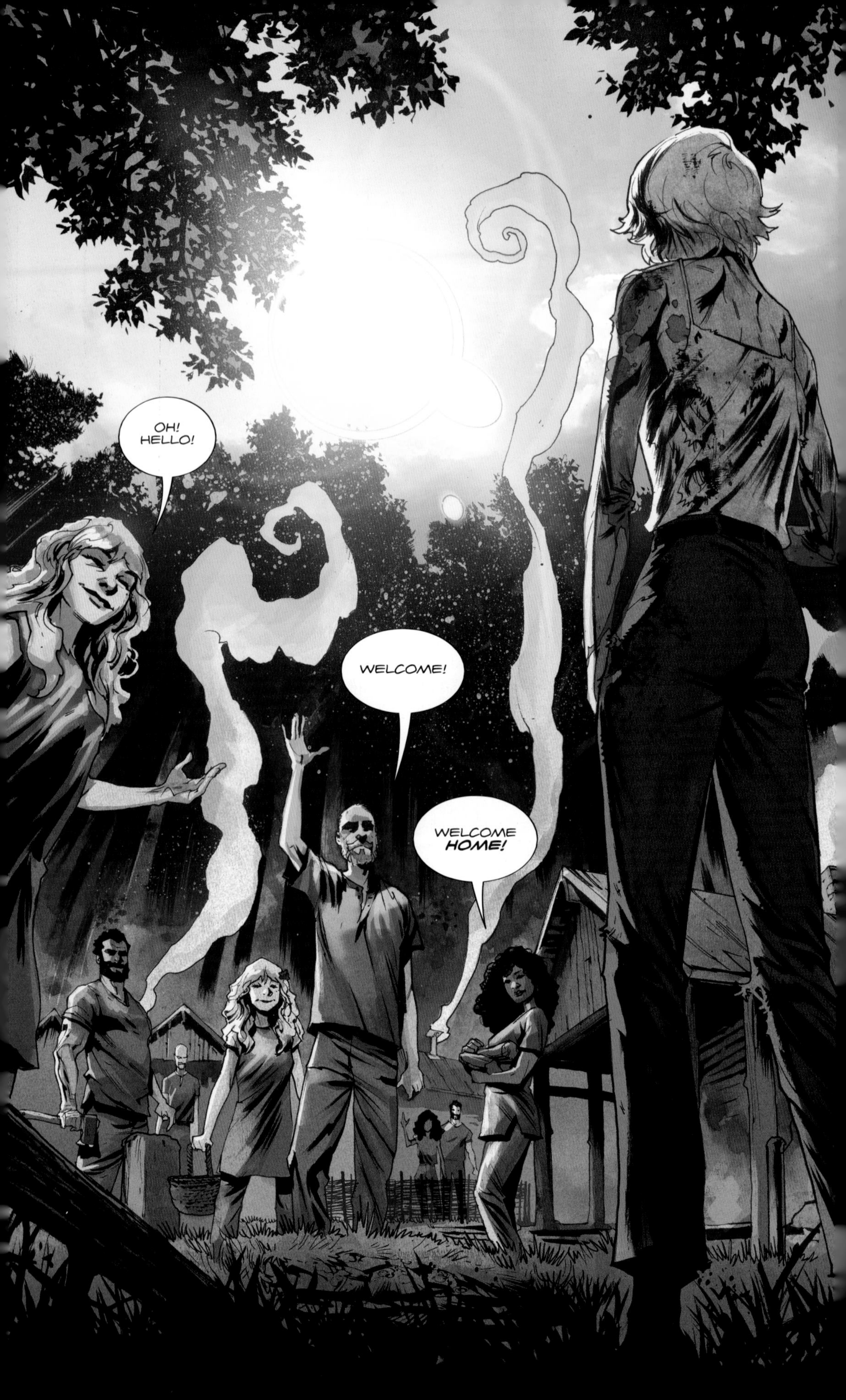
OH! HELLO!
WELCOME!
WELCOME HOME!

TO BE CONTINUED

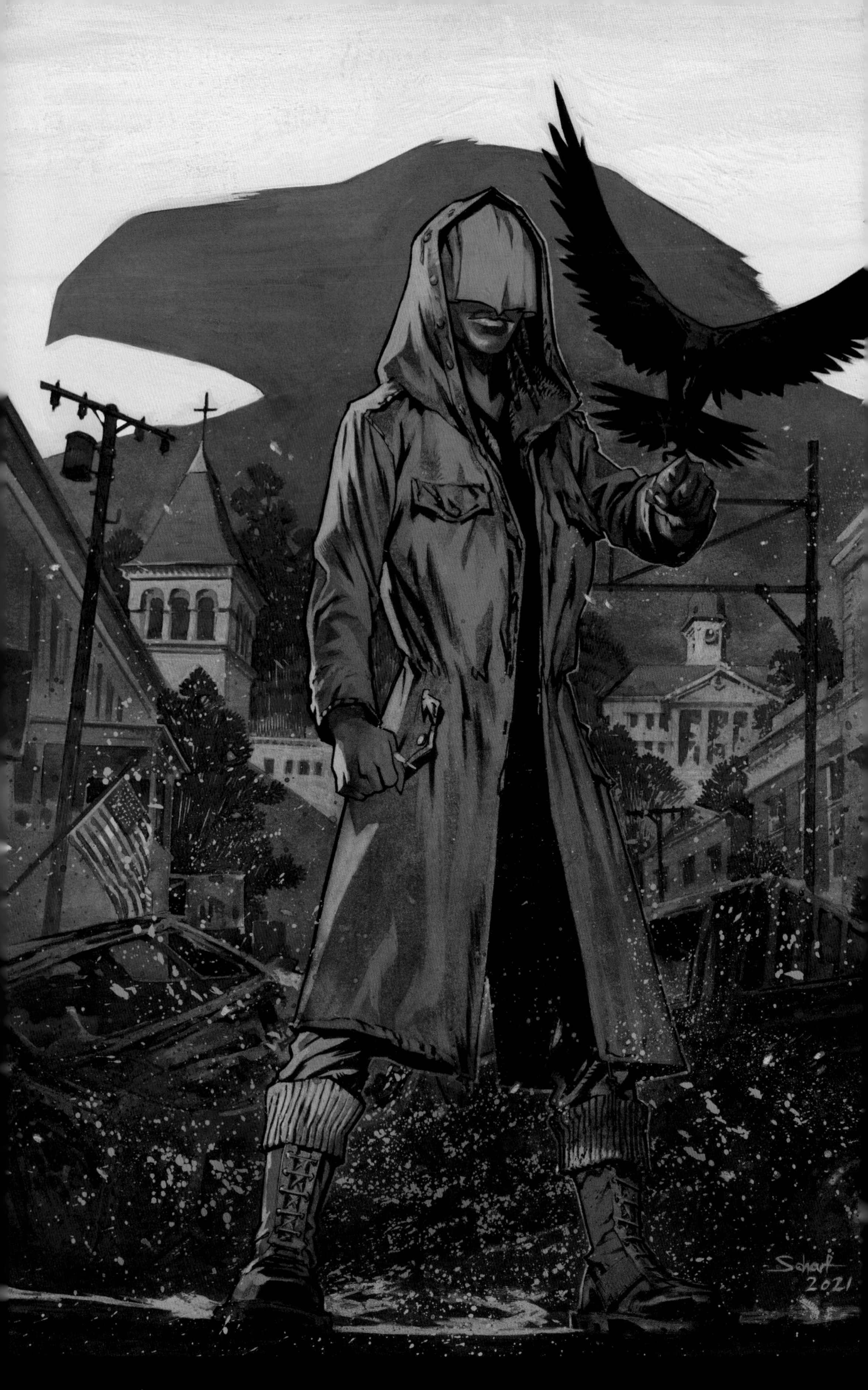
Scharf
2021

Issue Five Cover by **JONAS SCHARF**

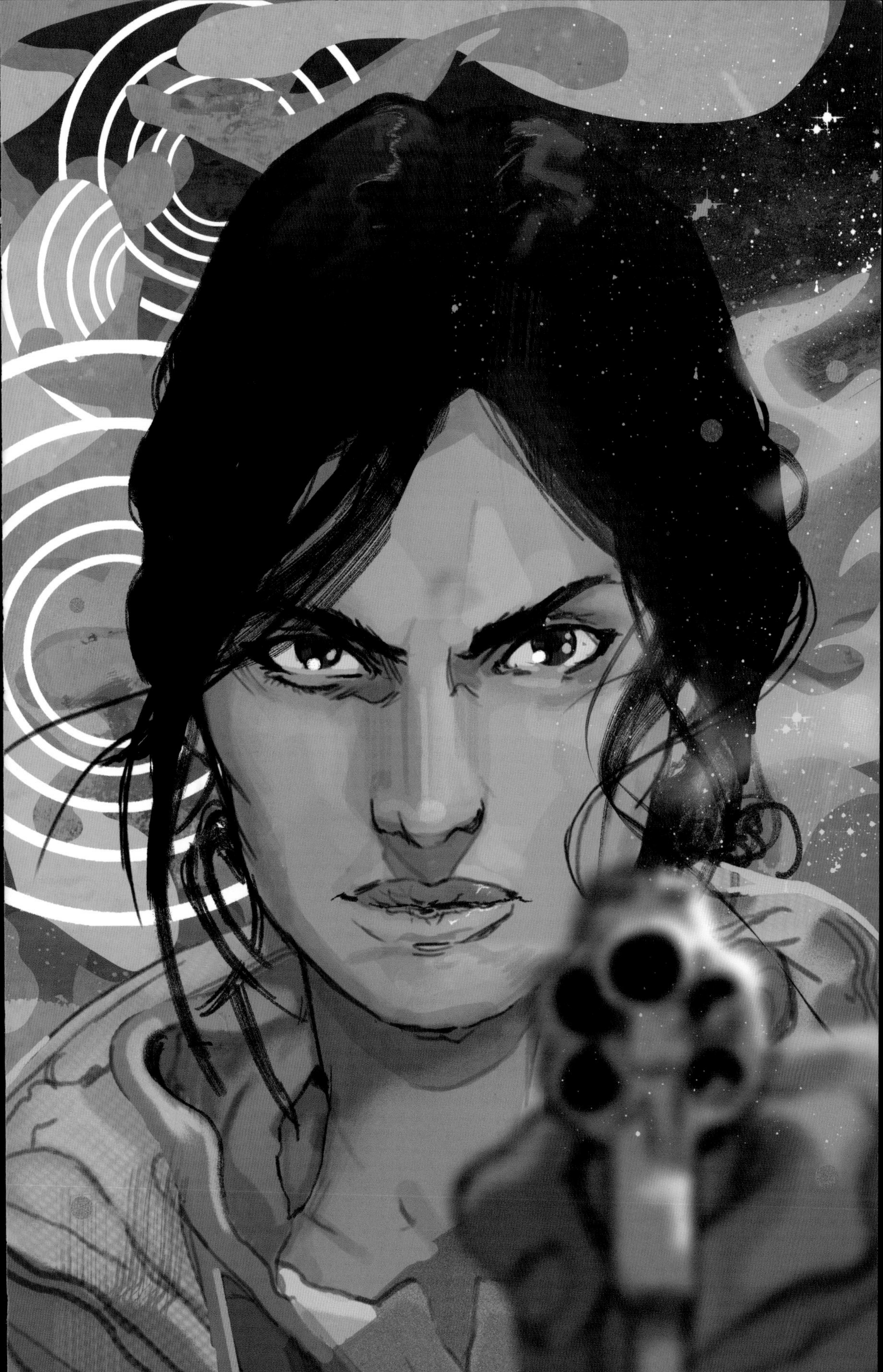

Issue Five Cover by **CHRISTIAN WARD**

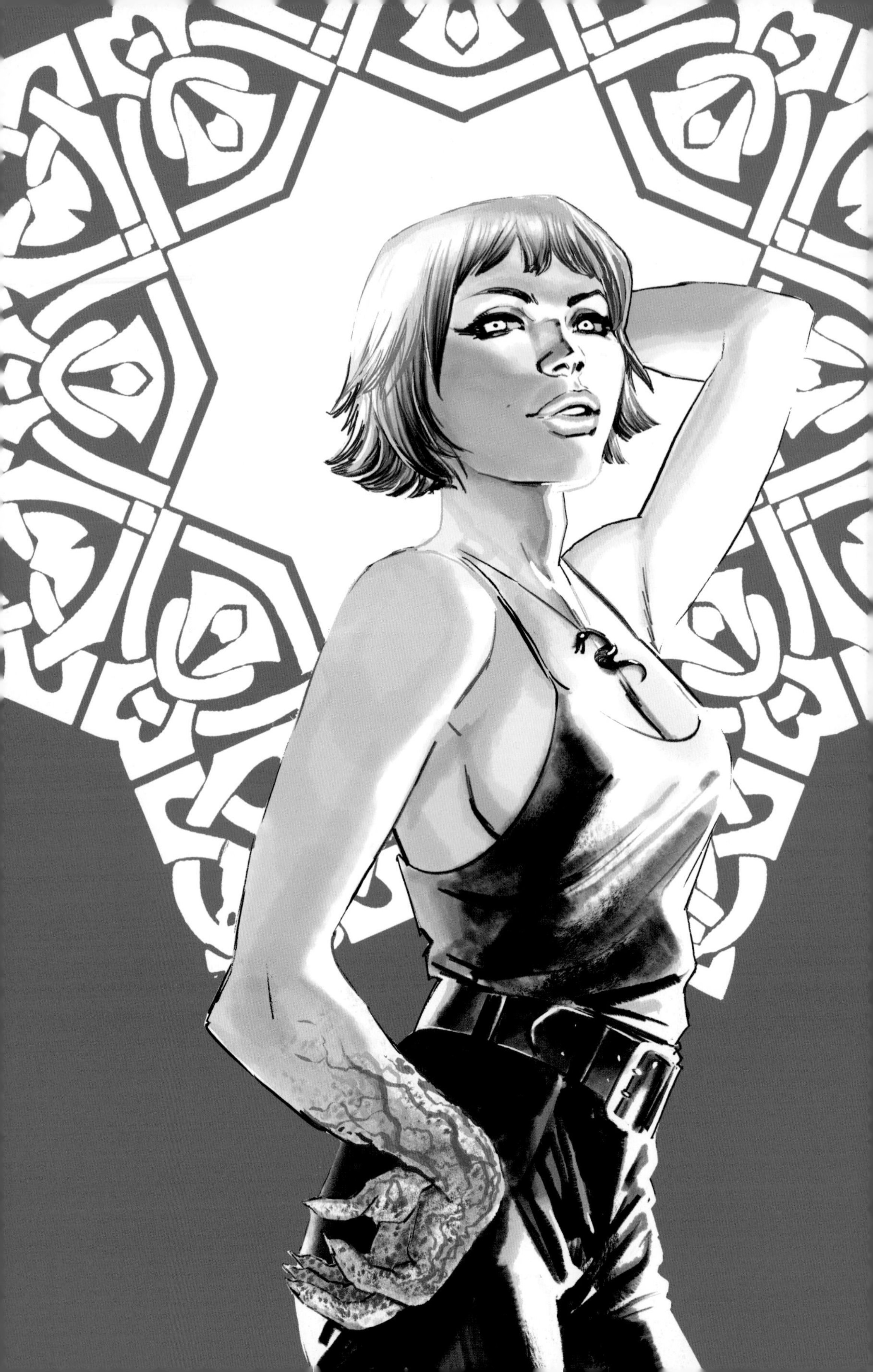

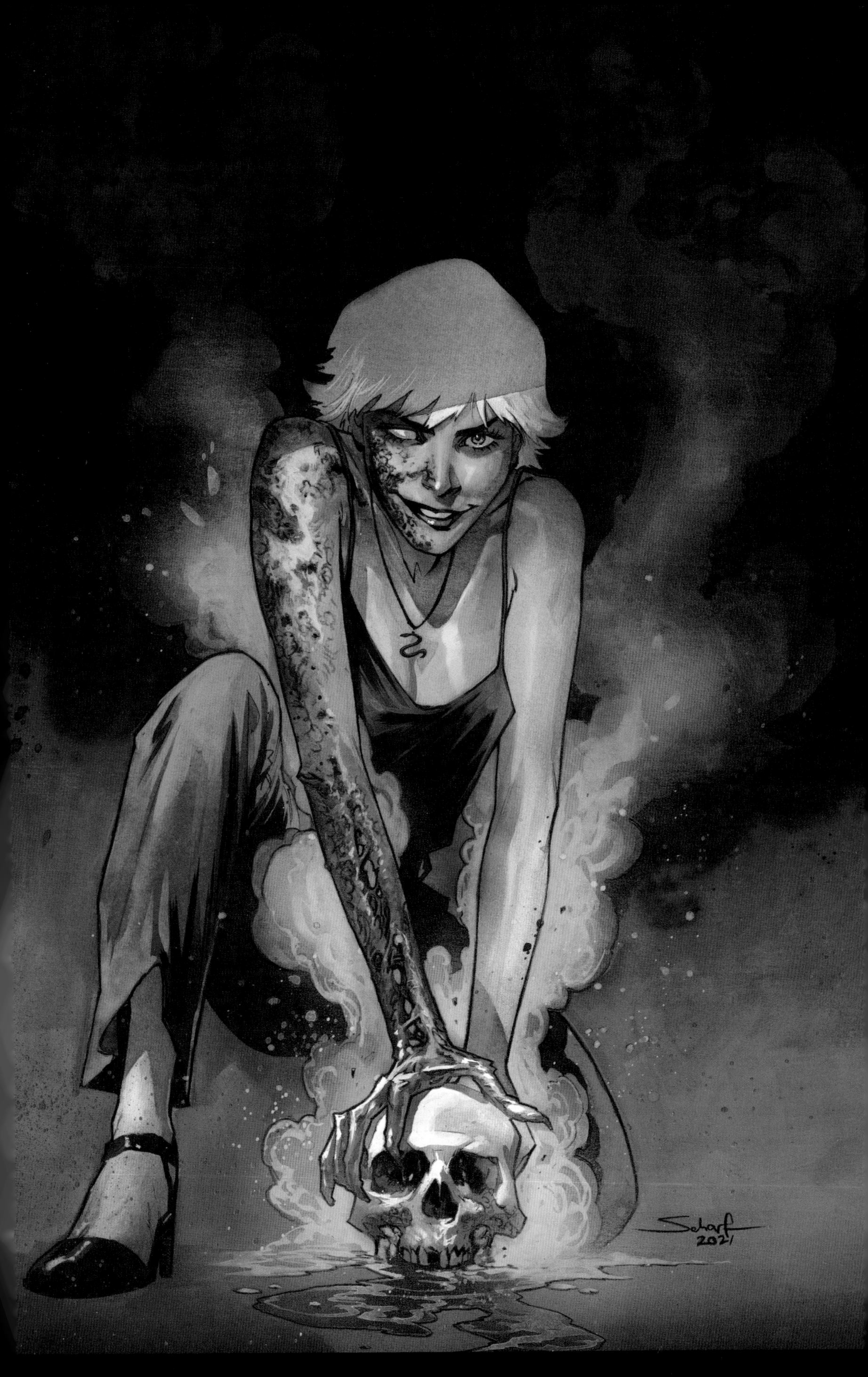
Scharf
2021

Issue Six Cover by **JONAS SCHARF**

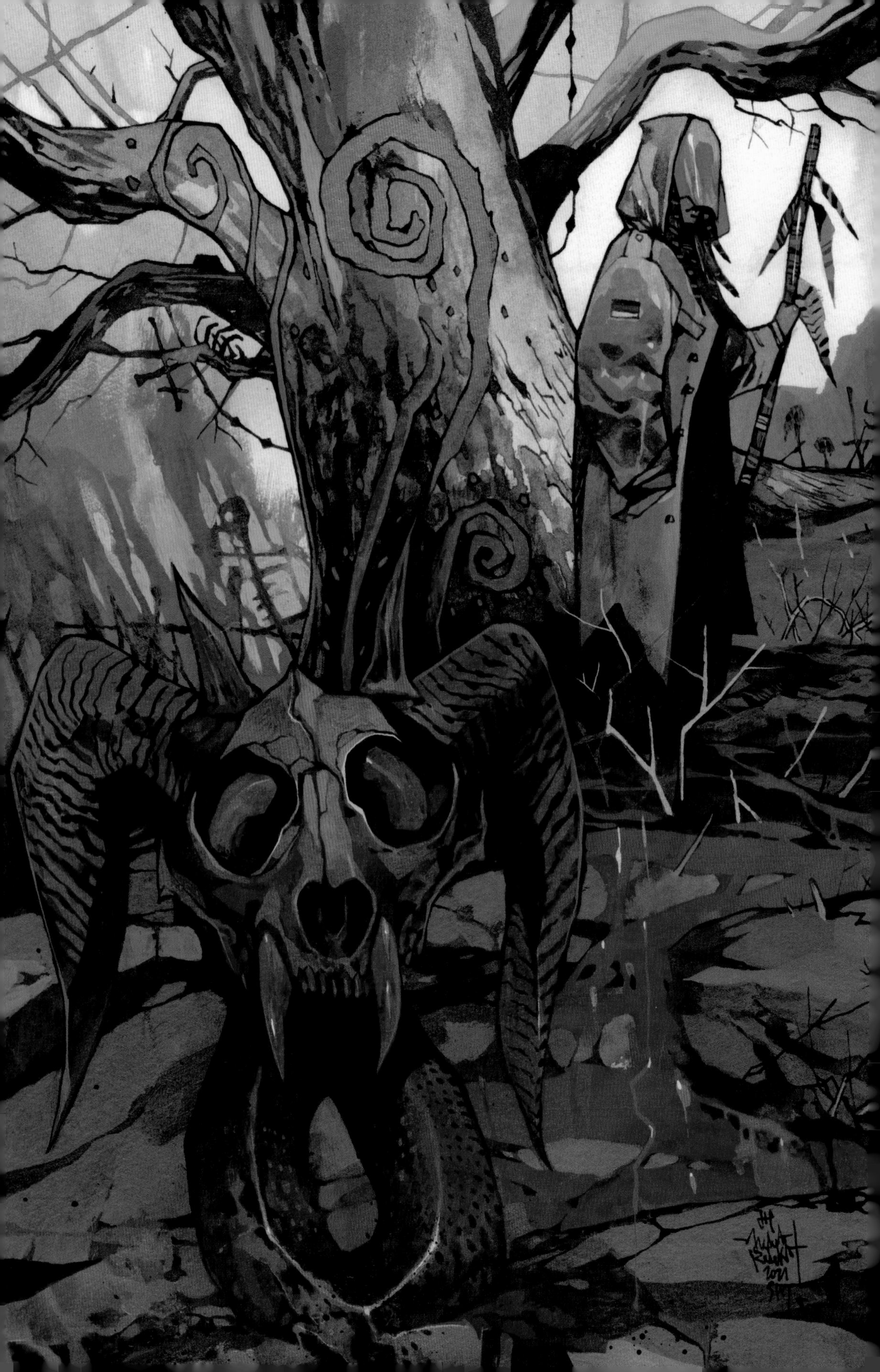

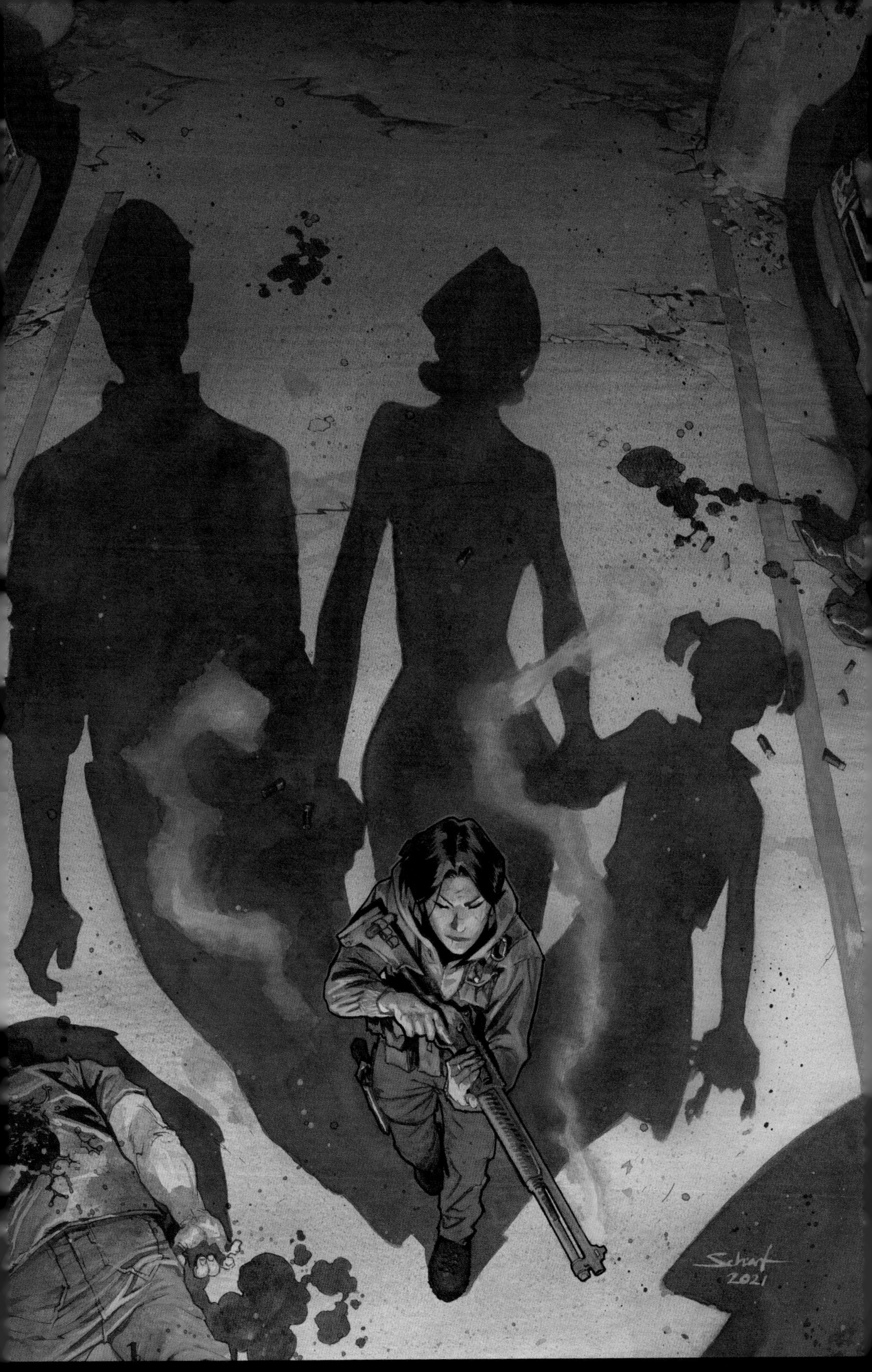
Scharf
2021

Issue Seven Cover by **JONAS SCHARF**

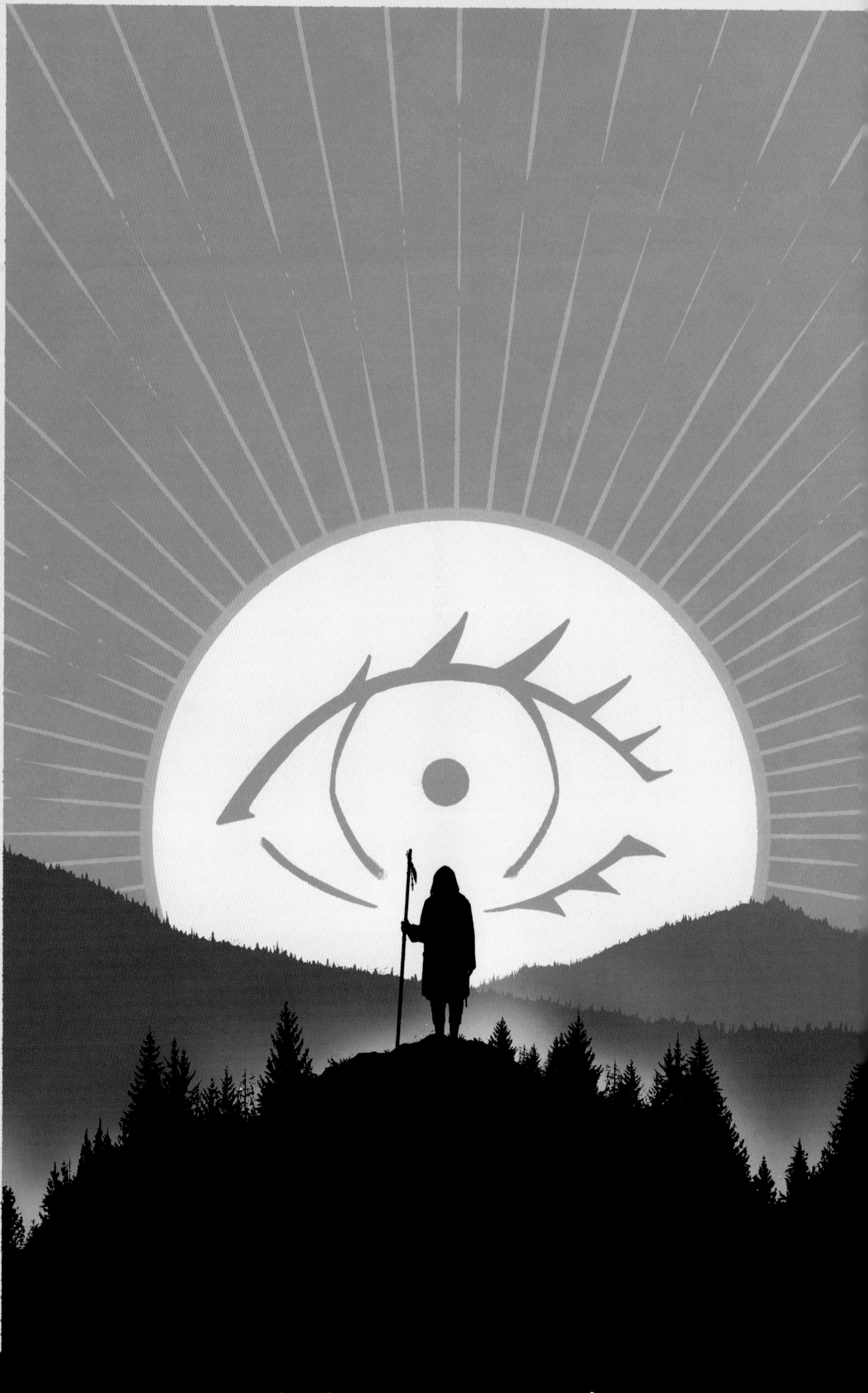

Issue Seven Cover by **JORGE FORNÉS**

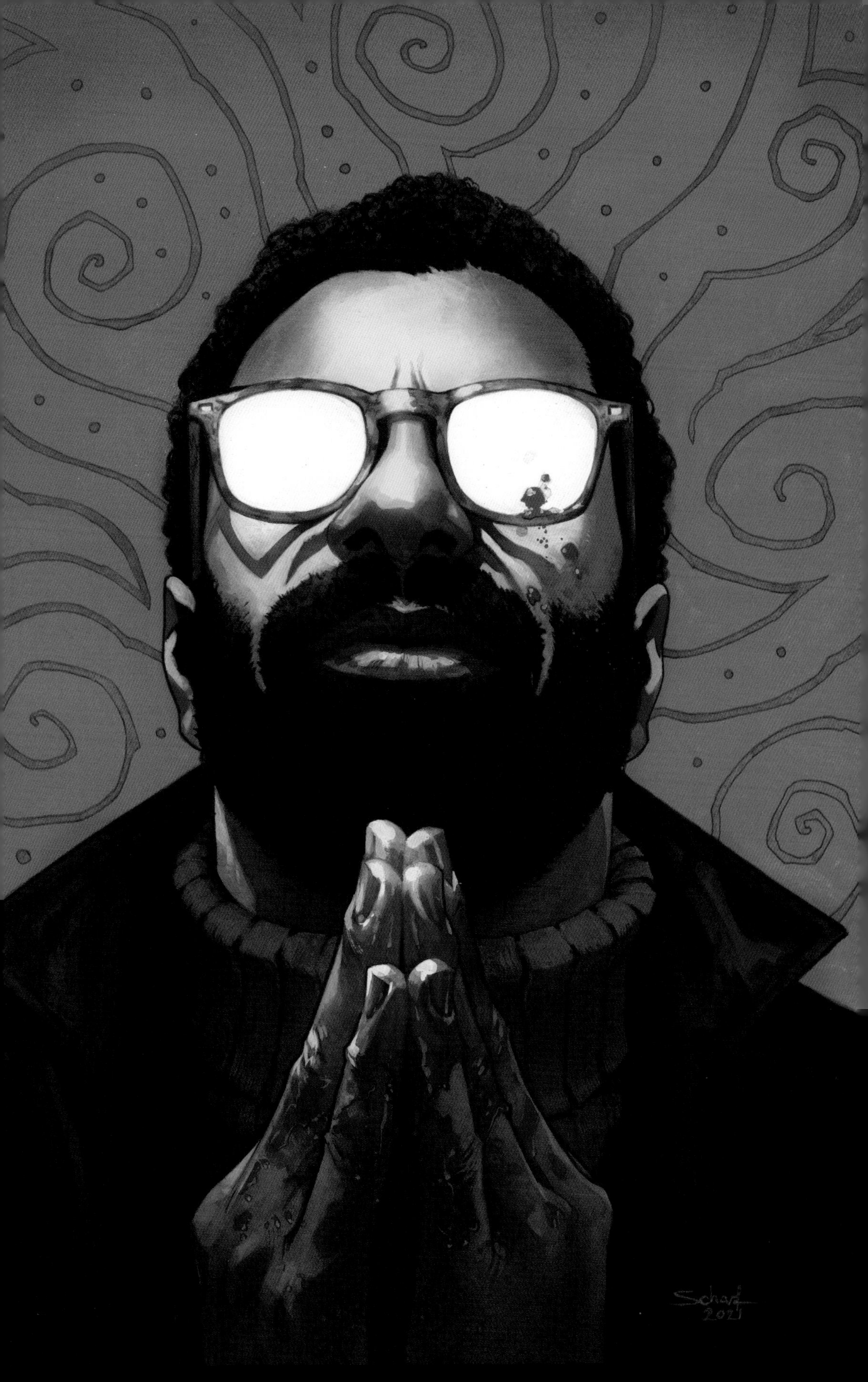
Scharf
2021

Issue Eight Cover by **JONAS SCHARF**

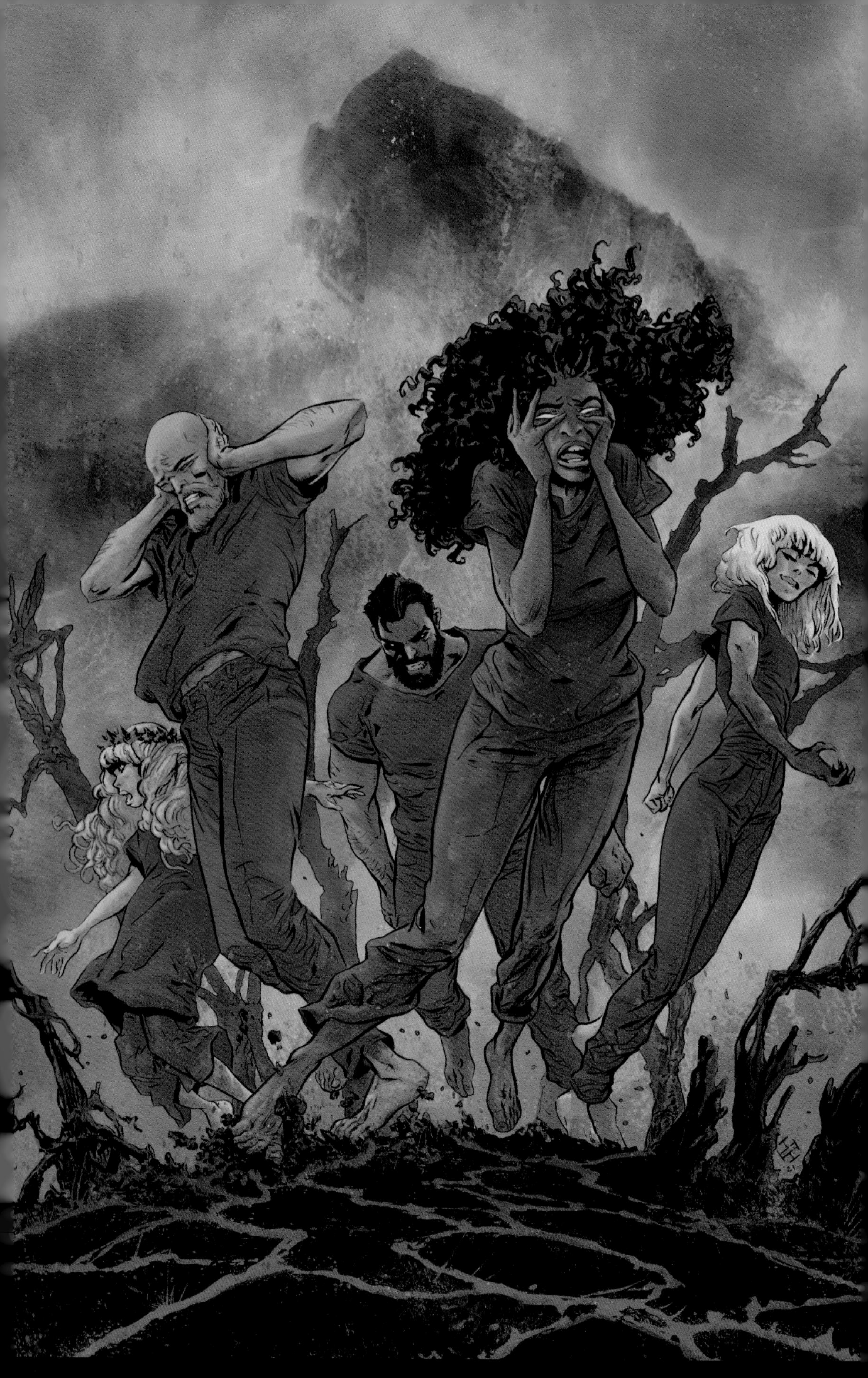

Issue Eight Cover by **MAX FIUMARA**

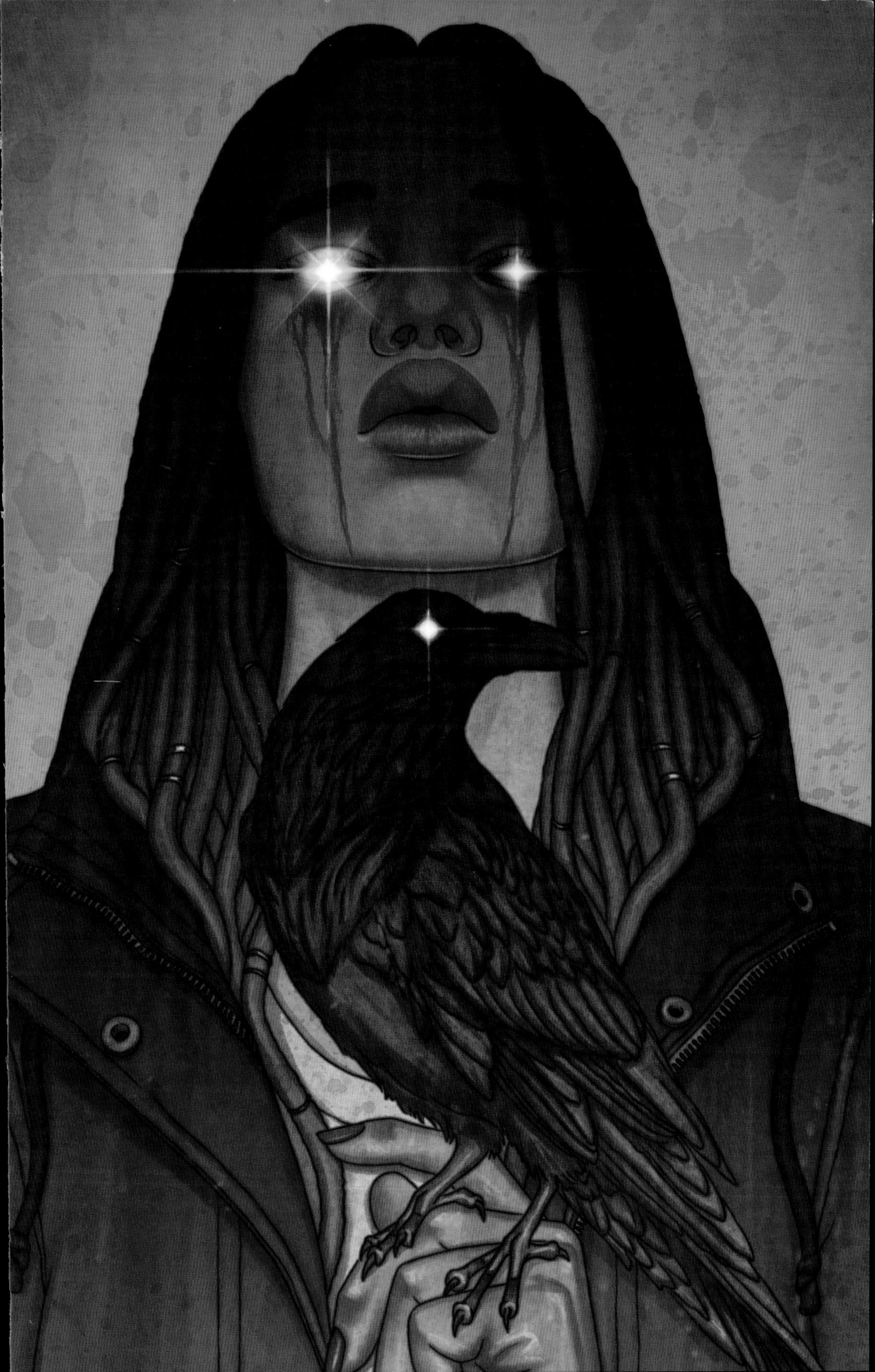

Issue Eight Cover by **JENNY FRISON**

CULLEN BUNN

Cullen Bunn is the writer of *The Empty Man*, *Bone Parish*, and *The Unsound* from BOOM! Studios. He is also the writer of *The Sixth Gun*, *Harrow County*, and *Regression*. You can find out more about his work at www.cullenbunn.com or by following him on Twitter (@cullenbunn).

JONAS SCHARF

Jonas Scharf is a comic book artist and illustrator from Nuremberg, Germany. Since his professional debut in 2016, his work has spanned many genres, from horror books like *Bone Parish* for BOOM! Studios to superhero comics for Marvel Entertainment.

ALEX GUIMARÃES

Alex Guimarães is a colorist from Brazil. He has been working in comics since 2000, with publishers like Marvel Comics, Dynamite, DC Comics, Image, 2000 AD, and many others. He started working with BOOM! Studios four years ago, and has had a lot of fun with the variety of projects and characters, from *Planet of the Apes* to *Bill & Ted*. In addition to *Basilisk*, he is also currently working on *Archer & Armstrong* for Valiant Entertainment.

ED DUKESHIRE

Born in Seoul, Korea, **Ed Dukeshire** is a graphic artist and Harvey-nominated comic book letterer who has worked in the biz since 2001. He has lettered titles from mainstream to creator-owned favorites. He also owns and operates the Digital Webbing website, a gathering place for comic creators. And you may even catch him playing video games once in a while.